ANYONE

Methodology and History in Anthropology

General Editor: David Parkin, Fellow of All Souls College, Oxford

Just as anthropology has had a significant influence on many other disciplines in recent years, so too have its methods been challenged by new intellectual and technical developments. This series is designed to offer a forum for debate on the interrelationship between anthropology and other academic fields but also on the challenge that new intellectual and technological developments pose to anthropological methods, and the role of anthropological thought in a general history of concepts.

ANYONE

The Cosmopolitan Subject of Anthropology

Nigel Rapport

berghahn
NEW YORK · OXFORD
www.berghahnbooks.com

First published in 2012 by

Berghahn Books

www.berghahnbooks.com

© 2012, 2014 Nigel Rapport
First paperback edition published in 2014

Library of Congress Cataloging-in-Publication Data

Rapport, Nigel, 1956-
  Anyone, the cosmopolitan subject of anthropology / Nigel Rapport.
    p. cm. -- (Methodology and history in anthropology ; v. 24)
  Includes bibliographical references and index.
  ISBN 978-0-85745-519-2 (hardback : alk. paper) -- ISBN 978-1-78238-526-4
(paperback : alk. paper) – ISBN 978-0-85745-523-9 (ebook)
  1. Anthropology--Philosophy. 2. Human behavior--Philosophy. 3.
Cosmopolitanism. 4. Globalization--Social aspects. I. Title.
  GN33.R35 2012
  301.01--dc23

                                                              2011047723

British Library Cataloguing in Publication Data
A catalogue record for this book is available from the British Library

Printed on acid-free paper

ISBN: 978-1-78238-526-4 paperback
ISBN: 978-0-85745-523-9 ebook

To my father and my mother

I cannot tolerate the fact that a human being should be assessed not for what he is but because of the group with which he happens to be identified.

—Primo Levi, letter to Heinz Riedt, 1961

CONTENTS

LIST OF FIGURES

ACKNOWLEDGEMENTS

The writing of this book was greatly assisted by the British Academy and the provision of a Research Development Award. Equally supportive has been the School of Philosophical, Anthropological and Film Studies at the University of St Andrews, affording the possibility to institute a Centre for Cosmopolitan Studies. In this regard I would like to thank very much Anthony Cohen and Michael Jackson, Ulf Hannerz and David McCrone; also Brian Lang and Louise Richardson, Peter Clark and Katherine Hawley.

Between 2004 and 2007 I held a Canada Research Chair in Globalization, Citizenship and Justice, and ran a centre for Cosmopolitan Studies at Concordia University of Montreal. For these opportunities I am especially grateful to Vered Amit and Christine Jourdan; also to Andrew Irving, Robert Paine, Katja Neves Graca, Max Forte, Kevin Tuite, Chantal Collard, Meir Amor, David Howes, Nelson Ferguson, Turid Satermo, Allen Young, Noel Dyck and Gerrie Casey.

Intellectually I owe a debt to all of the above: I would hope that the book evinces what I have learned from them. Likewise, I have been fortunate to have been able to debate cosmopolitanism with Ronald Stade, Morten Nielsen, Huon Wardle, Lisette Josephides, Hideko Mitsui, Laura Jefferey, Helena Wulff, Nina Holm Vohnsen, Jonathan Skinner, Peter Collins, Susan Lewis, Amos Goldberg, Keith Hart, Karen Fog Olwig, Pnina Werbner, Christer Norström, Maurice Roche, Caroline Knowles, David Zeitlyn, Elitza Ranova, Michal Buchowski, Tomasz Rakowski, Helena Patzer, Katarzyna Kaniowska and Ewa Chomicka. (The Polish Institute of Anthropology were fine hosts.)

Berghahn Books are what one would hope for from an academic publisher. I am indebted to Marion Berghahn and Ann Przyzycki, and also to David Parkin for a place in his series.

Morten Nielsen argues for the value that imagining an ideal future state of affairs can vouchsafe to the individual: 'inhabiting' that imaginative space can validate and redeem a life-project in the present which might otherwise appear impossibly difficult. Andrew Irving argues, meanwhile, that seeking what is impossible can in itself personify an individual virtue. The human condition entails imperfect and unfinished doings and beings, and the individual constructs world-views as works-in-motion without a point of certainty or rest. Yet the effort to see things as they are and to imagine things-in-themselves remains a humane and just, necessary thing.

Speculating upon cosmopolitanism as life-project and world-view, imagining the world of Anyone, I am especially lucky to have had Elizabeth, Callum and Emilie take me as I am.

NJR
St Andrews
February 2012

INTENT AND STRUCTURE

A Cosmopolitan Project

'Cosmopolitanism' has a certain momentum, in politics and academia equally: a 'growing intellectual movement', cross-disciplinary, confident, liberal (R. Werbner 2007: x). In anthropology we are witness to a flurry of research, writing and conferring. We meet 'plural discrepant cosmopolitanisms' (Clifford 1998), occupational cosmopolitanism (Hannerz 2007) and 'cosmopolitans' as distinct from 'locals' (Hannerz 1990); pre-modern and modern cosmopolitans (Stade 2006), urban Caribbean cosmopolitans (Wardle 2000), diasporic Chinese cosmopolitans (Ong 1998), rural Togolese cosmopolitans (Piot 1999), upper-class cosmopolitan Cairene youth (Peterson 2011), middle-class cosmopolitan Indian families (Lamb 2009), working-class Pakistani cosmopolitan migrants (P. Werbner 1999), heretical cosmopolitan Muslim intellectuals (Kersten 2011), 'instrumental, aesthetic, political and cultural cosmopolitans' (Hannerz 2004), cosmopolitan dancers and choreographers (Wulff 2009), cosmopolitan patriots (Appiah 1998), cosmopolitan cityscapes (Rapport 2006a), cosmopolitan civilities (Anderson 2004), cosmopolitan imaginations (Meskimmon 2010) and cosmopolitan emancipation (Rapport 2012a). Cosmopolitanism appears commonly as a theme of conferences, academic volumes and research centres.

Are these significant developments? Does 'cosmopolitanism' offer something new, distinct from 'multiculturalism', 'globalism', 'diaspora', 'transnationalism', 'hybridity', 'pluralism' or 'civil society'? Yes: cosmopolitanism usefully identifies a certain agenda in human science. Malcolm Bowie writes: 'Humanism certainly needs an infusion of audacity if it is to stand its ground against superstition, bigotry and fundamentalist rant' (Bowie 2000: 20); cosmopolitanism claims a particular history of inscribing the human, and a future project.

The worth of this book depends on the case it makes for three related notions. First, that 'humankind' represents a phenomenon whose universal condition and whose set of singular characteristics an anthropological science should determine to know. Second, that *Anyone* is a human actor who is to be recognized as at once universal and individual. Third, that one may conceive of a set of norms which serves as a universal ethic of polite human interaction: 'cosmopolitan politesse'. Here is a social medium which would everywhere afford Anyone the space to live according to the fulfilment of his or her capacities to author an individual life – individual world-views, identity and life-project – and the right and encouragement so to do; the right to be universally recognized and engaged as himself or herself, and not merely as a member of a social category or class. The 'cosmopolitan project' of the discipline of anthropology is, then, to provide evidence for treating humankind and Anyone as ontologies, as part of the nature of human being, a focus both of scholarly concern and of moral and political effort.

The cosmopolitan project is to know Anyone in terms of a universal human nature and at the same time an individual embodiment: to do justice to his or her universal capacities as well as to their singular expression. Humankind can be defined as the objective context of individuality. Individuality owes its unique nature to its humanity: humankind is ever instantiated as individuality. The evidence a cosmopolitan anthropology would adduce concerns seeing this relation plainly so that it is not obscured or distorted by cultural prejudices, social structures or historical contingencies. A cosmopolitan anthropology works to elucidate this dialectical relation: individuality out of humanity.

'Everyman' and 'Anyone'

Everyman was the title of a Christian morality play written in English around 1500 (and closely related to a Flemish production, *Elckerlyc*) (Cawley 1970). In an allegorical dramatization of what was taken to be a global moral struggle for humanity, the play portrays Death visiting a character called Everyman and informing him of his impending demise. The audience is then witness to Everyman's emotional journey from despair and fear to the final resignation that is a prelude to Christian redemption. We witness, too, a social journey as the play portrays Everyman being deserted by different false friends in turn: Kindred, Cousin, Fellowship and Worldly Goods. At first Everyman finds himself able to fall back on his own resources: Knowledge, Strength, Intelligence, Beauty and Good Deeds. In particular, Knowledge delivers the celebrated lines: 'Everyman, I will go with thee, and be thy guide, / In thy most need to go by thy side'. Together Everyman and his resources proceed to draw up a Book of Accounts for his meeting with God and the adjudication of his eternal fate. In extremis, however, when Everyman must go to his grave, his resources too all but desert him: we bear witness to Everyman's intellectual journey which leads him to the final realization that only Good Deeds can offer a faithful accompaniment to the soul. According to the play's Christian doctrinalism, the universal truth which the audience is to appreciate, and the moral drawn, is that the human individual is to progress from mundane life to a divine accounting equipped with nothing that he has taken or received from the world, only what he has given.

In terms which Hannah Arendt (1959) borrowed from Classical Greek philosophy, the allegory of *Everyman* turns on the difference and the tensions between *zoë* and *bios*. *Zoë* is bare life, a state of being alive common to all animals; *bios* is elaborated human experience, the bringing to *zoë* of consciousness and world-view. What makes a human life more than mere animal life, *Everyman* asks? Where does the intrinsic nature of human elaboration fundamentally lie? Not in kinship or friendship or property, nor even in wisdom, strength, intelligence or beauty. The key to a human life (*bios*), a humane life, that which fits it for a passage to heaven, is the doing of good deeds. The key is to recognize in human life the spiritual microcosm of Christian divinity.

A more recent meditation on the tensions between *zoë* and *bios* comes in the work of Giorgio Agamben, in particular his celebrated text, *Homo Sacer* (Agamben 1998). *Homo sacer* was an obscure figure in the law of Ancient Rome: a person who could be legally killed without retribution being levied but who could not be sacrificed. In other words, his death was not defined as a human death: it was not that of a social being surrounded by safeguards, and occasioning a sense of loss if lost. Agamben's argument is that the victims of the Nazi's Final Solution were reduced to mere embodiments of animal life: on their journey to Auschwitz, the Jews, Gypsies and others had their social and legal humanity officially rescinded by the Nazi state. More generally, Agamben depicts the concentration camp – whether that of refugees instituted out of humanitarian motives or the death camps of a totalitarian regime – as the paradigmatic space of modern life. Bare life is a human condition which many are forced to suffer: a kind of naked existence beyond the securities and elaborations of social being. We are witness to an expanded zone of 'irreducible indistinction' such that the bare life of the concentration camp becomes the 'hidden matrix' at the centre of our world (Agamben 1998: 166). Or, in the terms Walter Benjamin earlier made famous: 'The tradition of the oppressed teaches us that the "state of emergency" in which we live is not the exception but the rule' (Benjamin 1969: 257).

For *Everyman* and *Homo Sacer* alike, the key question concerns what it is to be human: Where does the particular dignity of humanity reside (cf. Redfield 2005)? According to *Everyman* it is in the practising of Christian virtues; according to *Homo Sacer* it is in a socially recognized life, a life accorded the opportunity of conventional engagement with others.

'Anyone' is distinct from both 'Everyman' and 'homo sacer' in that it collapses the distinction between *zoë* and *bios*. The human individual does not need to be or do any particular thing – whether engage in conventional exchanges or do good in conventional ways – in order to accede to a full humanity. Being human is Anyone's birthright. It is not the place of others to define what activities or what ideologies Anyone needs to practise in order to exhibit human dignity. Nor, indeed, can anyone else define for Anyone what dignity feels like or how it is to be interpreted; this is something that Anyone must know for himself or herself. Anyone's humanity precisely is this capacity to feel, interpret and come to know for himself or herself. Anyone's birthright, it might be said, is his or her futurity: the capacity to define the human in the context of his or her individual life. The tie between Anyone and humankind – microcosm to macrocosm – is immanent and irreducible.

Singular Values

That difference is an individual property, something that inheres ontologically in individual human embodiment and consciousness, has been the key insight I have drawn from my own ethnographic work (e.g., Rapport 1987, 1993, 1994, 2008), and which I have determined to privilege in the theoretical and analytical modelling of human social life. Cosmopolitanism is imbued with a comparable recognition of the intrinsic and irreducible individuality of human embodiment. But at the same time it trumpets the unity of humanity: all individuals can be recognized as manifestations of the same potentiality possessed by the species for self-expression and self-fulfilment. As an anthropological project, cosmopolitanism is concerned above all with this tension. What does it imply, ontologically and morally, that 'everyone is both identical and different' (Jackson 2008: 29)? How is it that individual human beings are irreducibly themselves and absolutely human? What are the moral implications of the fact that individuals are intrinsically different from each other and yet absolute examples of human capacities for self-expression? Each human being is capable of making sense of self and world – and does do so – and capable of effecting a life-project that manifests a personal version of self-and-environment – and should be free to do so. 'Cosmopolitanism' calls on 'anthropology' – both were words made anew and contemporaneously by Immanuel Kant – to furnish it with data concerning both the nature of the species and the specificities of individual expression. Indeed, anthropology dwells in this tension: What is it to be human, the capabilities and liabilities of the species? And how is it to be individual human beings, construing world-views and effecting a unique being-in-the-world?

Cosmopolitanism concerns, too, a philosophy of freedom. It is to be cherished, celebrated, that humanity is as it is, that individuality is as it is. One is to nurture those general conditions in which individuals might be so emancipated as to fulfil their capacities for making sense; one is to reckon their self-expression and creativity as a right. As a philosophy of freedom, cosmopolitanism can be said to compass a very particular and apparently paradoxical 'mathematics of value', focused on the one. Humanity is one. And the individual is one. The latter is how the singularity of the former manifests itself. Yet each individual instantiation of the human is unique: irreducible and unrepeatable, with a consciousness capable of encompassing an infinite set of potential connections, insights and realizations.

This is what I understand to be the meaning of the Talmudic judgement which might also have served as an epigraph to this book: 'Whoever destroys the life of a single human being – it is as if he had destroyed the entire world. And whoever preserves the life of a single human being – it is as if he had preserved the world entire' (*Jerusalem Talmud*, Sanhedrin 4: 8 (37a)). Each life is absolutely valuable: to consider the masses of human population is not to discover something of greater value or an overarching entity in which the individual existence is subsumed. The human population is a conglomeration of ones, an aggregation but not an integration. Nothing has greater value than a human individual because he or she is a 'perfect' embodiment of the human whole.

'No cry of torment can be greater than the cry of one person', supposes Ludwig Wittgenstein (1980: 45) for philosophy. For the novel, Graham Greene writes similarly: 'Suffering is not increased by numbers: one body can contain all the suffering the world can feel' (Greene 1979: 183). And not only suffering: the same may be said for happiness or a sense of beauty or fulfilment. These are qualities that pertain to, inhere and remain in, the individual body; there is nowhere but bodies that these qualities – the *qualia* or experience of life – *can* inhere. Hence, to claim that adding bodies in a social field causes suffering or happiness to be taken to another level is a category mistake: suffering or happiness cannot belong to a multiplicity, a society, community, culture or tradition. Individual experience represents a kind of absolute, entire in itself, whose nature does not lend itself to mathematical aggrandizement. 'Humanity' appears before us always and only as '*a* man', F.R. Leavis concurs: 'Only in living individuals is life there, and individual lives cannot be aggregated or equated or dealt with quantitatively in any way' (Leavis 1972: 53). The difficulty of such truths for a human science and a human society – apprehending subjectivity in objective terms, making policy for individual well-being in universal terms – gives on to the anthropological work of this book.

The argument to be made is that the only fundamentally real relationship is between individual and species. Differences of cultural convention and classification, and of social structuration and affiliation – differences of community membership, of nation, ethnicity, class and religion – are epiphenomenal, symbolic and rhetorical constructions as distinct from ontologies. The individual body, its species-wide capabilities and liabilities, provides both a beginning and an end both for a human science and a liberal society: What might the individual body be able to achieve, and what is it liable to suffer from (cf. Rapport 2003: 215–39)?

A 'cosmopolitan body' is that which practises a particular, localized life – including joining, making and leaving local relations and communities – and yet which continually embodies global entitlements and continues to be recognized as bearing universal capacities. The cosmopolitan project is to provide space for the flourishing of individual-human capabilities and to offer succour for its potential liabilities.

Cosmopolitanism and Liberalism

I deem cosmopolitanism to be a species of liberal virtue. 'The defining feature of a liberal', according to Brian Barry, is 'someone who holds that there are certain rights against oppression, exploitation and injury to which every single human being is entitled to lay claim; and that appeals to "cultural diversity" and pluralism under no circumstances trump the value of basic liberal rights' (Barry 2001: 132–33).

The defining features of cosmopolitanism as a political and philosophical programme, meanwhile, are amply set out by Martha Nussbaum:

> Whatever else we are bound by and pursue, we should recognize, at whatever personal or social cost, that each human being is human and

counts as the moral equal of every other ... The accident of being born a Sri Lankan, or a Jew, or a female, or an African-American, or a poor person, is just that – an accident of birth. It is not and should not be taken as a determinant of moral worth. Human personhood, by which I mean the possession of practical reason and other basic moral capacities, is the source of our moral worth, and this worth is equal ... Make liberty of choice the benchmark of any just constitutional order, and refuse to compromise this principle in favour of any particular tradition or religion. (Nussbaum 1996: 133, 136)

Nussbaum's conclusion coincides with Barry's: cosmopolitanism recognizes 'every single human being' as an instantiation of 'human personhood', an embodiment of human capacities, such as reason, and entitled to human respect. Cosmopolitanism regards the freedom of Anyone to choose a form of life and to form a world-view in accordance with his or her own lights as 'the benchmark of any just constitutional order'. It comes down to a question of the relationship between culture or community or tradition, and freedom.

Category-thinking and Politeness

In his study of the language of the Third Reich, written as a journal following his expulsion from the position of university philologist, Victor Klemperer noted the Nazi predilection for stereotypical labels, categories and classes. This language functioned, Klemperer observed on 12 December 1940, to 'strip everyone of their individuality, to paralyse them as personalities, to make them into unthinking and docile cattle in a herd driven and hounded in a particular direction, to turn them into atoms in a huge rolling block of stone'; '"the Jew", "the Englishman" – nothing but collectives, no individual counts' (Klemperer 2000: 21).

Symbolic collectivization – or as one might phrase it, the predominance of thinking and acting in categorial terms – is a deindividuating and hence dehumanizing practice with potentially tragic effects. At the conclusion of what he subtitled an 'alternative anthropology of identity', Anthony Cohen wrote how 'we must make deliberate efforts to acknowledge the subtleties, inflections and varieties of individual consciousness which are concealed by the categorical masks which we have invented so adeptly' or else we 'deny people the right to be themselves' (Cohen 1994: 180). Lisette Josephides concurs: beyond 'persons', those entities denominated from outside in terms of culturally ascribed characteristics, are the 'selves' that universally human beings know themselves to be (Josephides 2008: 23). The way selves

practise a physical and spiritual individuality is the existential testimony anthropology should provide.

Cohen's and Josephides' remarks are aimed at the social analyst but
they apply on a number of levels, including that of politician, policy
maker and fellow-citizen. Categorial masking includes the state's
formal incorporation of its citizens as well as those citizens' mundane
dealings with one another. The language of the Third Reich was not
an isolated incident, merely an extreme one. Reducing individual
identities to 'camp dust' also characterizes Stalinism and radical
Islamism at one pole to communitarianism and 'identity politics' at
the other (Amit and Rapport 2002).

If cosmopolitanism is a philosophy of freedom, then this entails
working towards the delegitimatization of category-thinking so
that the individuality of Anyone is never legitimately confounded
by classificatory, collective identifications or stereotypes. Public
identities and affiliations are to be treated as achievements not
ascriptions, seen to be voluntary and situational, and not to equate
to – or subsume, or exhaust – the identity of the individual as
such. No categorial placement is absolute, and rights inhere in the
individual, in Anyone, not in any particular affiliation: one cherishes
the human capacity to create and to go on creating self, society and
world – creating 'essence' out of 'existence', as Jean-Paul Sartre
(1956) phrased it – and not any particular manifestation of that
capacity.

But how does one go about construing social and cultural
exchange beyond the categorial? For Georg Simmel (1971), famously,
society is only possible by way of typical judgements and collectivistic
cultural forms. One cannot know a multitude of individuals in and as
themselves and therefore one relies on formalism and standardization
and the expectability these bring. In public life it is unavoidable that
the particularity of individual consciousness will be represented
(and misrepresented) by way of general categories and classes, of
persons, relations, situations and events. In this judgement, Simmel
looked back to Hegelian conclusions concerning the agonistic nature
of the human condition; in particular, concerning the strictures of
statecraft and the necessary distance between a normative, 'Prussian'
public sphere and a private home of personal exceptionalism (Hegel
2008). The conclusion also looks forward to what anthropologists
have described since as the 'indifference' of modern 'rational' society:
the ways in which bureaucratic structures, whether of large-scale
governance or merely of impersonal, non-partisan incorporation,
manifest themselves inevitably in a reliance upon the stereotypical and
classificatory which is indiscriminate, alienating and even inhumane
(Herzfeld 1993; Gupta 1995). Seeking an end to category-thinking,

cosmopolitanism must nevertheless come to terms with the need for a public discursive style, of address and exchange.

In Ronald Stade's formulation, the project is to presuppose the individuality of interacting citizens but not to presume an intimacy with them (Stade 2007). One can anticipate fellow citizens' individual natures but not expect to know their private selves – to read-off private truths from public expressions. This is a balancing act. As a philosophy of freedom, cosmopolitanism seeks to dwell in the tension between a public respect for the individual and a public ignorance of what is individual. The aspiration is to a means and a mode of social interaction which does not massify or stereotype the members of a polity, such that they are overwritten and overwhelmed by a collective category, but enter into public space as themselves – at least, as they would have themselves be known and met. The public space is not privy to the intimacies of personal selfhood: one does not presume that the radical particularities of personal selfhood – the 'gratuitousness' of difference (Rapport 2008) – should or could easily translate into a common code of expression. Rather, one imagines the individual being known, ideally, as he or she determines to be known. To return to Cohen's imagery, the individual in public space is known according to a mask that he or she fashions for themselves. The significant contrast, again, is achievement as against ascription.

'Politesse' is the term I employ to describe kinds of cosmopolitan 'good manners', comprising both a polite style of general public exchange and an ethic of individual dignity and freedom. In a lecture he delivered in 1885, Henri Bergson considered the possibility of traversing an 'evolutionary' path from politeness as mere formality to politeness as moral instrument. Can a set of rules and of civil exchanges – of mere etiquette – possibly serve as a guarantee for civilized dealings in a society? On the face of it: no. Politeness of manners or 'social politeness', as Bergson (1972) termed it, comprising ready-made formulae, catchwords, formal graces and habits, are not the same as what might be described as 'politeness of spirit': the empathy and sympathy involved in taking on another's point of view and imagining that unique life. Nor, finally, is such politeness the same as 'politeness of heart': the expectation that another is worthy of trust and will likely reciprocate one's own trusting engagement. The point for Bergson, however, was that the three politenesses, while analytically distinct, were mutually implicated in practice due to the continuity or flow that characterizes human experience. To practise a formal, social politeness was to become imbued over time with a politeness of spirit which gave rise to a politeness of heart. It was possible for civilitude to emerge from etiquette, and for a civil attitude to realize a commitment to human dignity.

Bergson's journey around 'social', 'spiritual' and 'hearty' politenesses comprises a set of zigzags between the universal and the particular. Social politeness and politeness of heart envisage the universal: the grace with which one greets and trusts a fellow interactant as Anyone. In between the social and hearty, a politeness of spirit is disposed towards recognizing the qualities and quiddities of particular others. The point is that the journey from universal ('social') via particular ('spiritual') to universal ('hearty') effects a dialectic which brings the universal and particular into relationship while retaining the integrity of each polar position. It is a balancing act effected by an a priori recognition: here is the universally human, and here is the individual particular; both are centres of value, ends in themselves.

Cosmopolitan politesse I would see as that act of zigzagging between difference which does not compromise difference but yet accommodates difference (cf. Rapport 1992). It will be elaborated upon in the book as a supple and subtle social practice which opposes category-thinking in universally affording Anyone a rightful public space while recognizing the particularity of Anyone's intrinsic difference.

Dead Dogma?

Politesse is a work, of imagination and transcendence: effort is always demanded if civility is not to descend to empty gesture and mere politeness. A more general warning against habituality comes from John Stuart Mill: 'However true an opinion may be, if it is not fully, frequently and fearlessly discussed, it will be held as dead dogma, not a living truth' (Mill 1963: 159). Truth itself can become old-fashioned and moribund – unfashionable – simply by becoming customary.

It might be questioned whether a project of humanist universalism is, in its entirety, not already dead dogma. However ambitious, necessary and new I would describe the cosmopolitan project of anthropology, I am also aware that harking back to a Western Enlightenment can be interpreted as anachronistic. This is the conclusion reached, for instance, by Alain Finkielkraut (1994) in his reflections on the question of Jewish identity in contemporary France and how the Jewish case serves as a kind of archetype. 'Be a Jew on the inside, in private, and a man towards the outside world', was the advice of the eighteenth-century Enlightenment philosopher Moses Mendelssohn to his diasporic fellows, on the eve of the French Revolution that for the first time would emancipate Jews en masse and grant them citizenship. Such a project of assimilation – and politesse – can now be seen to have failed, according to Finkielkraut. Called into serious question by the Dreyfus Affair in 1894, it was absolutely sundered by the Holocaust. The major trauma of these events, Finkielkraut (1994: 70) argues, was that the Judaeophobia was directed – not, as with the centuries of pogrom, against the ghetto and *stetl* – but against the assimilated: the Jew whose power was demonstrated by his invisibility, his proclivity to pass. 'It is impossible to exaggerate the formidable stature of the Jew as enemy', Adolf Hitler proclaimed, for this enemy is the man without qualities: at once Jew and invisible, traitorous and conspiratorial, plotting the worldwide heartless empire of capitalism.

In short, Auschwitz makes Enlightenment notions of progress and humanism appear absurd, irredeemably futile. Why assimilate to a liberal Europe if it is only to end your life as a 'free man' in a sealed-off train? And still, even at this distance from 1789, France has not begun to become cosmopolitan: to eschew the vain classificatory work that discriminates – joins and excludes – on the basis of nationality, locality, gender, age, class, lifestyle and language. Furthermore, if the Holocaust gave the lie to Jewish power and connectedness – 'Unique in 1940-1945 was the abandonment' (Emmanuel Levinas, cited in Finkielkraut 1994: 49) – then anti-Semitism has not been long in renaming itself, as anti-Zionism. The state of Israel, a dwarfish territory, is now the purported home of global power brokers, central to a colossal clandestine organization in imperialism and neo-colonialism. It is not coincidental that Theodor Herzl's idea of Zionism was born at the Dreyfus trial, Finkielkraut concludes: reason would never defeat anti-Semitism, Herzl feared, assimilation would always fail, and separation was the only solution.

Hence, Finkielkraut (1994: 82) reaches his own complex position. One must proclaim 'I am a Jew' so as to 'de-alienate' oneself from 'servitude' to the imposed categories and roles ('man', 'citizen', 'Frenchman', 'cosmopolitan') of all 'foreign powers'. In part this entails identification with Israel, vouchsafing its rights and security, since to identify with Israel is to transcend the discourse of the anti-Semite of all vintages: Israel becomes an 'inner kingdom' for the diasporic Jew, a source of a normalcy, a moral ease, a transcending of the haunting terror not to stand out, and a pride.

Ironically, however, Israel also becomes a source of anxiety. The state whose *raison d'être* was as eternal refuge for the Wandering Jew finds itself in the 'fundamental affective state [of being at] risk of death' (Finkielkraut 1994: 129), while the Diaspora, at least in the West, enjoys a relative peace of mind. And the irony is instructive, Finkielkraut finds. One proclaims 'I am a Jew' as part of a process of celebrating ethnicity as an intrinsically plural and non-essentialist phenomenon in a global public arena. One proclaims 'I am a Jew' and thereby lays claim to an equivocal label – at once diasporic and national – a label existing beyond the limits of category. One supports Israel, on the 'front line', embodiment of a millenarian Jewish destiny and a liberating vengeance, but one also distributes the 'weight' of Jewishness and affirms millennia of diasporic practice and civilization in which 'Jew' has meant more than simply one kind of citizenship among many. 'I am a Jew' bespeaks a precious and hard-earned refusal of definition.

Finkielkraut's discourse has a wider resonance: it pertains not only to 'the Jewish question' but to the place of 'culture' in a contemporary world of identity politics. If humanist universalism is a conceptualization and a project irrevocably tainted – not only by anti-Semitism or anti-Zionism but also by the histories of Western imperialism and colonialism, slavery and indentured labour, capitalist exploitation and underdevelopment – then a redemption (expiation and remission, reparation and empowerment) is to be found in a rediscovery and celebratory embrace of essential cultural differences. 'Whose "cosmos", and which "cosmopolitics"?', trumpets Bruno Latour: it is surely 'impossible for us now to inherit the beautiful idea of cosmopolitanism since what we lack is just what our prestigious ancestors possessed: a cosmos' (Latour 2004: 453). Recognition of and respect for cultural 'otherness' must now repudiate all claims to 'mononaturism': to there being one nature, one world and one humanity whose truths reason and science disclose. The 'awesome multiplicity' of the different perspectives revealed through ethnography mean that it is the very make-up of the cosmos that is at stake; there is no common world except one that is painstakingly negotiated and 'composed'. Global commonality might be an ideal project in peaceableness but it must be undertaken by a 'pluriverse' of earthly 'entities' who are at present 'owned' and inhabited by a 'freight of gods, attachments, and unruly cosmos [that] make it hard to get through the door into any common space' (Latour 2004: 454–57). One must admit the common constructed or 'cultured' nature of the diversity of worlds of the earth's entities before negotiations towards substantive commonalities can begin. Failing this, the 'fundamentalism' of scientific 'naturalizers' who appeal to an unconstructed 'Nature Out There' and that of radical Islam appealing to the revelation of the Koran and Sharia will war without end (Latour 2004: 459–60).

I find this line of argument to be invalid and unacceptable (cf. Wardle 2010). Rather than hoping to move from knowledge to morality ('Given the nature of life on earth this is how we should behave'), Latour's culturalist or perspectivist logic appears to endorse a reverse kind of causation ('Given the historico-political situation this is how we might know one another'); indeed, it collapses the distinction between knowledge and ethics. But the fact that all human knowledge is 'constructed' – in the sense of being made out, found out, using particular methods at particular times and places, by virtue of particular traditions of fabrication and production – does not mean that all such knowledge possesses the same factuality. The status of scientific facts is not the same as religious facts, for instance. The latter might fall into a category that Latour terms 'constructivist' – 'dependent on series of [human] mediations', '[apt to] fail and thus requiring careful maintenance and constant repair' (Latour 2004: 458–59) – but the world to which science provides insight has no need of our cultural 'life-support systems' and their histories. We can know it, we can adapt ourselves to it, we can even know how to adapt it to our desires, partially, but there is no way in which universal realities might 'fail' in the way that cultural paradigms of knowing might fail. Our 'construction' of knowledge gives onto different kinds of facts, in short; some are aesthetic in character, matters of taste, and some are empirical in character, matters of rational discernment. And while 'culture' might be a name we wish to give to a sum of aesthetic judgements, 'nature' is a domain of universal truths.

The distinction between natural and cultural worlds is therefore fundamental, and vital to retain, as is a conceptualization that 'science' is not equivalent to 'religion', or 'rationality' to 'taste'. It is in this way that one can hope for a progression in human knowledge, an improvement. As the aesthetic is distinguished from the empirical, so opinion ('We believe the world is flat') grades into fact ('We know the world is round'), and the particularity of specific historico-cultural world-views gives way to an overarching accumulation of universalizable insights one might know as 'civilized' (Rapport 2011).

I do not accept, then, that cosmopolitanism, as a project of humanist universalism, a species of liberal virtue concerning the global freedom of Anyone, is anachronistic or moribund. The point of Mill's warning is that a philosophy must be 'fully, frequently and fearlessly discussed' *because* it the truth. It might not do to 'defeat the anti-liberals by repeating the good old tunes', Keith Hart summarizes, but a valid project remains: to renew the classical liberal Enlightenment by presenting its philosophy in fresh language, as 'an inclusive invitation to contemporary debate' (Hart, personal communication 2009). It might not do 'innocently' to appeal to an Old World of Enlightenment and transcendental certainties, Natan Sznaider (2010) admits, since recent 'memory cultures' (including colonialism as well as the Holocaust) are so strong. But it must nevertheless be possible to imagine cosmopolitanism migrating from the domain of abstract philosophy so as to engage people in their everyday lives by inviting them to see its universal insights and values in the contexts of their personal constructions of identity.

Nor do I trust the discourse of ethnicity and multiculturalism – however much the likes of Alain Finkielkraut are assured that notions of essentialism and homogeneity can be exploded and eschewed. The fiction of culture, once written into systems of classification and habitual practice, however strategically, is a difficult discourse to transcend. Culture is a rhetoric of constructed collective sameness and difference which, however satisfying aesthetically and sentimentally, threatens to obscure the realities of individuality and humanity. The world of culture must be inhabited ironically if it is not to deliver 'grotesque' performances of discrimination and confinement (Kateb 1984: 351; Amit and Rapport 2002: 92–101). I conclude that the prevalence of category-thinking in contemporary 'identity politics' makes the issue of universalism all the more vital. Enlightenment advances in scientific rationality and social emancipation are so precious a legacy that a cosmopolitan project of anthropology is never untimely.

'We are all human', Ernest Gellner exhorted not long before his death: 'Don't take more specific classifications seriously' (Gellner 1993b: 3). The cosmopolitan project of anthropology provides a view beyond such classifications. Emancipating the individual and the human from symbols and structures that collectivize, homogenize and totalize, a cosmopolitan anthropology gives on to a science and a morality of Anyone.

Envoi

The book is divided into three main parts, each conceived of in terms of a key question. Part 1, 'Cosmopolitanism and Cosmopolis: Definitions and Issues', treats the question: What are the meanings of cosmopolitanism, past, present and future? Beginning with a historical overview of founding moments, I trace cosmopolitanism to a variety of contemporary voices and conceptualizations: as a kind of morality and also a normative programme, as a social condition, an orientation to the world and a kind of agency. Anthropological commentary has often remained sceptical, however. At best it would prescribe multiple cosmopolitanisms: the plurality of ways in which dialogue has been invited with worlds beyond particular cultural and communitarian boundaries. My intention in Part 1 is to show that such scepticism is misplaced. There is a viable cosmopolitan project for anthropology which involves carrying forward a Classical and Enlightenment tradition of thought. Not only should a cosmopolitan project be described as viable in theory, it warrants, too, serious attention as a practical alternative to varieties of communitarianism such as nationalism and multiculturalism.

Part 2 of the book, '"My name is Rickey Hirsch": A Life in Six Acts, with Marginalia and a Coda', treats the question: Is Anyone a feature of everyday social life and exchange, a real presence? I offer an ethnographic account of the life of one Rickey Hirsch, narrated in his own words, the intention being to evidence the individual consciousness that universally exists amid symbols and structures that might deal in essentialist classes and labels: the reductive machinations of category-thinking. Rickey, I say, personifies Anyone. While the particular substance of his life is his and his alone, the capacities he brings to bear as he inhabits social spaces and cultural symbologies instantiate human universals. Here is Anyone existing behind the role player, passing into, through and between communities, relationships, systems of classification and moments of interaction. In the testimony of Rickey Hirsch I wish to make Anyone visible as a concrete figure and not an abstraction: a real and constant presence.

In Part 3, 'Anyone in Science and Society: Evidencing and Engaging', the question becomes: How is the individuality of Anyone to be accommodated by an objective science and acknowledged by a democratic society? The issue is one of evidencing the personal in systematic terms and of engaging with the unique within a civil ethos that is universalist. The three sections comprising this part of the book have different emphases. The first uses historical case studies (in particular insights drawn from the works and lives of Kierkegaard and Nietzsche) in order to develop the notion of 'personal truth' and to explore how a science might treat this as evidence. The second section considers those models which are used, both in scientific hypotheses and in social policies, as prospective estimations of the human beings who will be engaged. Inevitably there is distortion between what is anticipated and the specificity of what is actually met: the radical particularity or 'gratuitousness' of Anyone. Interrogating those ways in which human beings are both the same and different I explore possible images (including the work of Stanley Spencer) of more ethical generalizing. The third section reflects on those norms of interaction which make for 'polite' or civil society. There are mannerly ways in which others are addressed that manifest and effect a recognition and an inclusion. If cosmopolitanism would recognize Anyone anywhere and everywhere, and include him or her as an equal member of a global liberal society, then interactional conventions must be in place of a special character. They would assure the individual of a space, by rights, but at the same time not classify that individual arbitrarily nor presume to know the particular qualities of their life. I compare interactional routines in different ethnographic settings and consider the ways and extents to which a kind of 'cosmopolitan politesse' might be legislated for.

In setting out to address the above issues I imagine this book as complementing and extending previous publications such as the articles 'An Outline for Cosmopolitan Study, for Reclaiming the Human through Introspection' (Rapport 2007), 'Apprehending *Anyone*: The Non-Indexical, Post-Cultural and Cosmopolitan Human Actor' (Rapport 2010a), and 'The Liberal Treatment of Difference: An Untimely Meditation on Culture and Civilization' (Rapport 2011; also see Rapport 2002, 2006c, 2009a, 2010b, 2012a; Rapport and Stade 2007; Rapport and Wardle 2010). I deem the project of cosmopolitanism to be speculative as well as empirical. A 'speculative philosophy', Mill wrote in connexion with nineteenth-century political liberalism, is in reality not remote from the 'business of life' given how the 'interests of men' manifest themselves (Mill 1950: 39). I certainly have an 'interest' in cosmopolitanism: my engagement is personal as well as professional. In the integrity that I find cosmopolitanism grants to the individual human being universally, and the dignity granted to the single human life, I find a personal vision of fulfilment: cosmopolitanism offers a global liberal emancipation. An Afterword to the book reflects on my interestedness, querying the elective affinity of 'Jewish cosmopolitanism'.

PART 1

What are the meanings of cosmopolitanism, past, present and future?

COSMOPOLITANISM AND COSMOPOLIS: DEFINITIONS AND ISSUES

'Cosmopolitanism', it has been noted, has gained wide currency in recent years.

For Seyla Benhabib it is a 'key word' of our time (Benhabib 2006: 17), once more a basis of debate in social science and social policy as well as philosophy and the humanities. 'Once more' because the term has a long and specific history – a long and painful history, in Ulrich Beck's (2006: 2–3) description, recalling its recent discrediting under Nazism and Stalinism. And yet, cosmopolitanism remains an unexhausted tradition, relatively untapped: cosmopolitanism retains the promise of encouraging a 'thinking of the unthinkable' (R. Werbner 2008: 194), of a humanity without frontiers. There is a protean quality to the term 'cosmopolitan', Ulf Hannerz (2006: 5) suggests. Its appeal is that it exists beyond any precise or consistent usage.

Certainly it is the case that while 'cosmopolitanism' comes down to us with a specific conceptual history, with meanings and inferences that are definitive, arguments in favour of a variety of cosmopolitanisms and critical of a definition dependent on Western philosophical and Enlightenment roots have come to be widely, and fashionably, made. Nonetheless, we should beware a promiscuous usage, as Pnina Werbner (2008a: 60) puts it: cosmopolitanism is not everything that is no longer purely local or parochial. It would be my view that the term's long-established, 'Western' significance should be preserved for current usage, and that there is no value in extending or transforming the definition of cosmopolitanism or inventing sub-types and versions. One states clearly that here is 'cosmopolitanism' and there 'multiculturalism' and 'pluralism', here is cosmopolitanism and there 'ecumenism', 'hybridity', 'creolization', 'transculturation', 'transnationalism', 'diaspora', 'globalization'. One may even say that here is cosmopolitanism and there is 'liberalism'.

The purpose of this part of the book is first to review the history of cosmopolitanism, including current writings and debates, and then to offer a prospectus concerning a possible future cosmopolitanism and its relation to anthropology.

A HISTORY AND OVERVIEW

Founding Moments

The term 'cosmopolitan' derives from a bringing together of two Greek words: *cosmos*, meaning the whole world or globe or universe, and *polites*, meaning a member of a local polity or society or community (a *polis*). A 'cosmopolitan' is someone whose perspective is global: he or she is a 'world citizen', belonging to the human world entire.

While a coming together of these two words, 'cosmopolitan' remains a site of tension: *cosmos* is dialectically related to *polites* and *polis*; global and local are brought together while insisting that one aspect cannot be conceived of except in relation to the other. One cannot comprehend a human condition except that local lives are regarded as versions of universal potentials, and give onto the possibility of global futures. One cannot be a world citizen except that one inhabits an individual consciousness which belongs both to localized settings and to global possibilities. Locality and globality, individual human being and humankind, are mutually constitutive and mutually implicated.

The term comes down to us from Greek because of its initial usage in Classical Greek philosophy. Diogenes claimed for himself the title of *Kosmou polites* (world citizen): he and his fellow so-called Cynics in the fourth century BC conceived of the paradoxical formulation of 'cosmopolitan' as a critique of the *polites*: the ones who were mired in the arbitrary customs and traditions of a *polis*. To be 'civilized', according to the Cynics, was to see beyond local community and place: Diogenes refused to be defined by his local origins and group memberships. The Cynics were, however, social outsiders, marginals in the Greek status hierarchy (Stade 2006). Their ideas foundered until the Stoics took them up a century later. Zeno and his fellows also described themselves as cosmopolitans and claimed that they were first and foremost human beings, living in a world of human beings, and only incidentally members of local polities. We inhabit at once two worlds, Stoic discourse promulgated: a local one assigned us at birth, and another global one, a human community deriving from, and guaranteed by, what is fundamental to all in the species: the equal worth of reason and humanity in every person. All 'wise men' should recognize that humanity constituted a single moral community, a 'city of the world' which was not spatially delimited or anchored; for all human individuals embodied the same 'sacred' or 'divine' spark, instantiated in their capacity for *logos* (reason).

More than simply recognizing human singularity, the Stoics urged an expansion in the practice of the circle of social inclusion so that it ultimately reached from the single individual to humanity as a whole: local laws, councils, currencies and temples would disappear in favour of a universal dispensation of reason, ideals, aspirations and argument. One should perhaps conceive of affiliations as a series of concentric circles: from self, leading through family and community, to species, the microcosm to the macrocosm. The aim, however, was always to 'draw the circles somehow towards the centre' (Hierocles): to live as an individual human being with an awareness of, and a rightful belonging to, the macrocosm.

Similar to the Cynics, however, Stoic philosophy occupied a marginal place in the Greek pantheon of metaphysical nostra; Stoical exponents were often *metics* (Semites or resident foreigners) rather than ethnic Greeks, and their credo – reason and the appreciation of humanity – offered what was felt to be a lonesome self-disciplined vision, and a remove from the rousing props of habit and locale. Homeric notions of primordial Greekness were brought to bear to paint Stoical philosophy as 'heartless' because it would transcend the 'timeless' law and tradition of the clan.

Resonances of Stoic ideas did nevertheless reappear among Roman statesmen and philosophers. Cicero's legal injunctions, in the second century BC, had a cosmopolitan logic: all human beings were subject to 'a single law of nature'. This translated into a necessary equality under the law in any local community (irrespective of wealth or learning), and also, ideally, into the universal recognition that they were thereby 'bound not to harm anyone'. There is one 'truly great and truly common' universal human society to which universally we should see ourselves as belonging, Seneca contended in the first century AD. Here, Plutarch concurred, 'we should regard all human beings as our fellow citizens and neighbours'.

These are somewhat isolated sentiments, notwithstanding, and it is not until the European Enlightenment of the eighteenth century that one finds a concerted effort to re-engage with Classical Greek cosmopolitan notions. Influenced by the rise of modern science and by the aftermath of the long religious conflict that followed the Reformation, Enlightenment thinkers combined a reappropriation of cosmopolitanism with a commitment to secularism and a confidence in human rationality – in the capacity of the individual to examine, discover and understand – as affording a basis for changing beneficially every area of human planetary life.

Foremost among these Enlightenment voices was that of Immanuel Kant (1724–1804) in his works 'Idea for a Universal History from a Cosmopolitan Point of View' (1784), 'On the Common Saying "This May Be True in Theory but it Does Not Apply in Practice"' (1793), 'Towards Perpetual Peace: A Philosophical Sketch' (1795/6), 'International Right' (1797) and 'Anthropology from a Pragmatic Point of View' (1798). Kant's ideas developed over the span of these writings, and not always in a coherent fashion; there is a wavering of emphasis, for instance, between internationalism and supra-nationalism (cf. Ree 1998). Nevertheless, these writings (see Kant 1991, 1996) came to represent the single most important source of nineteenth- and twentieth-century theories of civil society and normative globalism.

Kant begins by identifying three kinds of right: 'republican right' entails domestic laws within a state; 'international right' entails treaties between nations; and 'cosmopolitan right' entails the relations of persons anywhere – 'global citizens' – to one another and to states. Cosmopolitan rights were held by individuals by virtue of their humanity not their community memberships, and were to be regarded as superior to those pertaining to states; cosmopolitan right overrode claims of national sovereignty and could bend the will of communities since these latter were intrinsically sentimental manifestations: particularistic, arbitrary and non-rational.

Kant exemplified cosmopolitan right in terms of hospitality. An individual had the right to present himself or herself before others without harm, both within and across different communities, and to be heard. Whether a local or a stranger, the individual had the right not to be treated with hostility even though he or she placed himself or herself in the home space of another with a view to local interaction (such as commerce). Two duties attached to this right: not to harm the guest, and not to exploit the host. In our own terms, Kant can be seen to foreshadow a critique of identity politics: interaction not separation or the preservation of cultural integrity is the norm to be enshrined as a right, and visiting is not to be hedged about with restrictions or quarantine. The logic of Kant's argument derived from the limited space of the globe. We must accommodate one another, put up with being near one another, because as a species we possess in common the surface of the globe – and no other. All human individuals were attached equally to the globe. One was a world citizen, member of the Commonwealth of Nature, and entitled to enter into dialogue with any human others in an open and uncoerced fashion.

Kant envisaged a world where all of humanity would be participants in a global legal order of civil coexistence. 'Cosmopolitan right' here came to sit alongside 'cosmopolitan law' in a 'cosmopolitan order'. The arbitrarily defined local society or polis gave way to a global polis or 'cosmopolis': a world state or federation, with universal law and rational governance. Its practices would be 'enlightened', eschewing dogma and unvindicated authority. Predominant would be the public use of reason to generate critical vantage points from which to scrutinize and improve civil relations. Even the status of states would depend on their behaviour in terms of common human values and democratic and legal principles. The so-called 'Westphalian' political ordering, where states were sovereign over their territories and people, and engaged only in voluntary relations with one another on an ideal basis of equal might, gave way to a notion of liberal internationalism. Here, cosmopolitan law guaranteed the rights of every individual human being whether or not these individuals and these rights were originally or traditionally respected by their 'own' communities.

The cosmopolitan order provided a matrix within which all the potential capacities of humanity for creative expression might find fulfilment. The global society of equal citizens would represent a 'kingdom of ends' whose fundamental principle could be enunciated thus: 'Always behave so as to treat with equal respect the dignity of reason and of moral judgement in every human being'.

Kant's writings were coeval with the rise of nationalism in Europe, and were intended as a critique and antidote: insisting on the universal over the particular, the human as against the local community, the individual as end not means. The term 'cosmopolite' had already figured in the 1577 treatise by the English polymath John Dee, *General and Rare Memorials Pertaining to the Perfect Art of Navigation*. Here, a cosmopolite was: 'a Citizen, and Member, of the whole and only one Mystical City Universal' (cited in Knapp 1994: 102). Then, a 1738 French dictionary has 'a cosmopolite' as 'a person who moves comfortably in diversity: comfortable in situations which have no links or parallels to what is familiar' (cited in Sennett 2000: 42). In Kant's time, however, 'cosmopolite' would come to be contrasted, often unfavourably, with 'patriot', and 'the old home feeling' (Thomas Carlyle). Esteeming the cosmopolitan, for Kant, however, was not a matter of abstracting human beings from history and society but of recognizing the human capacity, disposition indeed, to transcend present and past in reaching for forms of life better informed by current scientific knowledge and the better accommodating of individual needs and desires. Focus was on the future and the potential for human betterment and individual fulfilment. In this regard it was not true, claimed Kant, that every existing tradition, culture, nation or society was equally deserving of respect: some were better placed to deliver the 'kingdom of ends', while some were more expressive of human sentimentalism, arbitrariness, cruelty and caprice than others.

Kant's faith in the possibility of a cosmopolitan order derived from his estimation of the human capacity for reason: a means for humanity to come to an enlightened appreciation of itself and its world. Reason was a universal capability, something inhering in the inner life of every human individual. Reason was the highest and most independent human faculty. It freed human beings both from instinct and from cultural traditions and social structures, and allowed for ends and laws which transcended the particularity of their origins. Moreover, human beings were equally rational, equally capable of directing their lives through reasonable principles, and this commanded respect. One respected the intrinsic potential for reason which all humans possessed, even if sickness, slavery or oppressive circumstance limited their practice of it in regard to their own lives. One hoped, nevertheless, for situations where individuals should fully exercise their capacities and realize the deliverances of reason. It was on the basis of reasonable action that the dignity of human beings was most and best espied: the dignity of human beings as absolute and incomparable worth as ends in themselves.

It was also the case, however, that dignity consisted largely in autonomy: each person determining for themselves versions of the good and the right. But then, since cosmopolitanism recognized the individual to be always an instantiation of the human species whole, in individuals acting as free agents Kant saw a human destiny as being ultimately fulfilled: the victory of reason in history. Human history was a natural process – 'Natural History' – and the end was the complete development of human faculties and dispositions, of which rationality was the highest.

Progress could be slow and painful, notwithstanding, and it was made not by violent revolution but via the spirit of enlightenment. 'Enlightenment' was that stage – an adolescence – when humanity broke free from nature and tradition alike and used reason to deliver law. 'Critique' was another name Kant gave to this turning point; and 'autonomy' a third. One adjudicated legitimate from illegitimate cognitive claims and critiqued those, such as religious superstitions, that based themselves on sentiment or sloth. One bound oneself, as rational beings, only by laws which reason had delivered.

Reason would cause a progress towards the 'end' of human history, Kant contended: a perfect civil union, an ideal community of mutuality, an organic whole. This would represent a universal cosmopolitan existence in which the capacities of the human race were fully developed and expressed. The foundation of this civil society would be justice and not loyalty – and the difference was absolute. Justice sprang from reason while loyalty was an expression of sentiment. Use of reason enabled humanity to conceptualize and impose universalizable and unconditional moral obligations. Loyalty was particularistic and ensured affectional relations and community attachments; loyalty dwelled in arbitrary differentiations (status, class, religiosity, geography). The indiscriminate commands of justice ought to give rise to a liberal politics that was 'blind' to arbitrary and accidental distinction (skin colour, gender, place and situation of birth) and see only the organic human beneath.

Clearly, cosmopolitanism was an idealistic project for Kant. He had written an outline, an intellectual ethic, but it was open-ended and it would be improved upon by its readers in historical course. He was confident, however, that knowledge and morality could alike be formulated beyond the polis or state, beyond tradition and sentiment, on a global human scale, by individual human beings, so as to give rise to a real political enterprise. Was not international trade a form of sociability between states? Was not the stranger in the midst, the alien, the trader and refugee, evidence of the universal capacity for hospitality and guesthood, for existing beyond the ontological security of the given? To guarantee peace, however, and to secure the cosmopolitan right of individuals to venture out as strangers and sojourn hospitably in other territories, one needed a 'league of peace': a constitutional universalism alongside localism. One needed universal procedures by which the rule of law could be seen to operate equally everywhere. What was called for was a world federation of states whose constitution transcended ethnic and racial values. This was the balance that might deliver universalism without despotism.

Kant's writings represent the clearest formulation of a cosmopolitan vision since the Cynics and Stoics, and the foundation of later elaborations. He aimed to outline binding principles of collective international engagement which might give onto a *ius cosmopoliticum*: all humanity recognized as a single, universal political community, based on universal human rights, and recognizing the universal state of the human that is embodied in each human individual. Kant saw his audience as humanity in general; he took pains to avoid Eurocentrism, and to distinguish between global rights to travel, interact and trade, and colonialism (cf. Wood 1998). And yet one finds a ready dismissal in contemporary communitarian and relativistic contexts of Kantian nostra; 'few are now convinced of a rational-universalist grounding' to cosmopolitanism, according to one commentator (Cheah 1998: 291). It is time to ask what the 'cosmopolitan' signifies now.

Contemporary Voices and Issues

Some have asserted that, far from being a known entity with a clear genealogy, cosmopolitanism, as a practice and a concept alike, is fuzzy or fluffy. It is an undelineated project which must ever remain thus: too positive and definite a specification would itself be 'uncosmopolitan' (Breckenridge et al. 2002: 1; Parry 2008: 327). There is, nevertheless, a burgeoning literature on things cosmopolitan: 'cosmopolitanism is back' (Harvey 2000: 529). There may not be agreement on the precise meaning of the term, its provenance, value and implications – there remains disagreement on how present-day 'cosmopolitanism' ought to position itself vis-à-vis Classical Greek philosophy and the European Enlightenment – yet contemporary phenomena such as globalization, transnationalism, multiculturalism, religious fundamentalism and pan-nationalism have provided a context for renewed cosmopolitan concern: a testing ground for an old ideal (Bauböck 2002: 111).

One might characterize contemporary literature on cosmopolitanism as an exploration of five key claims:

i)   Cosmopolitanism is a specific kind of morality;
ii) Cosmopolitanism is a specific kind of normative programme;
iii) Cosmopolitanism is a specific kind of social condition;
iv) Cosmopolitanism is a specific kind of attitude or orientation;
v)   The cosmopolitan is a specific kind of actor.

Let me elaborate on each of these in turn, surveying the literature by way of the voices of some of the main protagonists.

Cosmopolitanism is a Specific Kind of Morality

'Contemporary cosmopolitanism ... is a moral stance consisting of three elements: individualism, equality and universality. Its unit of value is individual human beings; it does not recognize any categories of people as having more or less moral weight; and it includes all human beings.'

—Brian Barry (1999)

'Cosmopolitanism is a moral perspective. The cosmopolitan standpoint is impartial, universal, individualist, and egalitarian, [and] individuals are the basic units of moral concern.'

—Charles Jones (2001)

'A cosmopolitan point of view [is one] that considers all human beings as individuals equally entitled to certain rights.' A cosmopolitan point of view imagines a moral conversation which potentially includes all of humanity: anyone whom my actions potentially affect and whose interests the consequences of my actions can impact upon is a potential moral conversational partner of mine, and I have a moral obligation to justify my actions to this individual through reason. We are now all potential participants in a global conversation, all moral agents to each other.

—Seyla Benhabib (2006)

As a kind of morality, clear links can be traced between contemporary assertions of cosmopolitanism and an Enlightenment heritage. Here is the Kantian project of creating a worldwide community of humanity which is committed to common moral values and opposes a communitarianism which would ground moral principles and attachments in specific groups and contexts. Cosmopolitanism entails a human respect, and duties to all human beings irrespective of origin. It negates any priority of compatriots or co-religionists, and refuses to place love of country (or ethnicity, race, class, gender and so on) ahead of love of humankind. A universalist devotion to the interests of humanity as a whole is born of the desire to emancipate oneself from narrowly local concerns, from unconsidered sentimental attachments, reserving allegiance to the worldwide community of humankind. One holds in abeyance – at an ironic distance – the hegemonic and totalizing claims of one's own religion, culture and community.

Cosmopolitanism as a moral focus owes much, too, to the major latter-day liberal text by John Rawls, *A Theory of Justice*, when he writes how 'each person possesses an inviolability founded on justice that even the welfare of society as a whole cannot override' (Rawls 1971: 3). But there can be a tension here, still, between philosophical and anthropological writers: for the latter, while cosmopolitanism is grounded in ideas of tolerance, inclusiveness, hospitality, personal autonomy and emancipation (P. Werbner 2008a: 17), a distantiation from local and national prejudices, what often comes to be the specific focus of tolerance are the different life-ways in which individuals are seen to be embedded, and an even-handed refusal to rank them or subsume them within a universal matrix (Parry 2008: 327–29).

Cosmopolitanism is a Specific Kind of Normative Programme

'[The cosmopolitan ideal entails] a world in which some fundamental principles of justice govern relations between all persons in all places.' The normative requirement is that commitment to these principles at a domestic level should be extended, to generate principles of cosmopolitan scope: a global justice.

—Catriona McKinnon (2006)

'Cosmopolitanism is concerned to disclose the ethical, cultural and legal basis of political order in a world where political communities and states matter, but not only and exclusively ... [A relevant cosmopolitanism must] build an ethically sound and politically robust conception of the proper basis of political community, and of the relations among communities.' The four first cosmopolitan principles can be summed up in the following normative statements. One: The world comprises of individual human beings deemed to be free, dignified and equal beings. Since the ultimate units of moral concern are individual human beings not states, humankind becomes one normative realm in which each individual is accorded equal respect and consideration, placing limits on the moral validity of certain cultural communities. Two: To accept the above as a universal is to recognize an individual human agency which compasses self-consciousness, self-determination and reason. Such agency is not merely the expression of a particular tradition or teleology; it must be afforded the capability of acting so as to shape the forms of community to which it voluntarily affiliates itself. Three: Individual human beings have different skills and competencies and accomplishments, and they will make different choices. These achieved differences, derivatives of individual agency, must be distinguished from unacceptable structures of ascribed difference. Four: For individuals to pursue ends of voluntary achievement a non-coercive political process is called for.

—David Held (2006)

As a kind of normative programme, cosmopolitanism envisages the universal application of human reason for the establishment of political institutions (legislative, jurisdictional, executive) with global normative reach, towards the end of universal justice, equality, freedom and peace. And it is also practical: how to create wider unity – the norms of a world order, even government – when faced with social and cultural diversity. Its most striking effect to date is international human rights legislation, which has been successfully applied so as to trump the international law of sovereign states, to liberate tyrannized individuals and to bring tyrants to book. Human rights legislation treats individuals as the universal bearers of rights not collectivities ('the people'; 'the state'), and irrespective of individuals' nationality, religion, gender, class or ethnicity. Also, human rights legislation treats individuals as universally responsible: since the Nuremberg trials, charges of 'crimes against humanity' can be levelled against individuals even should their behaviours have been legitimate in the states or regimens whose rules they were following.

Notwithstanding, the normative-cosmopolitan vision can be 'weak' or 'strong' (Brock and Brighouse 2006: 3). Should all society-wide principles of distributive justice automatically become global principles – so that our fellow nationals will have no special claims on us, and no right to use nationality as a moral trigger – or only some extra-national obligations come to carry moral weight? Furthermore, in effecting the normative project of building transnational and supra-national institutions which can supervene states, should structuration follow the model of the Kantian confederation or the super-state? More broadly, how should a global civil society that deals effectively with global debt, environmentalism, peace, women's enfranchisement or crime be modelled? On contemporary non-governmental global social movements? On inter-statal leagues such as the UN, EU and NATO; on the supra-statal; or even on the infra-statal (the world-city as a node in a global network, as well as regional centres of gravity, that supervene erstwhile state boundaries)?

Cosmopolitanism is a Specific Kind of Social Condition

'The human condition has itself become cosmopolitan ... Cosmopolitanism has ceased to be merely a controversial rational idea; in however distorted a form, it has left the realm of philosophical castles in the air and has entered reality. Indeed, it has become the defining feature of a new era, the era of reflexive modernity, in which national borders and differences are dissolving and must be renegotiated in accordance with the logic of a "politics of politics".' The era of the nation-state instituted a monologic imaginary of demarcation and exclusion, but the cosmopolitan condition initiates a dialogic imaginary: seductive insularity is replaced by global openness. Under the condition, the national internalizes the global. 'Cosmopolitanization' represents a change in the conditions of social and political life within nation-states: it is 'internal globalization'.

—Ulrich Beck (2006)

It has come to be commonly claimed that the human condition can now only be understood 'glocally': the global and local are not social or cultural polarities but mutually implicating and combined principles (Robertson 1995: 25–44). When cosmopolitanism is considered as a kind of social condition, it is intimated that social structures have themselves now become cosmopolitan. One refers not simply to cultural admixture, ethnic pluralism, political multiculturalism, an experiencing of global risk, terror and protest, large-scale migrations, cheap travel, global fashions, digital communications, catholic tastes and so on, but also to the way in which this has translated into a global public: a demos without borders. Now social relations within so-called bounded territories such as states are transformed, willy-nilly. Cosmopolitanism is globalization internal to the polis such that local life, social relations, identities and consciousness are inextricably implicated in and dependent on those elsewhere. 'The people' can now only refer to the human whole.

Cosmopolitanism is a Specific Kind of Attitude or Orientation

'Cosmopolitanism is a perspective, a state of mind, or – to take a more processual view – a mode of managing meaning ... The perspective of the cosmopolitan must entail relationships to a plurality of cultures, [calling for] first of all an orientation, a willingness to engage with the Other.' Cosmopolitanism is the competency to recontexualize oneself and one's sociability in different contexts. It entails a kind of reflexivity and an expansionist orientation towards cultural knowledge: one wants more and of more than one kind.

—Ulf Hannerz (1990)

'Cosmopolitanism is about reaching out across cultural differences through dialogue, aesthetic enjoyment, and respect; of living together with difference.' Cosmopolitanism is something that emerges from cross-cultural debate: a dialogical, collective creation grounded in a sensibility of hospitality and openness to difference.

—Pnina Werbner (2008a)

'["Cosmopolitanism"] refers to the idea of being part of a broad social project that exists outside the confines of kinship, ethnicity or nationality ... "Cosmopolitanism" envelops a consciousness of human diversity. It refers to a sense of living beyond the mundane collective boundaries of everyday life and is suggestive of a trans-communal society. In this society, people are conscious of the differences between themselves and cognisant of other patterns of obligations from which they may well be excluded.'

—Edward Simpson and Kai Kresse (2007)

'Let us define cosmopolitanism as an ethos of macro-interdependencies, with an acute consciousness (often forced upon people) of the inescapabilities and particularities of places, characters, historical trajectories and fates.' The ethos of cosmopolitanism is highly attentive to and respectful of difference but also wary of the tendency for differences to become essentialized.

—Paul Rabinow (1986)

As a kind of attitude or orientation, cosmopolitanism implies an openness to the world. One anticipates a 'cosmopolitan outlook' which queries boundaries within the global whole. But what does one do with the differences of which one becomes aware and of which one's cosmopolitan disposition and competencies allow one to appreciate and translate? There seems to be a range of expectations. For Hannerz the cosmopolitan orientation leads to an internalizing of the difference within the self. Such mingling of erstwhile separate identities overcomes boundaries between cultures as distinct entities. Either/or, friend/foe, compatriot/foreigner differentiations become old hat in a globalizing of emotion (Beck 2006: 4; Waldron 2006:

83); the cosmopolitan attitude is unbounded, unobstructed and unlocated, celebrating travel and the fluidity and evanescence of culture per se. For Rabinow, Simpson and Kresse, the cosmopolitan attitude accompanies an awareness of a global, interdependent, trans-communal society. Here, the seeming '"naturalness" of ethnic absolutisms' (whether of tribe, nation, or minority community) may be undermined, albeit not by non-location so much as multiple and complex relocations and reattachments (Clifford 1998: 365–69). One tries to live one's particularity without making it ineluctable, and to recognize the universal without making any one version of it compulsory (Pollock 2002: 48). But then again, for Werbner, one is still caught between own and other, home and away. Cosmopolitanism is an ongoing living with radical difference. One is orientated towards dialogue and one continues to negotiate over the disagreements that emerge; but even while 'thinking and acting beyond the local' (Breckenridge et al. 2002: 10–11; Narayan 2007: 62) and seeing the smaller place at the same time as the larger, one does not see cultural and communitarian differences being overcome.

The Cosmopolitan is a Specific Kind of Actor

'Cosmopolitanism signifies hybridity, fluidity and recognizing the fractured and internally riven nature of human selves and citizens whose complex aspirations cannot be circumscribed by national fantasies and primordial communities.'

—Jeremy Waldron (2006)

'Cosmopolitanism often has a narcissistic streak; the self is constructed in the space where cultures mirror one another'. The cosmopolitan constructs 'his own unique personal perspective out of an idiosyncratic collection of experiences'; or else he accepts otherness as 'a package deal'. Either way, he asserts personal autonomy with regard to culture: that in which he originated and those he samples. He never surrenders completely to any one, never swears absolute allegiance to any one, always knows where the exit is. The cosmopolitan prides himself on 'heterophilia': the aesthetic and intellectual competency to enter into and to participate in different (particular) forms of life; he aspires to contrasts not uniformity, and he disparages the tourist who merely spectates and does not experience divergent Otherness. Cultural competency affords a sense of mastery and expansion, controlling more of the world: 'he possesses it, it does not possess him'.

—Ulf Hannerz (1990)

As a kind of actor, the cosmopolitan is known by his or her multiplicity: simultaneously a member of different communities, standing beyond any singular locus (of birth, land, upbringing or conversion) and mediating traditions and loyalties. The cosmopolitan's production and consumption, sense of self, memory, pleasures, anxieties and wealth can no longer be tied to one social or physical locale: certainly, cosmopolitan experiential space no longer coincides with national space (Beck 2002: 29–30). And this applies to an increasing number of people: more people in the world today are more travelled, more catholic in their tastes, more inclusive in their cuisines, more attentive to global media and news, more influenced by global trends (Wilson 1998: 351). Even where social worlds are restrictive spaces, where ethnic and other absolutism claims a naturalness to closed notions of categorial collective identity, still we find individuals active in self-fashioning (Robinson 2007: 14). 'We are all cosmopolitans', Rabinow (1986: 258) concludes.

However, a range of opinions exist in the literature concerning the nature of the cosmopolitan's intentionality. The range extends from the description of him or her as liberally exercising lifestyle choices to warnings that the 'choices' of migration and strangerhood are not mere adventures in liberal self-invention and benign in neither cause nor effect. Is it that: 'The cosmopolitan feels the anguish of shaping a life and social relations under conditions of cultural extinction and threat'? Or is it that: 'The cosmopolitan is fated to experience a clash of cultures and rationalities and to compare, critique and combine contradictory certainties'? Or that: 'The cosmopolitan exercises innate competencies in border-crossing, translation and hybridity'? Or even that: 'The cosmopolite knows himself or herself to be a world citizen who shows tolerance towards those persecuted, wherever they might be, and takes responsibility for them'?

Anthropological Critiques

Given the above range of positions in the contemporary literature concerning the claims that can be made in the name of cosmopolitanism, is there what might be termed a standard *anthropological* perspective?

Ancient 'Homerian' prejudices against cosmopolitanism (deemed 'heartless' for its aspiration to transcend the law of the clan) correspond quite closely to later interventions on behalf of *la patrie*. Eighteenth- and nineteenth-century critique, such as that of Johann Herder and Joseph de Maistre, reacted against Kant's extolling of a humanistic holism by claiming that there was no such thing to know as 'Man' or humankind: only Germans and Frenchmen and Persians, and so on, in their ideal cultural-territorial primordialism (Maistre 1797: 102). For Georg Hegel, the cosmopolitan was an exile from the 'family of nations', that natural, human place in the world embodying an unconscious, organic and singular totality with a place; eschewing local contingencies and relativities and aspiring to global truths amounted to an alienation from self and from humanity: from love, trust, family and community, the natural and necessary environmental dwelling (cf. Steiner 1997a: 304–24).

Despite Kant's hopes for the discipline of anthropology – despite social science as such being born in the context of what Bryan Turner (1990: 344) has described as the 'universalistic' revolutionary movements of the late eighteenth century – the social sciences came to be instituted within nineteenth-century regimes of education and social policy which were nationalistic in ethos and intent on invigorating particular national traditions. While, according to George Stocking (1992: 347), a tension continued to exist in anthropology between an interest in 'anthropos' as against 'ethnos', it was the case that a study of particular groups of people – tribes, villages, communities, societies, ethnicities and nationalities – came to predominate in anthropology over a focus on global processes, a single and universal human condition, or the individual as a manifestation of a human nature (Rapport 2010c). Despite its abstracting and generalizing terminology, as Turner (1990: 343) concludes, the social sciences developed to explain and analyse, to sanction and delimit, local (at most national) not global destinies: local disciplines in the service of the nation-state.

'The *raison d'être*' of Durkheim's social-scientific project, for instance, can be seen as 'the welding of France into a well organized and well integrated nation' in patriotic response to the crisis of the Franco–Prussian war, German nationalism and then the devastation of morale following the First World War (Turner 1990: 347). French nationalism, rituals and symbols would provide a modern version of the traditional *conscience collective*: an integrative system replacing Christianity in providing significant moral bonds and curbing utilitarian individualism, hedonistic materialism and anomie. Likewise for Max Weber: German social science should serve a German-national purpose and commit to nationalist objectives, such as the development of a strong German state. Polish guestworkers in the 1890s could be seen as a threat to German cultural integrity, then, while the First World War had been 'great and wonderful' for its effect on German national life (Turner 1990: 354).

If these are partial assessments of founding figures, it would still be true to say that what many take to be the appropriate anthropological perspective on cosmopolitanism is coloured by a continuing privileging of local collectives and a suspicion concerning that which would claim to transcend the communitarian. Anthropologists have not been cosmopolitans, the philosopher Kwame Anthony Appiah (2007: 14) writes, because they spurn universalist discourses: their disciplinary signature is a fieldwork and ethnography whose end is comprehending 'native' difference. Cosmopolitanism can seem to be embedded in European notions of world consciousness which are those of an elite, remote from anthropology's subjects and not to be artificially imposed on them. There has been in anthropology a felt need to re-anchor talk of human rights and world citizenship to the real politics of countries and communities and the concerns of their local members. Anthropology theorizes global politics from the perspective of the post-colony (cf. P. Werbner 2008a: 1). More precisely, the anthropological critique of cosmopolitanism can be said to develop along two main avenues, epistemological and real-political, which I describe in turn.

Epistemological Critique of Cosmopolitanism

Following Foucault, explains Joel Kahn (2003: 404), we know that the category of 'the human' is a construct, not independent of cultural symbologies. We can further see Kantian constructions of 'humanity' to be exclusionary of those who do not demonstrate a particular version of mature reason. Women, the working European masses and non-Europeans are all variously disparaged or excluded from elitist Eurocentric notions of 'reason'. Likewise for the 'human being'. The Kantian (and Cartesian) slogan was *Sapere aude*: 'Have the courage to use your intelligence instead of blindly following traditional authority'. But the so-called enlightened individual who transcends the boundaries of socialization and tradition and gazes as if from nowhere is impossible – albeit that this figure plays an inextricable role in European modernity from the eighteenth century on. The universalist vision, reach and aspiration have been sham universalisms: a mask for white male privilege.

Maila Stivens (2008: 88–89) elaborates: Kant's privileging of the mobile individual cosmopolitan, with the ability to travel and live anywhere, is inexorably masculinist. Where is the female, contextualized in the domestic and vernacular? Singular personhood may be the fetishized icon of liberal individualism but feminist scholarship has identified the systemic nature of culture and social solidarity as something other than the mere coincidence of individual wills. Indeed, many of the key terms of cosmopolitan discourse – 'universal', 'theoretical', 'abstract', 'conceptual' – are implicitly masculine, eliciting properties of mastery, distance from experience, indifference to specifics and fixation on absolutes in human life. Stivens's preferred terminology to 'cosmopolitan', after Nira Yuval-

Davis, is 'transversal': here is a taking into account of interactants' different sociocultural and historical positionings so that one aspires to move towards a mutuality of acceptable agendas but without effacing one another's inevitably positioned identities.

No universalizing project can ever be culture-free, Kahn (2008: 271) concurs. Projects emerge in history and are applied by grounded cultures. Classical cosmopolitanism claimed to be 'open to the other' but its aim was a universalizing transformation of difference such that cultural specificity might be transcended in favour of a deculturalized, secular public and polity. But this is merely the imposition of one cultural construction: all universalizing humanism fails to apprehend the impossibility of culturally neutral practices, institutions and values.

Real-political Critique of Cosmopolitanism

Any cosmopolitan project must in practice be autocratic, hegemonic and violent, for cosmopolitanism is an outgrowth and ideological reflection of global capitalism, which remains its enabling condition, according to Danilo Zolo (1997: 40; cf. Hall 2008: 346). Cosmopolitanism is the latest phase of capitalist modernity, operating on a global scale; here is a new term to disguise an old form of Western engagement with 'the rest'. Overtly critical of the nation-state and nationalism, of the Westphalian dispensation concerning statal sovereignty, cosmopolitanism is yet tied to it: one of two poles in dialectical relationship which emerged together in the context of the capitalist world system. Cosmopolitanism is but another face of a universalizing hegemony whose ethos is neo-imperialist: bringing enlightenment to natives through colonialism. Its opposition to so-called provincialism is a refusal to countenance local sovereignty and rooted, radical otherness.

Cosmopolitanism makes him uneasy, Stuart Hall (2008: 349) elaborates, because, underpinned by Enlightenment conceptions of reason, it has never really understood or accepted difference and treated the alien simply as 'the childhood of Mankind' (John Locke). It is an ethnocentric conception, partisan and self-serving.

Richard Fardon (2008: 253–54) expresses similar anxieties concerning who is purportedly addressed by advocates of cosmopolitanism when they insist that cultures are not essences, that individuals' affiliations are plural and complex, that personal responsibilities do not end at national borders, and so on. In wanting to make the globe a 'better place', the great danger is the production of a Manichean world in which the other is excluded or disparaged as 'uncivilized' and 'uncivil'. But these are the cultural traditionalists or else aspiring modernists whom anthropologists are most likely to meet on the ground. However unimpeachable in principle may be the philosophical argument against cultural relativism, the latter might still be necessary in practice as an enabling rhetoric. Political exigency and the social logics of action may call for strategies of identity politics and strategic essentialism.

Cosmopolitanism is an elite concern, in short, of those with the security and wherewithal to pursue a refined global consumption, including a commodified ethnicity (Hage 1998: 212). For 99 per cent of 'world peoples' and 'world communities', cosmopolitanism threatens a deterioration in their welfare: deracination, depaysment and cultural detachment are less called for than 'durable cultural industries centred in their own life-worlds' and supported by international law (Legros 2008: 506–7). These peoples have nothing to learn from the West in regard to moral programmes, Scott Malcolmson (1998: 241) concludes. One can show a so-called 'cosmopolitan' concern for all humanity without ignoring difference or instituting a secular jihad which is Eurocentric, rationalist and parliamentarian. More than 1.3 billion people now live in extreme need, while the gap widens between rich and poor. Individualistic notions of identity, human belonging and human rights do not sufficiently address the questions of social justice and institutionalized exclusion which this situation represents (Bok 1996: 41).

Cosmopolitanisms

A point of overlap in the above epistemological and real-political critiques, as Malcolmson has observed, is the assertion that 'cosmopolitan' values and orientations characterize other cultural traditions in their own right. There is more than one way of being and doing the cosmopolitan, and non-anthropological literatures on cosmopolitanism have not taken sufficient account of this.

This is the explicit intent of Arjun Appadurai's statement that contemporary 'cosmopolitan' experiences do not necessarily derive from Western models or authority (cited in Robbins 1998: 1), and also James Clifford's claim that there are 'plural discrepant cosmopolitanisms' (Clifford 1998: 363–65). Cosmopolitanism can be loosed from Eurocentric and universalist moorings to become a travelling signifier, in the company of other partial equivalents such as 'exile', 'immigration', 'diaspora', 'pilgrimage' and 'tourism'.

One might nevertheless ask what the point might be of loosing 'cosmopolitanism' from a European, Enlightenment heritage? What is left of the term and the concept if stripped of this history and inheritance and taken to be synonymous with 'pilgrimage' or 'tourism', or even an anodyne 'respect for cultural difference'? But for a number of anthropological commentators, the concept is sufficiently powerful and prevalent to make such a translation worthwhile. Or perhaps the very point is to defuse the concept by making it so commonplace. Cosmopolitanism is not so different even to nationalism, then, Bruce Robbins (1998: 2–3) can conclude, because it, too, is shaped by particular collectivities, and is socially and geographically situated in its conceptual usage.

In short, anthropologists have anticipated, described and welcomed various versions and provenances of cosmopolitanism: 'weak' and 'strong', undeveloped and unprivileged, as pertaining to imagination and experience, to detachment and reattachment. This diversity of cosmopolitanisms will, as with any cultural discourse and trait, be likely formulated dialectically in relation to others within the class: one cosmopolitanism (one culture, one nation) is but a mirror of what it is not. Amid this diversity is also to be found a way for the Left to counter capitalist globalism, as Robbins (1998: 12–13) phrases it: a 'cosmopolitan' version of the global might recognize rooted belongings while still yet genuinely striving for common norms and mutual translatability.

The anthropological practice of field research is often to meet cosmopolitanism of a 'popular' kind as part and parcel of everyday local life, Kahn (2003: 409–11) explains. Albeit that it is permeated by time, place and culture, here is genuine 'cosmopolitan praxis': an attempt to mediate grounded and particularistic prejudices via universalizing aspirations; and here, too, is 'cosmopolitan knowledge': that which emerges out of encounters between representatives of different cultures. In her edited volume, *Anthropology and the New Cosmopolitanism*, Pnina Werbner (2008b) offers a compendium of studies in which anthropologists discover indigenous cosmopolitanisms. Indeed, indigenous activism is itself a form of 'cosmopolitics', according to Dorothy Hodgson (2008: 215), since it is located both within and outwith the nation-state. Or again, Melanesia is home to a 'defensive, cultural cosmopolitanism', Eric Hirsch (2008: 210) explains, where emphasis on difference coexists with its opposite, the surmounting of difference, in a process that continually creates the grounds for new distinctivenesses. There is stay-at-home cosmopolitanism in Cape Town, meanwhile, where African urbanites wait for the world to come to them while accepting that, universally, they are their brother's keeper (Sichone 2008: 310–12). All these examples evidence a 'cosmopolitan transcending of boundaries' (Colson 2008: 34).

Pnina Werbner's own contributions exemplify and justify this pluralizing ethos towards cosmopolitanism*s*. She begins by asserting that a differentiation which Ulf Hannerz would urge between true 'cosmopolitans' and mere 'transnationals' does not bear analytical scrutiny, and hides a class bias (P. Werbner 2008a: 18). That only cosmopolitans celebrate a hybrid in-betweenness (while transnationals put up with it until they can escape it) was an elitist construction which obscured the stratificatory dimensions to identity: where essentialism and ghettoization occurred, as for the urban poor, it was a matter of political economy not an orientation to difference and movement. Notwithstanding, working-class migrants could still 'open up to the world' in a cosmopolitan way. Take the example, Werbner (2008a: 19–29) suggests, of Pakistanis in the United Kingdom. By moving brides, food, jewels, clothes and cosmetics along global pathways, Pakistani migrants are successful in making their home places 'travel' the world, reconstituting moral, ethnic and social spaces ubiquitously. These unskilled and semi-skilled labourers learn foreign languages and also how to manipulate their foreign bosses. Should the women not learn English – remaining surrounded by kin, and engaging in rounds of Muslim rituals – then, still, the clothes they wore represented gifts from relations far away (thereby brought closer), and they acquired the cosmopolitan knowledge of how to browse in British department stores, becoming expert in British commercial material culture. Marriage in Britain between Pakistani Muslims of different castes and classes also represented a kind of cosmopolitanism; likewise, there was the cosmopolitanism of middle-class Muslims of different nationalities intermarrying – hybridizing a shared set of moral and cultural assumptions. In short, for Werbner, cosmopolitanism – which might be defined as rootedness plus openness to cultural difference – is something that arises plurally and vernacularly. Cosmopolitanism is always historically and spatially positioned, and politically contested, but it is not an exclusively Western idea or value. In our 'late modernity' one finds many different local cosmopolitan practices, each with its own distinctive world-view.

Hence, working-class cosmopolitanism need not result in the same modalities as middle-class cosmopolitanism. As well, one finds 'proletarian cosmopolitanism': the transcending of divisions of ethnicity, caste and nation by workers intent on uniting with trade unionists internationally. And one finds 'local-activist cosmopolitanism' that which would remake local, postcolonial worlds by engaging with post-liberal ideas and global rights-based movements (indigenous, multicultural and feminist). And one meets 'Marxist cosmopolites', who seek a brotherhood of workers, alongside 'gentlemanly cosmopolites' who oppose vulgar nationalism, alongside 'liberal cosmopolites' who intend universal moral standards, alongside 'Islamist cosmopolites' who would export a global *ummah*, alongside 'cosmopolitan patriots' who are rooted to a home culture but also take pleasure in others. And one may anticipate ever more versions: further 'critical', 'comparative', 'national', 'postcolonial', 'situated' and 'actually existing' cosmopolitanisms.

In short: anthropological engagement with 'cosmopolitanism' has often entailed a critical, indigenizing or localizing of the concept such that it becomes detached from a Western heritage and Enlightenment provenance deemed insufficiently sensitive to its own cultural biases, and also to radical difference, to history, to the masses, to realpolitik and to the social logics of community solidarity (Hollinger 2000: 228). Due to a discomfort with the concept and an abiding disquiet over the name, 'cosmopolitanism' comes to be multiplied and imaginatively reapplied, rendered vernacular, mundane, even banal (Vertovec and Cohen 2000: 4–16). Eschewing a 'cosmopolitanism from above' (Hall 2008: 346), an elite conception consequent upon pathways of global corporate power and circuits of global investment, one recognizes 'cosmopolitanism from below': people led through different indigenous practice similarly to come to terms with global otherness.

There is another possible version of 'writing the cosmopolitan', however, which returns in part to the ways in which Kant introduced 'cosmopolitanism' and 'anthropology' into modern intellectual parlance as a corresponding pairing. Anthropology was to 'write the human' in order to furnish a global knowledge; cosmopolitanism was the scientific and moral programme which deployed that knowledge in the securing of universal betterment for humanity, both in its collective (that is species-wide) manifestation and in its local (that is individual) manifestation. On this view, attempts to reconstitute cosmopolitanism and extend the term's provenance are misguided. Its meaning is both precise and ethical. Nor is there any guilt or shame that necessarily attaches to such a conception, albeit that its provenance is Western and 'enlightened'. The Enlightenment prescribed a rational freedom from the merely customary and traditional, from revelational and other sources of knowledge that did not bear critical scrutiny; it also prescribed a liberal freedom from social structuration and classification that ascribed individuals fixed, unequal and impersonal names and positions in closed communities. Here is cosmopolitanism as an asseveration of human identity and dignity and of individual integrity and liberty.

The cosmopolitan project of anthropology is empirically and objectively to elucidate the nature of human capacity, the workings of individual consciousness, creativity and accomplishment; morally to clarify the conditions whereby individuals may live out their potential for experience and expression to the fullest; and aesthetically to promote an appreciation of the dignity of human identity and individual integrity. It is a fact that human beings are everywhere capacitated to make sense of the world, to form world-views, in their own individual way; it is an aspiration that human beings everywhere should be afforded the space and the opportunity to fulfil this potential for sense-making, to live out the capacity to formulate individual life-projects. One imagines the individual human being looking out on the world *from anywhere*, rationally capacitated and legally sanctioned to view his or her life in the context of human life, indeed planetary life, as a whole. Also, from anywhere, here is the individual human being looked upon as a thing-in-itself, an instantiation of the whole class of humankind.

A COSMOPOLITAN PROJECT FOR ANTHROPOLOGY

'Valid knowledge ignores and does not engender frontiers', wrote Ernest Gellner (1995a: 8): 'One simply cannot understand our shared social condition unless one starts from the indisputable fact that genuine knowledge of nature is possible and has occurred, and has totally transformed the terms of reference in which human societies operate'. The modern scientific revolution that occurred in western Europe – consequent upon its Renaissance and Enlightenment – gave rise to a cognitive and technological superiority vis-à-vis the rest of the world. Scientific knowledge may remain provisional but the criteria of its rational method abide, and provide a distinctive perspective on the world and a distinctive power. Liberalism, individualism, open and civil society have been its social accompaniments. The moral issue now concerns how globally to share 'the fruit of our liberation from want and tyranny' (Gellner 1995a: 8): how to secure liberty and rationality globally, on surer foundations than capitalist consumerism, while anticipating a diversity of values and traditions that include the illiberal, intolerant and totalitarian (Gellner 1995b: 29). This work Gellner defined as 'the anthropological predicament'.

Gellner's stance on the particularities of this historical trajectory was, according to Chris Hann (2008: 73–74), to become something of an embarrassment to anthropologists who sought to come to terms with the politics of the post-colony. But I see nothing embarrassing here if it is historically accurate. The scientific truths concerning human singularity and individual identity, the potential for human control and improvement of the human condition, carry their own weight, one with which 'post-colonial sensibilities' must needs come to terms. The Gellnerian catchphrase, 'social tolerance always: intellectual tolerance never', anticipates the overturning of prejudices: not all cultural constructions are deserving of respect; customary practice is as likely to be despotic and straitening as liberating, if not more so. And yet. In a world of unequal power relations, even idealistic intervention in others' affairs runs the risk of being construed as Western hegemonic expansion (Beck 2006: 154). If an emancipatory cosmopolitanism risks being constructed as imperialistic, then what do the social logics of action call for here? How does one argue the cosmopolitan world-view in this context?

I have described as misguided attempts from within anthropology to deny a particular provenance for cosmopolitanism; and yet I have also outlined five distinct ways in which the cosmopolitan conception has come down to us from classical philosophy: cosmopolitanism as morality, as normative programme, as social condition, as attitude and as kind of actor. It is necessary to specify precisely what a cosmopolitan anthropology should entail.

What Cosmopolitanism Is and What It Is Not

Multiculturalism, Utilitarianism, Globalization, Pluralism

The keynotes of classical liberalism as a political philosophy are individualism, egalitarianism, universalism and meliorism (all human institutions and arrangements are correctable and improvable). Liberalism asserts the right of individuals to be the authors of their own identities, values and affiliations insofar as the expression or realization of these latter do not infringe upon the rights of other individuals; all in the polity are members equally, and no special rights are given on the basis of either ascriptive characteristics (gender, race, intelligence, strength) or achieved (religiosity, ethnicity, occupation, pastime). 'Cosmopolitanism' I would define as the assertion of a liberal ethic on a global scale: promoting the rights of individuals in any social, cultural and geographical locale. Citizenship in Western liberal democracies has been described as the equivalent of feudal privilege: an inherited status that greatly enhances an individual's life chances (Joseph Carens, cited in Jones 2001: 2). Cosmopolitanism embraces the ethical standpoint underlying modern liberal political theory but anticipates global justice: that every human being, irrespective of nationality and citizenship will have his or her vital interests equally met or protected (Jones 2001: 16–17).

Liberalism can be said to pass into cosmopolitanism as a modern political philosophy following the Nuremberg trials at the close of Second World War, and the United Nations Declaration of Human Rights in 1948. This was the point, according to Benhabib (2006: 15–16), when the evolution of civil society was characterized by the transition from international to cosmopolitan norms of justice: rights now accrue to individuals as moral and legal persons. Cosmopolitan norms endowed individuals not states or communities with rights and claims. Human rights law could henceforth bind and bend the will of sovereign nations, and dispense both with the extending and the withholding of rights on particularistic grounds (no special pleading on behalf of faith; no unequal treatment of women). According to liberalism in its universalist cosmopolitan colours – its 'revitalization' (Calhoun 2000: 93) – everyone you know or can affect by your actions is someone to whom you have responsibilities (Appiah 2007: xiii). One 'recognises humanity wherever it occurs, and gives its fundamental ingredients, reason and moral capacity, [one's] first allegiance and respect' (Nussbaum 1996: 7); all human beings have entitlements and therefore all have duties to provide them in a mutual dependency (Nussbaum 2006: 211).

Cosmopolitanism is not *multiculturalism*, then. Multiculturalism is based on the notion of homogeneous collectivities, clearly demarcated from one another and binding on their members: a collectivist or holist orthodoxy in which the individual is dependent on and reflective of his or her cultural home, the epiphenomenal product of its language, traditions, conventions and environment. Multiculturalism tends to reproduce rigid notions of culture and group belonging as zero sum, either/or and essentialist (e.g., Tully 1995). It envisages cross-cultural communication, interaction, toleration and respect on the foundation of supposed cultural homelands, conceived of as closed, sacrosanct, self-sufficient unities of language, land and heritage. Whether in bounded geographical spaces or in inner-city suburbs, these places are seen to house shared traditional cosmologies, normative certainties and hierarchies which are deserving of respect due to their very distinctiveness and claims to longevity. Multiculturalism, in Mario Vargas Llosa's critical summary (cited in Beck 2002: 35), wants 'dog, cat and mouse to eat from the same plate', as if human cultures represented sub-species of humankind. By contrast, 'cosmopolitanism *presupposes* individualization' (Beck 2006: 37, 67): it breaks open the 'social predetermination of the individual' and overcomes the ontological and epistemological pretensions of communities and groups and their discourses of identity.

Two moves characterize the distinctiveness of cosmopolitanism vis-à-vis multiculturalism. First, is the detachment the individual practises from his or her native and natal *polis*, from the traditions and conventions of family, community and nation. Second is the attachment the individual recognizes to *cosmos*: to humanity as it presents itself to him or her in the ubiquitous figure of Anyone. As Martha Nussbaum (1996: 7) expresses it, to be cosmopolitan is to be at once in a kind of exile from the comfort of custom and merely local truths, and also to see one's actions and choices of life-way from the perspective of universal possibilities, of justice and the right. One is loyal to no one section of humanity – a nation, a class, a religion, a *Volk* – but to all: it is to the moral community made up by the humanity of all human beings that one bears responsibility.

What is the basis of this universal human community? How does one recognize Anyone as an exemplar of humankind – as oneself – and why? We have heard Nussbaum talk of discovering in Anyone humanity's 'fundamental ingredients, reason and moral capacity'. Kwame Anthony Appiah (2007: xix–xx) emphasizes the act of meeting per se, and what this implies. There is a ubiquity to our encountering fellow human beings in interaction. We converse and trade, love and fight; it is very difficult to avoid our fellow human beings. Very often these encounters are habitual and conventional. They are the regular interactions with kin and neighbours and workmates, or else they take the routine form of their kinds: with strangers who are also 'bus-drivers' or 'students'. But the broader truth of our human encounters is that we make some kind of sense of and with our fellow human beings, stranger or otherwise. Our everyday habitual interactions and our 'strange' ones work alike because we recognize the signs of a commensurate human consciousness (Rapport 2007). We recognize a kind of human coexistence in space: the mutual interference that Anyone can cause and can experience from others. Nussbaum develops this into a kind of moral fellowship, a kind of natural human ecology reminiscent of the philosophy of Emanuel Levinas. She draws on the 'natural law' tradition of the seventeenth-century Dutch humanist, Hugo Grotius, to argue that human beings gravitate towards living together: there is, in Karl Marx's words, a 'rich human need' to live cooperatively with others (cited in Nussbaum 2006: 210). In short, we recognize our fellow human beings because we are predisposed to. Our everyday encounters and local communities are narrow versions of universal human necessities: there is no escape from our mutual human influencing and we desire such meeting.

'Natural law' is the thesis that binding moral laws and normative constraints naturally regulate the world of human affairs – given the characteristics of the species – even though these might not be written into a system of 'positive law' within particular states. The natural law tradition contrasts with the contractarian thinking of the likes of Thomas Hobbes and the assumption that beyond explicit human law there lay only a 'state of nature' of all against all. In opposing the latter tradition, Nussbaum is led to assert, too, that cosmopolitanism is not *utilitarianism*. Utilitarianism, the political philosophy that states one must pursue policies, laws and institutions that satisfy most people – 'the greatest happiness for the greatest number' – may share basic grounds with cosmopolitanism, as Brian Barry (1999: 36) argues, such as a recognition that every human being counts as one in any democratic calculation, and no more or less. However, for Nussbaum, cosmopolitan justice differs from contractarian notions of individuals coming together to cooperate on the basis of mutual advantage insofar as it begins from the dialectical assumption that individual and human whole are already and always mutually implicated in one another. The human instantiates itself as Anyone; Anyone is inexorably a member of the species and not someone party to a war of all against all. One recognizes Anyone because one is already and always his or her fellow in a human community, a species community. Moreover, one maintains a recognition of Anyone as absolutely himself or herself and does not massify him or her in calculations of benefit: in policies directed at 'more or less' human advantage. The purpose and aim of human encounters are seen as the protection of the one, of Anyone; he or she is approached as a fellow human being in a spirit of species-wide community rather than self-interest or profit.

The implications of this lead to a further distinction: cosmopolitanism is not *globalization*. Insofar as globalization has come to mean economic globalism and the 'neo-liberal' deregulation of global markets, cosmopolitanism entails a very different ethos. Again, in Nussbaum's (2006: 209) elaboration, the cosmopolitan aspires to a condition in which Anyone has equal opportunity: equally facilitated at birth towards the potential fulfilment of a life-project of their devising. But the cosmopolitan recognizes that, at present, individuals are not equal in life-chances even in the womb: there is no time in a human life when social inequalities do not now obtain. To set this right the cosmopolitan endeavours to institute global programmes of human care even when it is disadvantageous to the already advantaged, and to the members of his or her 'own' present or native polis.

Lastly, then, cosmopolitanism is not *pluralism* or perspectivism. The cosmopolitan distinguishes between the right and the worthwhile. It is Anyone's right to define his or her own version of what is worthwhile, and to put this in play in a collaborative enterprise: a local community of those who share in a notion of the worthful life. But there are notions of right that supervene upon the diversity of notions of the worthwhile. It may not be right to save Anyone from himself or herself, but it is right to save Anyone from another, and another from Anyone. It is not right that one imposes a notion of the worthwhile on another. It is not right that Anyone does not have the space or opportunity to fulfil a potential for self-creation. Cosmopolitanism effects procedures of right, therefore, in order to manage and regulate the perspectival diversity of human creativity and expression. One ensures, for instance, voluntarism when it comes to local community membership, so that inherited symbologies of classes, boundaries and identities do not place individuals in positions from which they cannot obviously extricate themselves. One would ensure the opportunity not to belong. One anticipates ever new conversations between individuals giving on to new world-views, new attachments, groupings and traditions. In securing voluntarism one can say that cosmopolitanism is wary of singular cultural traditions and emphasizes dynamism and multiplicities of identity, change and complexity (Hollinger 2000: 157–58).

Human Universalism and Cultural Diversity

There is no need to reconstitute the term 'cosmopolitanism', I have argued, and no need to widen its provenance, in order to render it a possible or necessary anthropological project. Its meaning is clear, as are its consequences. True, some have deemed it redundant: there is nothing in cosmopolitanism's universalist ethic, according to Michael McConnell (1996: 83), that Christianity's enjoining of care for strangers does not better accommodate. There is nothing in cosmopolitan conceptualization, according to Amy Gutmann (1996: 70), that democratic humanism does not already compass. I would argue that 'cosmopolitanism' is still useful for bringing together a specific set of assumptions and aims, as above, and eschewing others.

But there are also practical concerns: Is such universalism practicable, liveable? Many would doubt it. Gellner (1995c: 7–8) nicely sets the scene when he describes 'the triumph of rationality' as affording a more efficient satisfaction of human wants but also as draining social life of the 'mystification' necessary to afford efficiency any meaning beyond itself. Rational universalism is 'too thin, too abstract, too far removed from the earthy and the concrete' to support most people in a crisis. It may correctly give onto objective reality but it does not 'warm the heart, or help a man sustain a tragedy, or behave with dignity when circumstances become too much for him' (Gellner 1995c: 7–8). Science may have changed the traditional habit of employing religious doctrine to underwrite value but it offers little in its place. Continually changing itself, scientific knowledge of the world can be expected to furnish few foundations by which either rigid moral prescriptions might be legitimated or allegiance to a universal humanism be inculcated. What is needed to alleviate our global 'crisis' in morality, Gellner concludes, is a healthy amalgam of scientific order and truth on the one hand, and cultural, moral community and faith on the other, the latter affording social legitimation, aestheticism and comfort in ways which abstract universal realities of scientific knowledge, problem solving and decision making do not.

Commensurate suspicion of universalism and of those who profess it lies behind the disparaging which we have met that cosmopolitanism is heartless and anaemic, bereft of that 'old home feeling'. The cosmopolite is deemed untrustworthy, unloyal, irresponsible, privileged, elitist, abstract, unreal. Here is the lover of humankind who is impatient with actual living human beings, contemptible, even, of the messy parochialism, smallness, fixity and confinement of their lives: the cosmopolite is he or she predisposed to feeling comfortable nowhere while superior everywhere. At best, cosmopolitanism translates into rootless cultural dabbling, voyeurism, tourism and parasitism: a restless pursuit of novelty and sensation, while unable to commit to place and others, or to participate in a community for which sacrifices are made. At worst the cosmopolitan trading in human universalism translates into a totalitarian programme of imposition and imperialism no different in form from colonialism, fascism or religious fundamentalism.

The critique of universalism as a possible or appropriate morality is taken up by Richard Rorty. Rorty dubs himself a 'postmodern bourgeois liberal' in order to signal two significant dimensions by which he would distance himself from a Kantian cosmopolitan project. Firstly, he argues that there was no radical difference between justice and loyalty: between what is deemed right and what is felt to be worthy. We need to recognize, he argues (Rorty 1998: 47–49), that 'moral' is simply a shorthand for a concrete web of social practices and customs. 'Justice' is a name for attachment or loyalty to a community larger than our immediate everyday attachments. Moral dilemmas do not concern reason as against sentiment but conflict between different group attachments, different personal identities and social relations. If brave people during the Second World War endeavoured to save Jews from the Nazi Holocaust, say, then this was likely not because of abstract, universalist notions concerning humankind but because of concrete parochial notions: the Jews concerned were ethnically and religiously other but they were also from the same city or profession or neighbourhood. In short, 'common humanity' is a weak force which does not and will not generate solidarity. The latter works only within the bounds of ethnocentrism.

Secondly, Rorty (1998: 56–57) argues that the liberal West is not better informed about reason and justice than the Rest. The demands it would place on the Rest – in the name of universal humanity or rationality or morality – are in fact simply the West being true to itself. Not that this is any bad thing. The West should be arguing that the Rest should educate women, outlaw slavery, allow freedom of conscience, tolerate homosexuality and conscientious objection, separate church and state, regard innate differences between people as arbitrary and not fraught with moral significance, and so on and so forth, and thereby enter into a global moral community. But the logic for so arguing should be more self-consciously ethnocentric – 'loyal' and not seemingly 'just'. The West should declaim: The model of liberal democracy has been remarkably successful in ensuring individual rights and freedoms, peace, security and economic prosperity for an ever-increasing number of people. Look at what we have done over the past two hard-won centuries of Enlightenment; if you do the same you too might like the results. But the West should not declaim: Look at how much more rational we are, better at spotting which differences between people are arbitrary and which not. The West has an instructive history to tell the Rest but Westerners are not better exponents of the universal capacity for reason.

In short, as a 'postmodern bourgeois liberal', Rorty seeks to differentiate and separate Enlightenment rationalism from Enlightenment liberalism (cf. Kymlicka 2006: 129). He would be loyal to the latter and encourage its being taken up by (and taken to) others not because it is more rational but for pragmatic reasons: it works better than other cultural offerings. We in the West ought to try to persuade others not to be more rational but to be more successful – like us.

If Gellner saw a universal rectitude in rationality and its Western application but feared for an acultural life led solely in its terms, then Rorty sees a universal applicability of Western culture in whose success the construction of 'rationality' is but one rhetorical plank. Rorty's position is useful, however, for identifying the ways in which cosmopolitanism follows a more consistently Kantian route to the universal and to engaging with 'otherness', one for which rationalism is an inextricable facet of liberal morality. Rorty's postmodernism leads him to begin from difference, and there is no point at which the loyalties, moralities and accomplishments of different communities do not, for him, intercede between human actors. By contrast, cosmopolitanism starts, in Appiah's words, with 'what is human in humanity' (Appiah 2007: 134–35). 'My people' are the species, and a connexion is recognized not through different identities but over and against them. One recognizes this connexion, Appiah goes on, through an appreciation of a commensurate human consciousness. Here are similar skills and imagination; here is the potential that every human being anywhere has ever exercised to create which is also in me. And by the same token, one recognizes that a connexion through local identities is a subset of human connections: local identities are an imagination of sameness, nothing more; an interpretation of sameness across embodied human individual difference (Rapport 1993).

Other exponents of the cosmopolitan are equally existential in their arguments for a universal recognition of the human. Hilary Putnam (1996: 95), borrowing a Dickensian phrase, explains that one has a feeling for global others not as fellow community members but as 'fellow passengers to the grave'. For Bryan Turner (2002: 56), an awareness of the frailties and vulnerabilities of the universal human body, amid a universal global environment, 'fleshes out' the commonalities of human experience beyond socio-cultural differences. And most clearly in Martha Nussbaum: 'At birth, all an infant is is a human being. Its needs are universal needs for food and comfort and light' (Nussbaum 1996: 142). And however strange its guises as the infant matures, here remain common human aims and aspirations: 'the common in the concrete' (Nussbaum 1996: 141).

But Nussbaum does still emphasize the possibility rather than the necessity of this recognition: the existential commonalities of our condition *can* engage the human heart but it need not. To imagine one's way beyond the superficialities of socio-cultural difference calls for what she terms education and encouragement. Human matters may be differently organized, classified and normativized at different times and places, and we might never meet an 'abstract' human being, but we might still be taught and encouraged to admit to humanity whenever and wherever it is encountered. 'We are all born naked and poor; we are all subject to disease and misery of all kinds; finally, we are all condemned to death. The sight of these common miseries can, therefore, carry our hearts to humanity' (Nussbaum 1996: 132).

The universal human condition is an ontological reality, then, but admitting it as universal practice is a habit, a practice, a skill, a strength: being open to oneself and one's existential dispositions as much as to others. It is for this reason that the Avenue of the Righteous Gentiles at the Israeli Holocaust memorial, *Yad Va'shem*, in Jerusalem is, for Nussbaum, such a key trope. It is a commemoration, she asserts (Nussbaum 1996: 131–32) contra Rorty, to those who saved or defended the human other, the stranger, at the risk of everything. Imaginatively, they recognized and responded to the human and did not allow themselves to be overcome by powerful and pervasive local ideologies, categories and norms. They evince the possible moral basis of global citizenship, of world society, whose touchstone is not loyalty and communitarian allegiance but justice. The righteous recognition and the courage are, moreover, embodied qualities, Nussbaum suggests, which signal the individual bodily nature of the process by which the universally human may be encountered and engaged. The human body offers a basis of community beyond locality, also of life lived beyond the merely rational. The universal is practicable and liveable through an educated everyday recognition of Anyone: the embodied nature of the human condition and the bodily capabilities and liabilities of the human individual.

But if universalism is a human ontology, what of culture, the rhetorical differences by which we have thus far lived apart, and which, on an everyday and momentary basis, we may still be willing, content, anxious to reproduce? Ontologically, the cosmopolitan argues, these differences are, precisely, rhetorical: arbitrary and a superficial imposition. Cultural differences are, moreover, an ongoing manifestation of individual creativity, a projection and standardization of individual difference, an instance of 'the diversity of persons' (Nussbaum 1996: 136; cf. Rapport 2004). But they are lived far more essentialistically, as we know, when regarded as absolutes, attributes of divinity and destiny and collectivity, or deployed as frameworks of distinction, purity, hierarchy, ostracism, imprisonment and ghettoization. What should be the cosmopolitan attitude towards continuing cultural diversity?

There is a range of responses. For some, as we have seen, cosmopolitanism must be extended and newly conceptualized so that it reaches even to relativism. As Breckenridge et al. argue, the 'cosmofeminine' is a 'sign of an argument for a situated universalism that invites other universalisms into a broader debate based on recognition of their own situatedness' (Breckenridge et al. 2002: 9). In other words, there is a diversity of 'universals', particular to historical situations of interpretation, and cosmopolitan notions of truth (as of the feminine) must accommodate the plurality. The diverse ways in which 'we "world" the earth' (Chakrabarty 2002: 82) now mediates all universalistic assumptions about history or human nature, so that 'cosmopolitan knowledge' describes a translational process between cultures rather than something in pursuit of a transcendent universality.

Judith Butler (1996) is another exponent of this stance. The meaning of 'universal' is culturally variable, she begins, as are its specific articulations. Every current deployment is contingent, parochial and historical. The term might remain useful, substantively, as an open-ended and postulated ideal, if it is treated as the continual, difficult work of translating and transforming local terms: always incommensurate with conventional formulations, always opening up to the previously excluded. But 'the movement of that unanticipated transformation establishes the universal as that which is yet to be achieved and which, in order to resist domestication, may never be fully or finally achievable' (Butler 1996: 52).

For others, while relativism is not a defensible cosmopolitan position, either scientific or moral, some kind of accommodation with cultural difference should still be sought (cf. Turner 2002: 54).

In order to deliver some of the goods associated with nationalists, tribalists, populists, patriots and provincials, as David Hollinger puts it, echoing Gellner, 'new cosmopolitans' may see themselves acting as 'strategic communitarians' (Hollinger 2000: 229–31). Difference is not deemed a problem to be overcome, and local attachments are not something that will be grown out of. However much one hopes for a maximization of species consciousness and a treatment of problems in global terms, for Hollinger one will not 'grow the human' out of the ruins of the tribal.

Hollinger's approach, like Gellner's, is instrumentalist: the comforts of community are a necessary compromising of rationality given current global inequities of economic and cultural power. Appiah's position, however, is celebratory. One welcomes the fact that there is a diversity of local ways of human being and one does not aspire to a global homogeneity, so long as the different cultures meet certain general ethical standards, such as recognizing human rights and individuals' autonomy, equal dignity, elective freedoms and rights to action. Appiah is confident that a balance can be found between these two weightings: a diversity of cultures and a general ethical consensus. All cultures have enough overlap in their vocabularies of value and their ongoing interpretations of these to start a conversation, he urges. Such conversation might not lead to agreement but the point is not to persuade or to identify overall consensus or to score points: the point is the practice not the principle. Talking together across boundaries of identity, and exercising an imaginative empathy, gets people used to one another. One or two things will be found that one or two people can share: some values will become universal and some will remain local, never party to final agreements on how they are to be ranked. But then this, Appiah concludes, is cosmopolitanism 'in a slogan': 'universality plus difference' (Appiah 2007: 151).

And it is not difficult to find others who share his confidence. Charles Jones (2001: 174) imagines legal and rational universalist discourses sitting alongside a diversity of cultural moral codes shorn of those features that violate human rights. Ulrich Beck (2006: 176) foresees cosmopolitan continents in which an institutionalization of norms of toleration serves to constrain national, religious, ethnic and cultural difference. And Michael Ignatieff considers that a minimalist version of human rights, human agency, dignity and freedom could even gain widespread practical support among non-fundamentalist Muslims (cited in Turner 2002: 54).

I am not so sure. I am not sure that an instrumentalist stance sends a strong enough moral message, or clothes what is right in sufficiently respectable garb. Whether or not the message is destined for external consumption, one should not give the impression that right is negotiable, nor that the rhetoric of a 'strategic communitarianism', like a strategic essentialism, is acceptable as a matter of political expediency. Such habits can be hard to break.

Nor am I sure that conversation across the borders of different cultural rhetorics need encourage mutual respect and concurrence and so effect a minimalist version of universal rationality and rights. It seems as likely that conversation is schismogenetic: cultural identity is, after all, an ongoing matter of inventing tradition so as to maintain distinctions and boundaries against others, and to clarify the range of appropriate and expectable behaviour among co-members. And I am not sure one should allow universal truths and rights to be diluted in order to assist cultural traditionalists (or their community leaders) to save face.

Engaging the cultural traditionalist or religious fundamentalist would seem to be the paradigm case. In Zygmunt Bauman's (1998: 73) terminology we are presented here with the 'flawed consumer' of modern opportunities and freedom. Traditionalism and fundamentalism are defensive impulses born of the contradictions of modern life and a contemporary experience of human insufficiency. In a world of global trade and non-regulation, Bauman elaborates, the deprived and impoverished grow. This need not be conceived of as the result of deliberate exploitation, so much as some people being increasingly unable to take advantage of the goods of modernity now tantalizingly displayed. The flawed consumer resents the self-sufficiency of others, while life composed of risky strategies, difficult choices and unequal competition can seem more misery than freedom. The responsibility for one's life, amid the dread of personal inadequacy, becomes unbearable, nauseating. Hence the turn to a form of claimed insufficiency: the insufficiency of the individual vis-à-vis the group and the world and its causal forces. The message of fundamentalism is that the human individual is not self-sufficient and should not be seen as independent, a thing-in-itself, and therefore it provides legislation on, and regulation of, every aspect of life; abolishing freedom of choice, big and small, fundamentalism removes all risk. Religious fundamentalism and cultural traditionalism are, alike, contemporary phenomena, Bauman concludes: not a throwback or continuation of old irrationalities, ignorances or mystical cravings. The identity politics of tribe, race and ethnicity are commensurate with fundamentalism as forms of totalitarianism, offered as alternatives to the solitudes of individual freedom and the risks of opportunity. One must take the problem of insecurity seriously but not to the extent of kowtowing to its (culturalist) terms of debate.

The phrasing of Bauman's explanation – 'flawed consumers' – will be offensive to some. But the same point has been more empathetically made by Michael Jackson (2002). The discourses of culture and religion that emphasize bounded belonging and safety in numbers, he writes, reflect widespread contemporary anxieties among marginalized people concerning their ability to grasp and influence the global forces that intervene in their life-worlds. The politics of fundamentalist identity have become 'the catchwords for many of those disadvantaged by colonial and postcolonial inequalities in the distribution of power, [a means by which] powerless, dispersed, disparaged peoples imagine they can recapture something of the integrity and authenticity they feel they have *personally* lost' (Jackson 2002: 107). Embedding individual being in a transcendent field of Being, fusing the personal with the social and the biographical with the historical, is intended to empower the alienated through solidarity with others.

But what should be the cosmopolitan reaction? We have seen a range of offerings, construing cosmopolitanism so as to include relativist and instrumentalist as well as celebratory stances. Appiah describes fundamentalism as a mirror image of cosmopolitanism, a direct inversion of its values in its aspiration to build a global community of faithfulness to one religious cosmology. These 'counter-cosmopolitans', he says, operate out of 'an uncomfortable melange of resentment, anger, envy and admiration' (Appiah 2007: 143). And yet, he concludes, in finding out about each other and understanding each other, we can hope to find ways to live together, even if the others' choice is to continue to be fundamentalist. For Joel Kahn (2008: 266), global Islamism is itself to be considered a form of cosmopolitanism, merely dealing in a different but commensurate kind of normative universalism.

While the motives behind extending the definition and application of 'the cosmopolitan' in this way may be liberal ones, one recalls Robert Frost's cautionary depiction: 'A liberal is a man too broad-minded to take his own side in a quarrel' (cited in Mandle 2006: 219). One understands Gertrude Himmelfarb's (1996: 75–77) conclusion that cosmopolitanism can become a perilous illusion: unrealistic and too optimistic, too generous in its depiction of human hopes for forms of universalism across cultures. Islamic fundamentalism bespeaks despotic governments, caste systems and religious intolerance and persecution, female subjugation, child labour and illiteracy. For Himmelfarb, rational discourse, the rule of law, civil rights, humaneness, far from being variously instantiated in the cultures of the world, are more often violated or not even recognized as values. These are Enlightenment products. Democracy and liberty even more so. And they depend on a vigorous administrative and legal order whose authority is vested in a liberal state.

Global society faces intractable challenges arising from 'essentialising racisms, religious communalisms, fundamentalisms and castism, the tyranny of culture', as Pnina Werbner (2008a: 11) writes. Cosmopolitanism must fight on two fronts: against xenophobia and a fear of the stranger, and against cultural essentialism, traditionalism, relativism and a fundamentalist approach to identity (Rapport 2011). How cosmopolitanism remains true to its universalist vision and programme while treating the ongoing contrarieties of lived identity – the continuous rhetoric of difference and construction of boundaries, the agonism – is key to the cosmopolitan project of anthropology.

Voluntarism and Community Belonging

The keystone in a cosmopolitan understanding of identity and allegiance is their voluntary nature. For the first time in history, individuals do not need to represent and express a particular communitarian, ancestral, cultural rootedness in order to accrue the recognition of others (Fine and Cohen 2000: 159). The central characters of our time are individuals who can aspire to be the authors of their own public identities and life courses. For Ulrich Beck (1998: 28), the ethic of individual self-fulfilment and achievement is the most powerful current in modern society.

Adherence to a culture, a set of behavioural forms and sanctions, need not be a life sentence. Rather, membership of a cultural community, a religious congregation, an ethnic group or a local set should be a choice of lifestyle. Everyone has the capacity – and should enjoy the right and the space – to create their own cultural home, and the opportunity to join with others (or with none) in furthering a particular way of life – and to secede and to create and join again, and again.

There is, in short, no duty to follow the cultural or communitarian choices of anyone else, including (especially) those of one's parents, and there is no right to expect or pressurize or force someone else (including one's children) so to do. Cosmopolitan order would enshrine a voluntaristic ethos to identity. There is an institutionalization of Anyone in law: he or she becomes the original and basic repository of rights.

What ought these rights to include? There is no more consensus among cosmopolitan thinkers than there was among liberals concerning the balance between 'positive' and 'negative' liberties in this regard (Berlin 1990). That is, one first and foremost enshrines individual freedom of choice, and freedom from coercion ('negative freedom'), and one does not have in mind to what particular vision of a worthful life that freedom of choice might be put. One leaves

individuals alone to make their choices so long as they do not affect
the liberty of others; particular choices can be argued with, even
criticized and satirized by others, but coercion is always illegitimate.
At the same time, there are aspects of freedom of expression ('positive
freedom', freedom to do) that one hopes will be availed of by all:
freedom to enjoy the benefits of medical science, nutrition, a broad
education, travel, a comfortable home space, and so on. For Beck
(1998: 28), then, while people are 'invited' by cosmopolitanism to
constitute themselves as individuals – to plan, understand, design
and blame themselves as their own persons – he also envisages a
welfare society where entitlements translate into actual enjoyments:
of education, employment and mobility. For Brian Barry (1999:
52), the overriding importance is to make no concessions to cultural
relativism – to tolerate no communitarian intolerance or injustice –
to ensure absolutely no dilution of freedom from coercion. One also
recalls in this connexion Paul Feyerabend's forthright phrasing:
'cultural peculiarities are not sacrosanct. There is no such thing as
a "culturally authentic" suppression, or a "culturally authentic"
murder. There is only suppression and murder, and both should be
treated as such, with determination if necessary' (Feyerabend 1995:
152). The foundational premise is that cosmopolitanism grounds itself
in individual freedom. As Appiah expresses this: 'the fundamental
idea [is] that every society should respect human dignity and personal
autonomy' (Appiah 1998: 108), and this is 'more basic' than a
celebration of cultural variety per se. Variety is not to be valued for
its own sake – if it goes against individual choice – and many kinds of
cultural variety constrain more than they enable. Individuals cannot
be expected to maintain communitarian diversity at the expense of
their autonomy: children should not be made to stay within a tradition
in the name of protecting its authentic reproduction or heritage.

Cosmopolitanism entails the ability to stand outside any one
communitarian scripting of the course of a proper, worthful, necessary
or traditional life, to draw selectively on a variety of such discourses
and to write one's own. Cosmopolitanism envisages multiple, uneven,
non-exclusive and unfixed forms of belonging (Caglar 2000: 180),
each person with a variety of cultural attachments which are theirs
to command: they stand apart from them, reflect on them, dispense
with them.

The key cognitive position, perhaps, is irony (Amit and Rapport
2002: 97–101). One recognizes the traditional ways in which life is
given value, and the variety of these, and one respects the comfort,
certainty and security these can afford. But one also recognizes
the individuality of one's own life: its finite nature and its creative
possibilities. What has suited others may not suit oneself, and vice

versa. One will treat ironically individual choices, others' and one's own. What is of ultimate value is the freedom with which a choice is made, and remade, not the particularities of any one choice.

Voluntarism entails a particular attitude to culture and community, then. First, that the latter are morally derivative (Jones 2001: 208). Cultures and communities have no interests in their own right and deserve ethical consideration only insofar as they secure and promote the interests, the moral worth, of their individual members – indeed, of any individuals, of Anyone. Individuals' moral worth – as ends in themselves in a cosmopolitan 'kingdom of ends' – exists quite apart from their community memberships, and it overrides the latter. Cultures are to be taken seriously, as Appiah puts it, only because the choices and desires of free and autonomous individuals are to be taken seriously. But it is the individuals – not nations or tribes or peoples, or football teams or mosques or pubs – who remain the sole objects of moral concern.

This does not mean that one does not recognize the need that community belonging might represent: that they 'warm the heart, help a man sustain a tragedy and behave with dignity', as Gellner phrased it. But one wishes for communities to survive only through the free allegiance of their members, and having been subjected to rational and moral critique, however much it is to be admitted that belonging and inheritance will offer significant context to many lives (cf. Putnam 1996: 94–96).

Martha Nussbaum refers to this as cosmopolitanism's 'capabilities approach' (Nussbaum 2006; cf. Anderson 1999). Treading a fine line between negative and positive freedoms, Nussbaum suggests that, as a minimum of justice, a set of basic human entitlements must be met. These are those 'capabilities' necessary to function as an equal citizen, enable the individual to avoid, or escape being entangled in, oppressive relationships and have the opportunity to fulfil the rich human potential. Nussbaum has in mind the aforementioned benefits of nutrition, education, bodily protection, and so on, but her point is that different communities can be looked to for having the role of supplying these entitlements. It is in part a matter of scale. Human beings often live better on a smaller scale, as Appiah (1998: 97) puts it: they need neighbourhoods, towns, streets, businesses, professions, and so on as communities. Cultural fundamentalism may be 'a pathology of community' (Barber 1996: 36) but the solution, for many, may not be the 'soullessness' of globalism – the deracinated world of contracts, markets, bureaucracies and legal personhood – but a humane and neighbourly means of civic identification. In part it is a matter of variety: the benefit of communities derives from the example that their variety provides. 'Different people require different conditions for their spiritual development', for 'the cultivation of their higher nature', John Stuart Mill wrote in his *Essay on Liberty* (Mill 1963: 192), the foundational document of nineteenth-century political liberalism. Not all can be healthy in the same moral climate, he elaborated, and what helps one individual might hinder another. Fulfilment attached therefore to a diversity of ways of life through which individuals were afforded the options to shape their own lives. A diversity of life-ways supplied them with exemplification that they could themselves adopt or foreswear, themselves join, parody or critique. Mill's argument was made in the context of national societies, but as cosmopolitanism extends liberalism worldwide, Appiah (1998: 97–98) would adapt Mill's conclusions: preserve a range of human conditions so that free people globally have the chance to make their own lives amid a situation of greatest choice. In other words, cultural and community diversity serves as a tool-kit for individual self-creation. Here are ready-made identities, norms and expectations, stereotypes and demands, rights and obligations which operate ideally as facilitating resources. The expectation may be that these will not satisfy the new individual and the new life-project, but the range of previous human ingenuity and creativeness is nevertheless instructive. The attitude towards this existing diversity may be one of appreciation but also of irony: one may oneself act differently again, even if not better .

Whatever the family, ethnicity, religiosity, cultural tradition, heritage and community into which the individual is born, the cosmopolitan ethos is to endeavour to make these as much accidental and temporary attributes of the individual as possible. We may not come into the world as free-floating individuals because our parents and their wider society made choices. But their choices should not define the new individual. They must not serve as a given. As soon as the individual is intellectually and emotionally able he or she should be accorded the space to define himself or herself. It is this individual right that the cosmopolitan order enshrines.

Indeed, the same goes for any human being, adult too. Current identifications, cultural and community belongings, do not exhaust individual rights; they do not cover all that an individual is or is capable of willing and fulfilling. The identifications pertain only until the next choice is made. Any community represents not an abiding or homogeneous assemblage but a gathering of individuals who agree that for the moment this is their choice, or one of their choices, of behavioural expression and exchange. Here are individuals who have come together on distinct life trajectories because, for a time, and in certain respects, this is how they would choose to practise their self-fulfilment. The community is a meeting point of mutually served, individual and ultimately independent, life-projects. The cultural forms of any community, as living phenomena rather than relics, are animated by the meanings, purposes and interests of the individuals who use them for self-expression in the moment (Rapport 1993). The cultural forms are rightly maintained to the extent that they serve current individual interests – and for no other reason.

The Fluidity of Experience

A cosmopolitan anthropology denies the notion of primordial or essential cultural identities, whether based on territory or religion. The *Volk* and the *ummah* – organic, inviolable and constitutive of overarching collective identities and values – are ideological constructs. Appiah (1998: 99) has called them 'fantasies'; for Robert Pinsky, 'insofar as the chauvinist refers to any human group or making as a static purity, the chauvinist elevates an illusion' (Pinsky 1996: 86). But such illusion and fantasy are by no means harmless. Whether couched in terms of the romantic nationalism of Johann Herder or Joseph de Maistre, the historic organicism of Georg Hegel, the racial ideology of the Nazis, the religious dogma of Irish bishops or Iranian mullahs, the political expediency of Soviet or Chinese communists, such 'organismic diversitarianism' (Stocking 1982: 214) delivers a pernicious mixture of relativism and absolutism: a cultural apartheid where 'members' are constrained to accept a common sense of the meaning of life and each collective is its own unique centre of gravity and experience.

By contrast, cosmopolitanism defines experience as intrinsically fluid. This is the nature of experience, for individuals inexorably and inevitably find themselves in different moments of being, different moods and motivations, different world-views and identities (Rapport 1993). It is not that these differences bespeak individuals ever acting and interpreting as less then themselves – as the pawns of contexts and situations, discourses and epistemes, which cast them hither and thither – but rather that individual interpretations are momentary creations, even random creations (Rapport 2001). Between these interpretations there can be enormous diversity. Aggregated together they amount to a mosaic consciousness.

There may be radically different evaluations of this fluidity and orientations towards it. On an individual level, reactions span an arc from a celebration of internal contrariety to an embarrassment and attempts to eradicate any inconsistency of behaviour (Rapport 1997b). In terms of collective ideology, Hannerz (1990: 241) suggests the polar terms 'transnational cultures' and 'territorial cultures' to describe the arc from rhetorical acceptance of fluidity and an opening up to global difference, to denial and attempted negation of contrariety in favour of consistency of world-view and homogeneity of life-way.

Hannerz's thesis is that cosmopolitanism as a global social condition now entails these opposed orientations becoming themselves more closely intertwined: transnational cultures supervene upon territorial cultures such that the dialectic of their difference is more an everyday feature of life everywhere. There now exists a 'world culture' (Hannerz 1990: 237) which operates as an 'organization of diversity': there is one global conversation between all structures of meaning and expression distributed round the world which accompanies the one global movement of people, meanings and goods. 'Territorial' and 'transnational' orientations become themselves subcultural characteristics within a wider whole. The absolutist denial of contrariety and fluidity, in other words, exists as an ideology *within* a cosmopolitan world.

There was a time, Hannerz (1990) elaborates, when territorial cultural orientations predominated. He recalls a famous study by the American sociologist, Robert Merton, of small-town North America in the 1950s. Those orientated towards living their lives within the broad ambit of the nation as a whole were outnumbered by those who lived their lives according to far more circumscribed and localized social structures. The value of transportable knowledge and expertise – a decontextualized cultural capital – was overshadowed by the value of knowledge grounded in the locale. Since the 1950s two things have changed, according to Hannerz. First, the scale of human social exchange: those orientated towards not living 'local' lives now see their stage as a transnational or supra-national one rather than a merely national one. Second, the preponderance of orientation has changed: the small-town Americans – and to which one might add the 'romantic authochthonists' (Malkki 1995: 52) who trade in organicist notions of nationalism, race and religion – now find themselves in less of a majority, even a minority. There are more globalists today than ever before, Hannerz considers, because of the growth and proliferation of transnational social connexions; close and direct involvement in more than one national-cultural sphere is now not merely an idiosyncratic aspect of biography or a by-product of war, famine or oppression. Furthermore, a transnational orientation has, in recent decades, been more institutionally promoted and legitimated. The West, for instance, has had a need to know more about Japan or the oil-rich Middle East.

One implication of the temporal shift which Hannerz describes is that one might anticipate – hope for – a change in the general awareness concerning culture as a concept. If there is a preponderance of 'transnationalism' as an orientation on a global scale – a desire to move, a liberty to move, and with no necessity to rejoin a bounded community – then the ideology that culture is something innate, tacit, taken for granted, unconscious, implicit, irrevocably habituated, ought to be an exploded rhetoric, and widely challenged at least. In a cosmopolitan world it should become clear that closing off individuals as culture members in totalized social worlds is a rhetorical stance, a strategy of essentialism and socio-cultural determination. It should become clear that cultural differentiation is actually formed as part of an inexorable dialectic of boundary making and marking which is contingent and contextual: an invention of difference and a simulation of essential identity. Cultural distinction is, in Beck's (2002: 7) words, transparent not ontological.

Reflecting ironically on the transparent, translatable and transportable nature of cultural knowledge and difference can be an emancipatory practice, Beck (2002: 67) continues. Individuals are set free by the plural possibilities, even the competing demands, of differently constructed communitarian identities, albeit that from small-town America, say, and small-town Arabia, individuals enter into this emancipation with different resources at their disposal. But even the subaltern has his or her new-found opportunities, as Benedict Anderson (1998: 131–32) observes: here is the young Javanese girl, for instance, now able to imagine herself escaping identitarian conceptions of her gender and ethnicity and enrolling herself in the unboundedness of the world; here is the working-class Jamaican able to imagine effecting an adventure of travel and reinvention (Wardle 2000: 84).

The situation may remain one of 'mixed feelings', of 'complex, unfinished paths between local and global attachments' (Clifford 1998: 362). Tensions remain between the 'transnational' and the 'territorial'. Hence the so-called 'culture wars' and the rise of identity politics. Cultural fundamentalism is a reaction to the cosmopolitan, and an often violent response, forcibly reinstitutionalizing and imposing a home space of 'natural' and 'necessary' absolutes. Even the ironist, willing to reflect on the arbitrariness of cultural norms, can find himself or herself nostalgic for the 'remembered' simplicity and the innocence of boundaries. Indeed, the clash between radically different orientations to fluidities of experience, both at the level of the individual and the collective – the nation-state, the pressure group, the profession, the church – can manifest itself as crisis ('war') on a global scale. It may be the case (after Hannerz and Beck) that transnational cultures represent our cosmopolitan social condition, but it is also the case that Bauman's 'flawed consumers' make fundamentalism a violent reaction that is a threat to all.

Experience is fluid and incoherent, individual, but we are party to one global human community of risk and fate (Beck 2002: 7). A cosmopolitan order delivers fluidity of experience as a possible

emancipation for Anyone, but an accompaniment of this freedom
is that, 'nothing is guaranteed, except contamination, messy politics
and more translation' (Clifford 1998: 369).

Cosmopolitan Hope

Human Rights, World Cities, Worldwide Issues

If nothing is guaranteed by freedom, then cosmopolitanism has
its anticipations nevertheless. In Martha Nussbaum's formulation
(Nussbaum 1996: 133), the cosmopolitan hopes for a society in
which 'the Norm of the Righteous Gentile' is realized as widely as
possible: legally and institutionally promoted. That is, one promotes
the factual and imaginative prerequisites whereby the human is
recognized in the significant other, the neighbour, the stranger and
alien alike. A cosmopolitan world is one where the particularism of
communitarian attachment is routinely superseded by a universal
humanism. Particular memberships dissolve, to be replaced by a
global public which rules itself democratically, interacts civilly, and
recognizes Anyone as an individual embodiment of a human whole.
Individualism becomes an ethic of global social integration and
cohesion.

Beck (1998: 28) insists that a global liberal-cosmopolitan
democracy is a realistic ideal. Caroline Humphrey retorts that,
however enlightened and utopian, cosmopolitanism has referred,
from the time of its founding, to 'persons not yet known in the world'
who will ever exist in an 'unattainable' political order (Humphrey
2004: 138). For to free oneself from bounded, classificatory and
essentialist identifications and manifest an infinite openness and
universalism is a conceptual imaginary which bears an 'inverse
analogy with the real space of society' (Humphrey 2004: 152). Why
should cosmopolitan hopes be taken seriously?

Beck et al. commonly cite three portents for maintaining
cosmopolitanism as a living hope. The first concerns the spread
of human rights as a global discourse. Second is the emergence of
'world cities'. Third is the rise of worldwide 'issues' which eventuate
in global moral campaigns and protest movements, and the spread
of non-governmental organizations (NGOs). Let me elaborate briefly
on these and their interconnexions.

In the past few decades the spread of international human rights
law, as well as a wider public discourse of rights, has been rapid.
'International human rights is the world's first universal ideology',
David Weissbrodt (1988: 1) suggests. Normatively, human rights law
disconnects the holding of rights from membership of nation-states

(which are no longer the sole subjects of international law) and 'holds out the promise of a global language that is capable of commanding loyalties in a post-national political environment' (Turner 2002: 46). Difficulties indubitably remain: the issues over enforcement, the association of a set of Western ideas and institutions with elitism and interventionism, and the purported foreignness of individualism as a value. Nevertheless, proponents of such law can take succour from the Enlightenment argument (following Hume) that 'ought' implies 'can': if a state of affairs is one which a moral requirement would seem to demand, then the very conceptualization implies that it is possible to create that state. This is the essence of cosmopolitan hope.

Human rights have been anthropologically recognized as one of the most globalized political values of our time. They challenge the fantasy or illusion that humanity is divided into essential collectivities with clear frontiers of culture and hold out the promise of a 'post-cultural' world of liberal openness (Wilson 1997: 10). They offer a vital ingredient for a post-national, global cohesiveness.

The ethos of citizenship as against subjecthood, slavery and alienage was originally a product of the European Renaissance and its humanism: part and parcel of an urbanism which was open and inclusive. The 'citizen' of the Renaissance city state possessed rights to equal treatment and self-expression whether he or she was originally native born or an asylum seeker and refugee (Kwon 2008: 23–25). Only with the rise of nation-states in the nineteenth century, after a long period of rivalry, did the autonomous city come to be subordinated to national sovereignty, and the urbane cosmopolitan ethic of hospitality was replaced by a communitarian one of exclusiveness and closure. Nationalism effected a separation between the local and global.

Recent decades, however, have witnessed a buffeting, even withering, of nation-states under the influence of global capital and global crisis (environmental and governmental). With the inability of the nation-state to engender consensus, deliver democratic demands or end violence, commentators have seen the return to prominence of the city as a global social form. For Verena Conley (2002: 127), then, the 'cosmopolis' emerges: the world city (or world-as-city, city-as-world) which exceeds the state and circumvents the national by way of a global net of alliance and exchange. Rather than bounded territorial units, here are urban spaces which act as points of interaction in a network of global processes which transcend boundaries. The world city is a site where fluid or contrarian and diasporic identities find refuge (Rapport 2006).

World cities have, according to Conley, the power to resist economic, social and political forces that would tend towards totalitarian structures, and remain flexible and open. Beck (2006: 88) agrees:

globalism becomes an everyday reality in world cities, with people becoming more sceptical about the rhetoric, the pretensions and the myopia of cultural fundamentalism, communitarianism and the nation-state. Living in world cities – working transnationally or for global companies and institutions or merely existing in the shadow of global markets and international trade – inculcates a self-consciousness which is global, at least post-national. People get used to the pervasiveness of dealings across state boundaries: such dealings become ordinary and everyday, as if already instantiations of a supranational framework. Out of the 'demotic dailiness' of interaction in world cities, Jeremy Waldron (2006: 97) concludes, 'cosmopolitan norms' of according the alien reciprocity and respect, recognizing all human beings as equal repositories of certain entitlements, gradually crystallize.

A new global sociability and societalism has already emerged, according to Beck, which includes a sense of responsibility for the whole world, and a concomitant openness and civility. Witness, he writes (Beck 1998: 28–30), the moral and political passions with which members of the purported 'me generation' have prosecuted worldwide ethical issues, from gender and racial inequality to the environment, AIDS, Third World debt, and human and animal rights. These issues originally by-passed the agendas of nation-based politics and politicians, but people globally have transcended national apathies, working together to bring about certain global futures.

Moreover, there are new political players: NGOs, lobby groups and campaigners, grassroots voluntary associations. These might be regarded as precursors of a worldwide civil society and participatory democracy. Not implicated in a state nexus, and outwith present government structures, these new political entities engage globally with structures of authority and demand global accountability. Here is a 'globalization from below' (Falk 1996: 58). It is people- and nature-orientated, ethically motivated, and generative of a new global public sphere of debate and advocacy.

Beck has penned a manifesto for those he dubs 'Freedom's children' (Beck 1998: 29). According to this we live in a world of more moral cosmopolitanism than we might realize: there are already indications that many are operating effectively on a global scale so as to create a politics of *human* concerns. This suggests that we are living under the preconditions of a radically new democracy whose next step might be transnational political parties representing transnational issues. Working, initially at least, within the arenas of national politics and polities, these parties could be multinational in their organization. They would appeal to human responses to worries over universal problems.

The task of opening out a transnational electoral domain will be difficult, Beck admits, as will the organizing of global campaigns between people of different political traditions over sensitive issues to do with food, hygiene and disease, with liberty, diversity and toleration. But then, broader than any particular set of cultural discourses, according to Josephides (2003: 229–37), are implicit moral attitudes towards human ontology ('What is due to human beings?') that are shared across cultures. It can be inferred from existing human action that perceptions of human dignity and expressions of human commonality are universal. Hope can be drawn from this 'implicit moral stance that transcends cultural particularities' (Josephides 2003: 246).

There is an allure in the very act of proclaiming that 'culture is change, it is movement [and not essence]', Pinsky (1996: 90) attests: cosmopolitanism conveys an eros as well as an ethos. The allure is of openness: global communication and consumption. Also the allure is of futurity. Released from the tyranny of material want and from the closure of classes and identities sanctioned only by tradition, one finds hope in the possibilities of becoming: new knowledge that one secures; new meaning that one creates.

Global Governance

Beck admits (1998: 28) that world citizenship as a cosmopolitan project progresses at present with the wind of global capitalism at its back. This is one of the reasons that cosmopolitanism or global liberalism, human rights and democracy, can be disparaged as avatars of Western neo-imperialism and colonialism, elitism, Orientalism, and so on. But they are not the same. What is called for, again as Gellner exhorted, is an assuring of global individual freedoms on better foundations than those at present provided by the power of capital.

Beck is of the opinion that, however paradoxical, anti-globalization movements represent the start of an institutional cosmopolitanism. Here is a basis of actually existing, 'urbane' global relations between individuals who come together to campaign on worldwide issues such as rights. Intensifying these, it is not too fanciful to envisage a supra-national legal order with human rights as its civil religion (Beck 2002: 37; 2006: 9).

But what will be the constitutional arrangement of this global order? Anthony Smith (1990) is mindful of how theorists of modernization have for some centuries now presaged larger and larger, more inclusive, societies, moving from nations to continents to the globe as such. These included nineteenth- and twentieth-century liberals – Mill, Spencer, Parsons, Smelser – and equally socialists who looked forward to a transcending of humanity's boundaries in a proletarian and then classless whole: Engels spoke of a cosmopolitan culture within which national cultures and creeds would be residual folk forms. Yet Smith is of the opinion that the prominence of twentieth-century totalitarian movements (Stalinism and Nazism) and latter-day versions of fundamentalism and terrorism show the emptiness of such hopes. History continues to put paid to Enlightenment visions: contemporary socio-political life continues to be dominated by renascent particularisms, militant religions and resurgent ethnicities. In Michael Walzer's terms, people are tribalists still who enjoy to bear communal memories, languages, customs, beliefs and commitments; the concept of humanity has 'no memory, and so it has no history and no culture, no customary practices, no familiar life-ways, no festivals, no shared understanding of social goods' (Walzer 1994: 8).

Smith elaborates: the obstacles to a constitutional global order are both institutional and sentimental. While the Second World War launched the idea of a 'United Nations', in Franklin D. Roosevelt's phrasing, it was from the outset an *inter*-national collaboration for maintaining peace and security, and economic stability. Moreover, what the era more significantly gave birth to was continental superpowers: the USA and the USSR, and latterly the EU, Russia and China. These macro-institutions have proved both jealous of their own spheres of influence and sovereignty, and the continuing focus of antagonism from institutions they superseded or sidelined. How can one envisage global institutionalism of any significance that would be acceptable to existing power brokers, and then not be bedevilled by constant claims to secede? Sentimentally, a global polis is bound to fail because loyalties to flags, myths, heroes, values and even constitutions are inherently agonistic. 'Global citizenship' is an impossible misnomer because belonging is based on bounded separation from the foreign. In other words, cultural identities – nationalities, ethnicities, religiosities – are based on invented differences and upheld differentiation from others. During the great era of nationalism in the nineteenth century, distinct and separate national cultures of invented traditions, symbols, ceremonies and artefacts, of territories and borders, of conflictual and heroic histories, memories and destinies, were often painfully forged. But what differentiation (agonism) and what continuation (heritage) could globalism promise? There are no common global memories that could do anything but divide. Global culture would be difficult to construct, not even possessing the premodern mythology of ethnic primordialism on which nineteenth-century national elites could carefully draw.

At best, Smith concludes, one can anticipate competing versions of the global, beginning in different existing homelands and drawing on divergent cultural traditions, and attracting different bands of followers so that the ethnic-cum-national will continue to live in the global. One sees this already in the phenomenon of so-called pan-nationalisms, which seek to unify in a political community contiguous nation-states: part of one family of cultures, Arab, Latin American or European. But these attempts to conceive wider regional alignments and institutions are a far cry from cosmopolitanism. Indeed, their ethos of global particularity, a globalized ethnicity, is a contradiction. 'We are still far from even mapping out the kind of global culture and cosmopolitan ideal that can truly supersede a world of nations, each cultivating its distinctive historical character and rediscovering its national myths, memories and symbols in past golden ages and sacred landscapes' (Smith 1990: 188).

So how might one proceed? Cosmopolitan scholarship appears divided. A common starting point is the original Stoic conception of human identifications as a series of concentric circles from self to species, microcosm to macrocosm. According to Nussbaum (1996: 142), the aim should be to know that all the spheres can be, and ought to be, experienced immediately and as one. All are interlaced, mutually implicated. We are born human just as we are locally situated. To know of our particular parents or family or locale is to know of the human commonality of distinct human bodies and wills and fates; we are dependent on, close to and yet separate from parents, family members and locale precisely as we are from all human beings. Love is everywhere contingent; support and good fortune can everywhere disappear. Our hunger and apartness as individual bodies tie us in with all of humanity. For Nussbaum, in short, the cosmopolitan begins with the hard lesson that those nearest us in the set of concentric circles – including our very selves – are absolutely equivalent to those apparently farthest. What we are owed by and owe to the most distant and foreign should be seen to be precisely the same as we owe to and are owed by our familiars. The legal arrangements of a cosmopolis must constitutionalize this moral truth.

For many commentators, however, the seeming disregard – demotion, certainly – of the familiar and parochial is misguided: impractical, even unethical. They recall that even Kant foresaw a cosmopolitan order as a federation of states not an overcoming or dissolution of the local polis in a world state or government. For it is to be feared that world government might easily degenerate into a soulless despotism even as it seeks to rationalize dealings with and among the human species as a whole. World government might accumulate uncontrollable power, outlaw opposition, remain unresponsive to local needs, and reduce the amount of institutional differentiation which offers an insurance scheme of checks and balances.

In drawing on the Stoical image of concentric circles, then, most commentators see a global cosmopolitan order as arriving out of an extension from near to far: from the polis to the cosmos. But even here, five distinct positionings can be identified. They differ, for instance, according to whether they define 'the near' of our human identifications in terms of emotional attachments or rational institutions. Is a cultural community or a liberal state to be taken as the starting point or paradigm case from which one plans to reach the global constitutional order or cosmopolis? I would depict five distinct positionings as follows:

i)   Reach out to cosmopolis by extending the cultural community;
ii) Reach out to cosmopolis by allying the cultural community;
iii) Reach out to cosmopolis by multiplying the liberal state;
iv) Reach out to cosmopolis by civilizing the liberal state;
v)   Reach out to cosmopolis by regulating the liberal state.

Let me briefly outline the differences between these and refer to some of their chief exponents.

Extend the Cultural Community

A global community of citizens, according to Rainer Bauböck (2000), cannot be constructed from above. Global institutions and the rule of law must be preceded by the existence of a *demos*: a sense of belonging to a historical community enjoyed by a specific group of people. Cosmopolis will be an extension of a cultural community and of existing social reality. For the spread of globalism as ethos cannot simply appeal to reason – against existing identities, loyalties and interests. One should not underestimate the difficulties of organizing institutions of governance that do not have secure historical and territorial bases. Institutions are empty shells without the motivations that underwrite their authority; there needs to be a community that corresponds to the political structuration. Common sympathies and common belonging underwrite a willingness to share and respond to the same government.

What of morality, then, and the weighting of one's moral duty between the local and the global? One must begin where people begin: not with a 'thin' or abstract notion of the human but with the 'thick' notion of local attachments (Walzer 1996). Morality starts out as a relation of reciprocal trust among a close-knit group: to behave morally is to do what comes naturally in dealings with familiars. It is a detailed and concrete story. To accede to global morality is to enlarge the group: one is loyal now to the species (Baier 1995).

Cosmopolis will never be a matter of a reasoned approach to an abstraction like humanity or the dignity of Anyone. A collective life free from the 'irrationalities' of religion and traditional local and ethnic loyalties and solidarities is never likely to come about (Calhoun 2000).

Ally the Cultural Community

A global human fellowship, Appiah (2007) explains, will best be served by an approach via local sympathies. As Edmund Burke long ago realized: 'To love the little platoon we belong to in society, is the first principle (the germ as it were) of public affections. It is the first link in the series by which we proceed towards a love to our country and to mankind' (Burke 2005: 5). Cosmopolitanism is a kind of principle, reason and conscience that sits alongside feelings for one's own locality but which is minted in another currency: not all values are measurable in one and the same terms. To move between community and cosmopolis calls for translation and alliance. It is like a marriage that sits alongside relations by descent. If cosmopolis is to represent a more peaceful future then it will be reached as a conglomeration of communities, their pasts distinct but their futures now married together (Simpson and Kresse 2007: 3).

But the cosmopolitan commitment to do one's fair 'human' share remains secondary to those commitments to one's nearest and dearest, and epiphenomenal upon them. One continues to view the wider world to which one is allied through the lens of what is one's own. It is because one cares about one's own culture and religion and heroes that one comes to care about the attainments and attachments of those in other communities with whom one shares the globe (McConnell 1996: 80–81). One loves the real people with whom one has real relationships; one learns to value in one's own community and then one rises to the cosmopolitan challenge of recognizing other values.

Multiply the Liberal State

The foundation of liberal democracies, Barry (1999) begins, is autonomous individual actors who feel themselves free of ascriptive identities and willing to extend a generalized trust to other members whatever their other identifications and affiliations. One knows, however, that this foundation cannot be taken for granted, that elsewhere identity and solidarity remain ascriptive and communal. This 'elsewhere' represents what might be described as a sentimental, 'pre-political stage' with which it is hard to engage and impossible to imagine an inter-governmental arrangement. And when one recalls the amount of hammering that particularistic identities had to take in the process of forging nineteenth-century nationalism, it is difficult to conceive of how this might be repeated on a supra-national level. But one goes back to Kant and the original conception of a cosmopolitan confederation of sovereign republics each responsible for upholding the rights of the global citizen, rights both to reside within their own territory and to be welcomed as a sojourner and trader in others. Cosmopolis is brought about by multiplying the model of the liberal state.

One might name this 'cosmopolitan civic nationalism'. Basic to it is an education in a kind of citizenship that is intent on occupying democratic (as against communitarian) spaces and institutions. Such cosmopolitanism promotes universalistic moral tenets based in the global equality of persons. International courts of justice and courts of human rights then ensure that conditions local to each civic-nation are equal; also that one works towards an equal, global distribution of resources.

In this way one might hope to solve the conundrum, the tension, between a discourse of morality and ethics which is universalist in character – what Anyone is owed as a human being – and a discourse of law and politics which remains largely a consideration of memberships of bounded states (Post 2006). One continues to practise an ethical commitment to the transcendent and equal dignity of all human beings as distinct from a legal commitment to one's fellow citizens. Law continues to root itself in a circumscribed liberal polis and is made binding, enforceable and accountable by way of institutions attached to the state. It claims legitimacy and authority by attaching itself to the will of the 'people' of the state whose consent and opinion has been formally signalled. However, treaties between a federation of such liberal states importantly translate the national into the international, the political into the cosmopolitical, the legal into the ethical.

Civilize the Liberal State

Cosmopolis is to be reached by deploying emerging norms that tame or diffuse nationhood, such as its proclivity to exclude minorities, both indigenous and immigrant (Kymlicka 2006: 142). One does not transcend nationhood, and one becomes a cosmopolitan only through the state, but one engages in certain civilizing mediations by which the boundaries of the state become permeable and its *demos* flexible and expansive in definition.

The notion of cosmopolitan norms began with the Nuremberg trials and the Eichmann trial after the Second World War, Benhabib explains (2006: 20–21). As Hannah Arendt foresaw, the legal system of the nation could no longer serve as its own moral foundation. Citizens of liberal-democratic states became increasingly aware of and convinced by the independent validity of certain moral standards. What is also fundamental to democracies, however, is the principle that the views of citizens translate into the state's laws via a transparent public sphere. What has to happen, therefore, is a 'project of mediations' whereby cosmopolitan norms acquire legal status via a public contribution to law-making processes. Cosmopolitan law thus emerges and progresses through an incorporation into the laws of liberal states. It is a process of 'democratic iteration', of public pronouncements; and it is a form of 'jurisgenerative politics', of majoritarian democratic constitutionalism (Benhabib 2006: 49).

At the same time as democratic iteration changes the internal law of the liberal state, it also extends the boundary of that state to include more and more aliens as equal members. The 'nation-state' as container of an *ethnos* is finally fully replaced by the state as embodiment of an enfranchized *demos* whose boundaries are a matter of legal convention not essentialism (shared history, memory or fate), and which allows for free entry and exit. One finally unbundles or disaggregates civic rights and national-cum-ethnic belonging. Citizenship becomes a matter not of collective identity but of political membership and social rights and benefits whose entitlements are granted on universalistic grounds.

The discrepancy between universalism and particularism may only slowly and painstakingly be overcome. However universalistic their principles, liberal states begin from distinct cultural, historical, legal, institutional and memorial traditions. But cosmopolis is a project of mediations. Moral norms of cosmopolitan range can effect the legalization of rights in liberal states such that individuals, regardless of their original and ongoing ethnic or cultural memberships, become full members of the demos.

Regulate the Liberal State

The no-longer-sovereign state is faced with a vast array of networks and organizations established to regulate international and transnational activity, David Held (2000) explains, and this can be viewed as the birth of a normative cosmopolitanism. It also signals a shift from singular, central government to 'multi-level governance': layered systems of power and authority at a number of levels and sites which function both as a territorial division of government and as a process of checks and balances (Jones 2001: 229). The variety of political and legal arrangements also serve to secure the citizen a diversity of entitlements. The institutions cross-cut and need not be seen as subordinate one to another or even as beholden to one overarching institutionalism.

In practical terms, one can imagine there being a global citizenship as well as national citizenships. One can describe there being a fundamental duty owed to the human whole while not insisting this is an exclusive duty (Sen 1996). At the same time, the state is regulated to the extent that there are supra-national procedures for grievances. There are different sites of a comparable level of importance and power, all of which promote a sense of global belonging and cosmopolitan rights, and none of which has exclusive claim to being the fount of freedom.

Cosmopolitan Politesse

If global governance refers to formal procedures by which cosmopolitan norms may be constitutionally instituted, and by which Anyone is to be everywhere assured of human rights and freedoms, then cosmopolitan norms should also compass the informal. One hopes for a kind of politeness or set or manners by which Anyone might be everywhere recognized as themselves, an individual human being, and admitted into interaction on this basis. One might name this interactional ethos and style 'cosmopolitan politesse'.

Cosmopolitan politesse is a proportionate figure: it attempts a very difficult balancing act, on a global scale. Cosmopolitanism cherishes the capacity of Anyone to make sense for themselves and to fill their lives with personal value, and it celebrates the diversity that ensues: the variety of what individuals will choose for themselves when at liberty. It is a global liberalism which denies communitarian notions of society where all are constrained to accept a common framing of the aims of life. Social structures should not constrain individuals beyond what is necessary to enable their ongoing assemblage and free expression.

But this *is* a constraint. One constrains intolerance and illiberalism and selfishness. One cannot impose one's will on others, even one's children, to the extent that one writes their lives as a version of one's own or treats them as a means of one's own, or in any way other than as an end in themselves. Some expressions of diversity cannot be tolerated at all. There is a point at which diversity threatens the very existence of liberalism and here the necessary procedures of effecting balance and maintaining free expression must take precedence over the right to decide for oneself the nature of life's goods and values. In Jon Mandle's (2006: 219) terms, notions of 'right' (matters of justice) take final precedence over notions of 'good' (matters of taste). A broad range of concepts of the worthful life can be welcomed but some 'unreasonable' versions will remain, such as those which would negate the very liberal structure of society as such. These versions must be addressed and contained, so that they do not threaten the structure of justice.

Part of the liberal balancing act, then, is being sufficiently tough-minded to defend liberality, and recognizing that some illiberal expressions will always occur: that liberalism is not going to satisfy all world-views. For David Held, what is important, at least as a foundation, is not to anticipate, or even work for, agreement on meanings and values but to find a language of engagement and debate. This represents 'the necessary background conditions for a "common" or "basic" structure of individual action and social activity' (Held 2006: 16). One might never agree, Held posits, on the moral status of persons, the conditions of agency, on collective decision making, about just difference, but cosmopolitan norms can ensure a free expression and a space for democratic dialogue.

What Held's extreme divergences – no agreement necessarily even on the moral status of persons and the conditions of agency – recall is the diversity of cultural rhetorics and cosmologies that one can anticipate continuing within cosmopolis. One intends a situation of global cosmopolitan normativity and a universal free space for Anyone, but one cannot anticipate the demise of cultural agonism, competition, contrast and exclusionism. Cosmopolis is 'post-cultural' in terms of the scientific and rational understanding of the human condition on which it is based, including the universal conceptualization of individual capacities, rights and freedoms, but it remains cultural in the likely continuation of sentimental attachments, of tribalism and neo-tribalism. One hopes to meet this in two ways. First, legalistically and constitutionally, as we have seen: through enshrining universalist concepts of human rights and their embodiment in Anyone. Second, through engendering a form of discursive engagement, a language of expression and debate, mechanisms of politeness, by which on an everyday basis different world-views and life-projects, different individuals and collectivities can come together and agree to differ, respectfully. As Appiah sums it up: cosmopolitanism does not anticipate all being cosmopolitans, or patriots, or anything else but 'only to share the political culture of the state', engage in 'the political culture of liberalism and the constitutional order it entails' (Appiah 1998: 107).

Appiah ends the above quotation, however, by asserting that 'the essence' of liberalism lies in 'respect for the dignity and autonomy of individual persons'. And we are back with the question of balance. How far do we expect the cultural divergences to which Held referred to go before the rhetoric of anti-liberalism – of some version of communitarian holism, say, or religious essentialism – translates into demands for an illiberal space? Beginning with a broad language of engagement does one end with shariah law?

Elaine Scarry warns against what she calls 'an unanchored good will of generous imaginings' (Scarry 1996: 99). Constitutions are needed to uphold cosmopolitan norms and values, and 'the work accomplished by a structure of laws cannot be accomplished by a structure of sentiment' (Scarry 1996: 110). She frames her words in the context of a consideration of the limits of human imagination, or rather empathy. Our capacity to injure other people is so great, she considers, because our capacity to imagine them is so small; one may not even know that a familiar, or a nearest and dearest, is in pain. Parts of her argument could be contradicted – 'our capacity to injure other people is so great precisely because our capacity to imagine them is so great' – but what holds is the need to have a rational social sphere of legal-constitutional guarantees which is distinct from the domain of sentiment, culture and imagination. Second is the need to recognize an ambiguity in human exchange, in the languages of our engagement, which is actually very precious. It is part of the condition of freedom of Anyone that one does not know the reach of empathy and imagination. Am I imagining another aright? Is a loved one in pain? There are never guarantees here. The language of cosmopolitan engagement, the politenesses by which difference is anticipated and accommodated everyday in cosmopolis, must be an ambiguous space in which one meets on a surface but is never certain of depths. And the allowed-for distance between surface and depth is an assurance of freedom (as well as anxiety).

But one could almost say that it is also an assurance of threats to that freedom. It is because of the ambiguity of human communication, the uncertainty of interpreting another, the difficulties of knowing the individual, that the individual is so easy to make up: to imagine as essentially the same or essentially different, as having these and these innate characteristics, as needing this scrutiny and this discipline, and so on. Theorists of civil society, most famously Jürgen Habermas (1989), have put great store by the benefits of a 'bourgeois public sphere' for the free exchange of opinion. The caveats here are the space this seems to afford and the insights claimed not for a rational exploration of the 'other' – which, as we have seen, cannot proceed that far into another consciousness – but for a sentimental or ideological construction of the 'other'. Cultural classifications and determination of identity will continue to be forged in the dialectic of public exchange. Discourses of communitarian solidarity will continue to be enjoyed and enjoined, albeit that global spaces of individual passage and free expression now offer themselves. When Terence, in the second century AD, penned the lines that have since come to stand as a sometime slogan of humanism, and also of cosmopolitanism, 'I am human: nothing human is alien to me' (*Homo sum: humani nil a me alienum puto*), the context, Appiah (2007: 111–13) reminds us, was a comedy, *The Self-tormentor*, in which Chremes, a nosey neighbour, was justifying his inquisitiveness and gossiping. Nothing human was alien to Chremes and so he could claim to be able to know, and justify needing to discover and domesticate, everything that his fellows were about. A common language of public engagement, in short, can eventuate in intrusion as much as in equal expression, in being invented by others as much as in making meaning towards one's own personal fulfilment.

Politesse is a matter of proportion. It is a surface beneath which individual lives are led in personally meaningful ways; it is a surface upon which the balancing act of social life is carried out. Too little politesse, too dense a social environment or too regimented, and Anyone is threatened by the designs of others, and may not have the space to lead an individually determined life. Too much politesse, too rarefied a social environment or too anomic, and Anyone is not given the support or nurture necessary to lead an individual life and can succumb to the schemes of others by default. Formal and constitutional procedures and informal norms of mannerly exchange must balance each other in cosmopolis.

Cosmopolitanism is the science of Anyone, that universal human actor who is not epistemologically constrained by the cultural traditions and communitarian mores into which he or she at present (perhaps accidentally) or in future dwells. Cosmopolitanism is also an ethic of Anyone: securing those conditions, local and global, formal and informal, by which all human individuals may be respected for who they are – as ends in themselves – and afforded the space to exercise their capacities for creating personally fulfilling selves and worlds. Having outlined what I would see as the rubric of cosmopolitanism as an anthropological project I turn, in the next section of the book, to Anyone as an empirical figure to whose individual life story ethnography gives testimony.

PART 2

*Is **Anyone** a feature of everyday social life and exchange, a real presence?*

'MY NAME IS RICKEY HIRSCH': A LIFE IN SIX ACTS, WITH MARGINALIA AND A CODA

Figure 1. Rickey, Andrew and Nigel

Act One

I'll tell you my story. My name is Rickey Hirsch, I am 84. I was born in 1924 and I grew up in Bucharest, Romania. My wife died five years ago. She was convinced she had arthritis and I could not persuade her: she refused to see how all the different symptoms in her body were connected. And then it was too late. The cancer had gotten into her bones. Now, I volunteer once a week at the hospital, visit patients with cancer. Part of an organization called 'Hope and Cope'. Trouble is, when people see you coming they say: 'Not you! I must be dying!' Ha ha. 'Hope and Cope' want you to go in and say that you're representing them – like you're selling their product or something! Fuck that! I'm representing no one but myself! I'm giving my soul, not selling anything. So I just go in there and say: 'Is there anything I can do? If I can help I will'. Anyway: who's to say what's a hopeless case and what isn't? Everyone's metabolism is different. How everyone reacts to a disease is different. I was a patient in the Jewish General myself, for my hernia operation. Then I was at the Royal Vic. for my throat cancer, and the McGill Health Centre for my prostate cancer. I beat them all ... so far.

Notes in the Margin 1

In this part of the book I want to present the life story of Rickey Hirsch. I came to know Rickey in Montreal in 2007, through a friend and colleague of mine, Andrew Irving, who was collecting information on the life-projects of immigrants to the city. Together with Andrew, I met Rickey in his apartment, in a café, and in his car as he showed off to us the city he had come to call his home. The interviews were recorded, and formalized by the clutter of the recording process: dictaphone and camera. But Rickey needed little prompting, and soon Andrew and I were relating to him with an informal immediacy. Some months later, when my wife met Rickey and we both met Rickey's girlfriend in a café they frequented for its Middle Eastern cakes, it was the same: it was easy to be at ease with Rickey.

Rickey's life and the way he recounted it were remarkable, but his life was also immediately accessible; the details of his life are precise and complicated, but they also speak centrally to the subject of Anyone. My intent here in bringing Rickey into focus is also to encounter a human life that points beyond the particularities of time and place. 'The accident of where one is born is just that, an accident; any human being might have been born in any nation', was how Nussbaum (1996: 7) phrased it.

The ethnographic practice of a cosmopolitan anthropology is so far as possible to identify and provide testimony of the individual life: that localized life-world that is imbued with a global nature. Anthropology's particular methodology, and its unique value as a modern science, has been the ethnographer's insistence on the possibility, and the propriety, of establishing elaborate relations with individual human beings in any and every life-world. As fieldworker, the anthropologist considers any human being met in 'the field' to be a potential 'informant' or research subject. This is intrinsically a cosmopolitan ethos. Here is the informant as Anyone. What distinguishes a fully cosmopolitan anthropology is for this ethnographic engagement not then to be translated (reduced) as the interaction with a category: the engagement with a member of a class, a tribe, a lineage, a caste, an ethnicity, a religion, a nation or even a gender. One preserves the informant's individual integrity. There is an individual story to be investigated and a human one: What is the particular substance of this life? What general capacities does it evince? The substance of that life may well include involvement in collective discourses – of class, tribe, lineage, caste, ethnicity, religion, nation and gender – but these are not the determining constituents of that life. On the contrary, these discourses will be animated by individual interpretations and intentions: exchanged for individual purposes, maintained, made and remade by individual wills; the discourses exhibit an inertia, one might say, but not a momentum (Rapport 1993). The anthropologist may chart the location and transition of individual lives in and across collective discourses but the animating consciousness of those lives remains attached to individual informants, and the anthropologist's sympathies too: How has this life expressed itself in these discourses, manifested itself in these situations, been acknowledged or denied? How do these stories add to the human record? Engagement with an individual informant at a particular time and place is undertaken with a view to a potential elucidation and celebration of human individuality and of individual humanity.

Let me return us to Rickey's apartment, and his story.

Act Two

So, I grew up in Bucharest. Before the Germans came, Romania was still a free country. People from Poland came there when Germany invaded Poland at the start of the Second World War: all those who had money, they ran to Romania to escape. To Constanza, on the Black Sea, where there is a harbour for big ships. People went wherever they could, to escape the Germans. I was still in school.

And then, all of a sudden, Romania gave in: became an ally to the Germans. Because they didn't want to be occupied, I presume. It was very confusing. Especially when you're a youngster: you don't know what's happening.

They introduced a law that all the kids, all the boys, when they reached the age of sixteen, they had to come to work – Jewish people, I mean. And what jobs they had for us! Either cutting wood for fire or else cleaning up the streets. We went in twos: one boy had a big broom almost the size of himself – for me it was a gigantic thing – and then you had to brush the streets. But because this was too hard for me, they put me to – they had public toilets in Romania, so this was the job of the weaker people: to clean up the toilets. Only Jewish people. We had to do that.

But then, even among the Jewish people there were some with connections. They could connect to somebody who was in the military or wherever. At that time, my father, through a connection, was hired to work for the Postal Office. And working for the Postal Office, he had a uniform – distinguished that he is! So when they brought in new rules that we have to wear a sign that we are 'Jew', my father was exempted because he had a uniform.

I am not sure what my father was doing before the Postal Office. I think he was an interpreter but I'm not sure. He left my mother when I was three and my sister was four. He left us and remarried. I had about two mothers, two fathers, four grandmothers and four grandfathers! It was very confusing! Ha ha. Nobody was really taking care of me or my sister. We were stranded: nobody wanted to take us.

I still have some memories from that time, because there were attachments, and they keep the memory working. For example, I remember my father came with a car to kidnap me and my sister from my grandmother. We were playing in the street, and he brought my sister a golden chain with a little medallion, a little black rat. And for me he brought a dog: like a savings bank, to put money in. As a child you are enchanted to see a toy like this, so we got in the car and he drove us away! He drove us to his mother. But his mother didn't want to accept us. So he made a commitment that he was going to pay for us, to stay there. This was my understanding – whatever I remember at my age. What I used to hear was: 'If your mother comes here and brings you some chocolates, don't eat them because it's poison'. Also they used to tell us a devil lived at the end of the street, and if we strayed too far or we did something wrong, he was going to come out! They keep us frightened! We didn't know what to do, where to go...

My father kept us there until my sister went to school; she had to be seven. So, three years he kept us. Then at the end of the first school year, the school made a photograph of all the students. And coincidentally, the daughter of a neighbour of my mother's was in the same school. And my mother saw the picture and recognized *her* daughter, my sister. So she came to the school; but my sister didn't want to talk to her, she was afraid. And then, I think – I just try to connect the events, how that happened – my mother came to the area where we were living with the grandmother: she came to take us away. The only conversation I remember her having was that she gave my sister her address, and said: 'Anytime you can escape and get free, take a horse and carriage (a cab), take your brother, and give the driver the address and he'll bring you to me'. Well, it took, I don't know how long time, but my father's mother – the one who we'd been staying with for a long time, since we were kidnapped – did not receive the commitment, the money, which my father had promised her. And she threw us out. Remembering that my sister had that address of our mother's, I said: 'Let's go there'. But the distance! I don't know how to evaluate it for you so you'll understand, but there were miles and miles between the houses. And two little kids. We'd been given a stick, and a bundle of whatever clothes we had, and one end of the stick I was holding and the other my sister. And we were walking in the direction of my mother's, asking directions!

They were poor, they were workers, my parents. In my memory I don't see anything rich there. My mother was working, and I don't know what my father was doing. 'Existing'. I don't know what. Anyway, we reached there, my mother's, and even though she had committed herself to our coming to her, she had a boyfriend, and the boyfriend didn't want us. Again we were stranded! Where to go? We don't know, we cannot take decisions, we're just children. So my mother made another commitment, to her mother, to take us in, and that's what happened. She took us in and she lived till she was 104, my grandmother. And what I am, who I am – how I am, how I survived – I say it's thanks to her. She was really our mother, our parents! That one woman.

Notes in the Margin 2

I have shortened Rickey's account: the life of an individual in his eighties is an extended affair, even in the retelling. The edited narrative that I present is above all a story of character and of capacity for perseverance. I find Rickey Hirsch being Rickey Hirsch as if circumstances were secondary.

An observation of Nietzsche's was that, 'everything decisive comes about "in spite of"' (Nietzsche 1979b: 100). I find that Rickey lived his life 'in spite of' or 'without respect to'. And here is Rickey's integrity. Rickey continues as himself, central in the intending of his own life even if rarely in a position to be a central 'historical' actor; Rickey passes through world-historical events and eras, as we shall see, while living only and always his own life.

I would posit the capacity to lead one's own life – to make sense in one's own way and to give shape to a life – to be a universal one. Indeed, it is a human necessity since the individual must think for himself or herself. What I see in Rickey's life is substance that is all his own – this is his life and no one else's – that instantiates in a remarkable way a capacity that is species-wide. Rickey's life is, in this respect, also Anyone's.

Act Three

I don't have the reason for why my mother and my father behaved like this, because it's not there. I think their marriage was not solid to begin with. I think we children came unexpectedly to them and they could not handle the situation: they were probably young and wanted to make their own lives. I don't blame them.

But I do blame my father for ... he made a grave error towards me. He's dead now. I respect his name because I carry it, but there were moments where I wanted to kill him. Because, when he was working at the Postal Office, and he knew that I had to go to labour work – as 'Jew' – he said to me: 'You should run away, escape. If they catch you, the policemen, get them to bring the case to me and I'll arrange it with them and you can run away again'. So I escaped. And they caught me. They put me – they didn't have a jail at the time, they had a basement where they were keeping tomatoes, potatoes, wines, and all this stuff, and they closed it with two shutters and with a lock. Any air you had to breathe was just from the shutter openings. Anyway, I convinced a sergeant, a policeman in the gendarmerie, a soldier: they were supposed to take me to a court martial – because I had escaped – but I promised them that if they took me to my father, that my father would take care of them, make it worth their while just to turn their head and I'd disappear. So, when we came to my father – he was already married to another woman by then – I knocked on the door. Finally he came, opened up, and I remember my words to him: 'Dad! You promised me: I've come now. Help me.' And he said: 'I don't know this person. I don't know who he is!' I got a slap in the face from the policeman! He thought I was the liar. I began to cry: I didn't know what to do.

They took me away, this time to the court martial, and they condemned me to twenty-five years of hard labour. Now there was another guy who was in the same situation as me: he was arrested, he was condemned, and we both decided we had to escape. You're young – we were both about 17 at the time – you dream, you have all kinds of inventions in your head that you're going to apply, and it's all going to work out well. What can you do? So we dreamed of escape. Now, at the time, for transporting prisoners they didn't have trucks like now: if there was a distance to go, you travelled by train. And the trains were all full with soldiers – it was during the war, the war had started – and they were going towards Crimea, to Russia. And they didn't have any handcuffs for prisoners at the time: they had rope and a small piece of wood to secure it; and the hands were tied in front, not in the back. So, we travelled – I don't know where exactly – by horse and cart and by train. Not electric train, coal. And with all the smoke and the fumes and everything, we were black! Ha ha. We reached the place where we had to change trains for our destination – I don't remember – we'd been condemned to go and work wherever bridges had been destroyed by bombardment from the air. We were going to stand in the deep water and carry whatever it was to try and rebuild the bridges. So, when we reached the stop to change trains, we had to go from one station to another station, through the streets. Me and the other guy who was handcuffed, we walked first, with the soldier behind us. Suddenly, a lieutenant came towards us, an officer. And the rules were, whenever a soldier sees an officer, he must salute. This guy who was guarding us, he was so tired – his eyes were closed, I think – he didn't see him. So the lieutenant stopped him, slapped him and put him under arrest! Took him away! So we were free! Ha ha.

But we were still handcuffed. So, we walked the streets, looking into people's yards, storehouses, and there we saw a woman peeling potatoes: we didn't realize there was a restaurant there. So she was peeling potatoes and we saw she had a knife, and that's what we needed to undo ourselves – it was just rope. So we went and said to her: 'We'll do all the potatoes, you just go and sleep – do whatever you want – and when you come back all the work'll be done'. And she agreed! She left: we got the knife, we cut the handcuffs. *And* we peeled the potatoes! We did that for her. Ha ha!

I think we slept in the courtyard that first night. The second night or the third night on the run, we were so tired. We were in the train station, looking for empty cars that we could sneak into and sleep. We did that, but then I had to pee! And with the silence there in the big empty car, when somebody makes a sound there's an echo. And it so happened that the soldier who was on guard duty heard it. He whistled immediately, and another soldier came, and another: three soldiers for two little kids like us! So they opened up the big car-doors, sliding doors, and got us.

They took us to the railway station – they had a house there, a room, I don't know – and there were other people sleeping there. So, they put us there until the morning, when they were going to arraign us – what they were going to do with us, I don't know. But as soon as those three soldiers left us in that room, we started thinking already about how we were going to get out of there. Then, my friend took an army coat from one of the other people sleeping there, put it over himself and walked out. And nobody stopped him, and nobody said anything, because he had an army coat! They thought he was part of the crowd waiting for the train or something, I don't know. But I see that, and I *do the same thing*: put on a coat. And so ... we meet again! We are out again! And there was a train going to Constanza, and we went on it.

And now again we have to survive. In Constanza.

Now, there was a boxing gala. I remember the name of one of the fighters: Checho Morizon. He was a black guy, fighting in I don't know what category. And they were selling tickets to people outside in the street, at a table like this. So I said: 'Wait; maybe we can make some money'. So we asked the guy to give us a little table, too, to sell the tickets. We did that, we made some money, three dollars, towards our survival. But when you're a kid and you have three dollars, you spend it right away! Because you don't know the value of it. Ha ha! What can you do?

So, we go into a bar and we see a sign for Liberty Ships. Because it was still possible to get out of Romania at that time, from Constanza, if you have money. Aristocrats, even rich Jews going to Palestine – it was still 'Palestine' at that time. And Liberty Ships were taking them. And Polish people, too ... Well, I don't remember how, but I ended up in one of those ships, as a dishwasher. And there was a homosexual guy working there in the ship – I don't know, as a waiter, or whatever – and he told me they would hide me in there, and I could go to America! I was the happiest man in the world! But my friend was not with me.

Anyway, I don't want to be 'dirty', but this man asked me to sleep with him. I was a kid: I didn't want to do it, so he began to get angry with me. In the morning, when the other sailors came to eat breakfast, they all looked at me – because they knew him – and they already made me out to be guilty. I was innocent! I just wanted to escape: my dream was to go to America. I was just trying to figure out exactly how to do it. (I remember, when I was maybe ten, eleven years old, and a friend lived across the street who had a big back garden – his father was a butcher or something. Anyway, we decided one day that we wanted to go to America. So we looked on the globe and we saw that America was below Romania, so we began to dig, in the garden! Made quite a deep hole – we reached stone. And what were we going to do there, in America? Shoe-shine boys! Ha ha. But that's how it was then: a totally different life to now.)

So: Liberty Ships were an American company, merchant marine, and they were still sailing. They had access to Europe, because America hadn't entered the war yet. This was '40, '41. Something like this. (I don't remember dates, years.) But if they had merchandise to deliver in Romania, or wherever, they had access. And they were taking passengers as well – Europe, America – there was an arrangement.

But I didn't go. My father found out about me somehow – that I was on the ship – and he came with the police to take me off. I had no relations with my father then, but I probably did some things when I was on the ship that he heard rumours about. For a time I wore the American uniform with the other sailors: the little white cap and blue pants. A coloured sailor had drowned himself by jumping into the sea and an acquaintance of mine took his chain, with the number and name on it, and gave it to me. So that I appeared like a – so that nobody was going to stop me. I did other things too: I used to take bed sheets from the ship, tie them around my body, take them out of the harbour and sell them. And with the money I bought guns, revolvers. I found a policeman who was willing to sell guns – not knowing that I was a Jew and a Romanian, but thinking I was an American who had learnt

Romanian. He sold me revolvers but no bullets. So then I had to buy bullets. With an empty gun the Romanian soldiers at the port would let you through to the ship, but not with bullets. So how are you going to smuggle them through? I used to buy grapes in a paper bag, put the bullets in the bottom, put the grapes on top, and walk through the checkpoint eating grapes, like nothing happened! So, say I got one hundred dollars for the bed sheet, then I bought a gun and I gave it to the sailors: I was getting nothing – I didn't make any business – I was just making the exchange for them. But they were hiding me and keeping me. I guess I was doing the sailors a favour and they were doing me a favour. To the point where I think there were no more bed sheets in any of the cabins! Ha ha.

The guts I had as a child! Until my father discovered all this...

But before all this, of course, I had to go to school. When my grandmother was taking care of us: the mother of my mother. My sister and me: we were brilliant in school. We had this gift of learning very quickly. Not because we were Jews, but because the other Romanian children were not so smart: about understanding a lesson; how to learn; how to provide yourself with information from the teacher. At the time we had one teacher for practically the whole day, teaching math, English, all subjects, and they would grade you – where you sat – according to your intelligence. If you were in the first row of benches, you were okay: if you were put in the last one – then you know how bad you are! So one day, the door is opened and a lady with a kid comes in. But the kid looks a little strange to me. And I see the lady talking to the teacher, and the teacher pointing to me, and it was decided: they brought this child to sit by me so that I could help him at anything. His name was Levio Edelstein. I didn't know but he had polio. I saw the way he was moving his body and his legs – and when you're a child you're afraid of somebody who is not as normal as you think *you* are. But my fear disappeared because he made a great exchange: every day he brought me a ham sandwich. Which was unheard of! Because he was the son of a famous engineer (Jewish), and his grandfather was a colonel in the army; so they were very rich. And this friendship continued for about three years. Every Saturday, also, I was invited to their house for lunch, where I learned my manners: learned how to behave, how to eat with a fork and a knife. Meanwhile it helped them that their son absorbed what they were teaching *me* in school – so, not minimizing *his* potential but the opposite. And me: I couldn't eat any more! ... You know, Nigel and Andrew, I think I might make your life bitter: all these stories of mine! Ha ha.

So: my father found out about me being on the ship in Constanza, washing dishes and what have you, and he came with the police and they took me off ... So I went to find my friend again, and he was still hanging around the boxing arena where they were still having fights. Sleeping wherever. During the wartime you sleep in any hiding place you could stay in. I slept in a bordello for a bit – hidden by some of the girls who were sleeping with German soldiers! One of them brought me a Parabellum [pistol], and I said: 'With this I'm going to kill my father'. And I wanted to. But I didn't find him. Maybe it was his luck and mine both, because my conscience would have been even worse. But, like this, now: I'm happy the way I am. I went through all this ... Ehhhhh... when I take you back now, I grow up again myself.

So: my friend and I decided to go back to Bucharest together. We took the train – no tickets, no nothing, two kids – and when we see the comptroller coming we go the other way, and we reached Bucharest okay. But now at the station, we don't know where we're going to go. Bucharest train station seemed to me immense. (Maybe it wasn't actually as grandiose as I thought it was.) There were several steps – I don't know – maybe twenty or thirty, going down to the street, and I was sitting on the steps, with my friend. I still had the Parabellum with me. And a taxi stops, and a man gets out and shouts: 'Help! Police! Help!' It turned out he was the taxi driver and there were two bandits inside the car who had killed a man and were forcing him to drive them away! They ran away, too, at this point. Finally a policeman arrives, and he and a group of people start searching for the runaways. And I went with the group. We caught one and circled him. I had the Parabellum and I could have just 'silenced him' or something, but the thought just didn't pass through my head. But he had a gun, too, and he escaped again. Then the second one was caught, and the sergeant, or the policeman, took him away. And this is another episode which I cannot forget: it was so exciting!

I don't remember where I went after that. Vaguely, I remember places. I slept wherever there was a hole that you could put your head in and hide.

And then the Russians began to advance. 1944. Into Romania to get to Hungary. So I decided to go towards the Russians, so that I could come back with them. And I got affiliated with another guy: a plain-clothes police agent who wanted to escape too, to America. We were going to go together. And being a policeman, he had an identity card. On one side the identity card had his picture, and his status as a secret agent – or whatever you want to call him – and the other side was like a pass for all the street cars and the buses. And he also had a little insignia on his lapel, showing that he was a policeman. So, to cover me, he gave me the bus pass and the insignia, and he kept the other identity card. And we reached the Russians that way and they accepted us. Because it was part of the military code, or whatever, that policemen were under protection – whatever it was. Anyway, we reached a place near

Transylvania somewhere – in that region somewhere – the policeman and I. The houses had big gates: you couldn't even climb over them when they were closed. It was a monastery. So this guy, the policeman, the agent, he knew how to handle the situation. He banged on the door and finally one of those sisters came out and he identified himself as the police. He said: 'We want to see the injured soldiers here, people who are sick or have been shot: who have had difficulty in finding their families, or whatever. That's our job'. I didn't know what he was up to, but in the meantime, we had a cover over our heads, we had food, and he was going round questioning people! I don't know what he was asking them! But we slept there.

You see, Romania was nothing then, militarily. The Germans were retreating, causing what damage they could, trying to leave everything destroyed. The English were bombing. Romania was just a disaster area. So, in just a very short time, I think, we reached Budapest. And next to the place where we stopped there was a prison, holding some parachutists, American soldiers who had been captured; they were in that jail there. Two of them. And so we arranged with the Russians – the policeman and I – that we would go and liberate them. And we did. And we had a party! Oh, did we have a party! I knew a few words of English by then. How to ask for a cigarette, how to ask for a drink, how to ask for money, how to provide the Americans with girls: that's all that you needed!

So, now we were two Americans and two bums. How are we going to live? We need money. We found an empty school to stay in. In the school was a gym, with all this parquet flooring. We took out all the parquet and went and sold it, and made money! And then, all the money we made – we destroyed a whole class-room! – we spent in one night! With girls, with music, with everything! Yeah, they knew what to do, the soldiers! Ha ha. But we didn't hang out too long in Budapest and we went on to Vienna. In Austria there were four territorial divisions by then, made by the Allies – English, Russian, American and French – and you needed a pass to go from one area to another. If you were located with the Americans then you were restricted from going anywhere else. So we were restricted to the American zone, and I become sort of a translator for UNRA: United Nations refugee stuff.

There was a captain, a woman captain, who got to like me, and they needed information on all the people who were now floating around Austria, from all countries. To know if they're really not intruders, or whatever. So they offer me a job like a spy, CIA. But I was young, stupid, and I immediately went and told all the other boys, and on the first day of my appointment there was a long line-up of people, all saying they want to be spies like me! So they realize that I am too young, too stupid: they cannot rely on me for anything. But

she kept me, the captain, just because she liked me; she kept me there
and I used to get coupons for rations. Everybody with a coupon got a
food package every day, and I had several coupons. I could sell some
of the packages to make some money on the side. There was a lot of
contraband about.

There was a store for the American soldiers, with supplies of
cigarettes, sugar, everything. And the American soldiers were corrupt;
they would take the cigarettes and sell them on the black market. One
day, I find out that a Hungarian guy was also selling this merchandise,
and I told the Americans – I am a spy after all! – and the Americans
arrest the Hungarian, but then they also sequester all his merchandise
and take the money for themselves! But now all the fingers are pointing
to me: I'm suddenly the spy who did all this, destroyed the Hungarian
guy! Ha ha. So I have to escape, get away from the American zone.
Because I didn't want to be part of it any longer. But how do you get
out of there? I find out that the only way to get out is to join the French
Foreign Legion, who were sending people to Belabes. The French
Foreign Legion put you in locked and sealed train cars, and then when
they go through Austria, nobody stops them. Nobody checks them. So
I got together all my possessions and went to the French Legion. Sidi
Belabes, that was the place I was supposed to go to. Algeria! Ha ha.
When I think of it now, it's a laugh, it's a joke. At the time it was very
serious: now it's just so funny.

So we went the next day, in the morning. We were supposed to get
on the train and go to Bregenz. Bregenz is a little small village on the
border of Switzerland and Austria. And it was also the headquarters
of the French Legion, from where they were sending people to Sidi
Belabes. So I came to Bregenz, and they put us up there in a very
nice house. But before getting on the train that transported us from
Vienna, I had spent everything I had, all my money. All I had left was
my luggage, a few German marks, a watch, things like that. Next
thing I know, I come back to the house in Bregenz and everything has
disappeared: stolen! After all, who were in the French Foreign Legion?
Bandits, criminals, all kinds of guys! I was just a puppet there. What
was I doing there! I was happy to be accepted, and to get out of Vienna,
but the next day, in the morning, when they came to do a medical and
see how strong you were, I said: 'Listen, I'm a Jew. I just came from a
concentration camp. Do you think I'm going to another one? I'm not
going anywhere!' So they sent me down to sweep the courtyard with
another guy, a Hungarian, while they discussed it among themselves.

So I'm working with this guy Tibi, the Hungarian, in the courtyard,
by these big iron gates that you could see through. And all of a sudden,
outside, we hear voices speaking Hungarian. I look up and I see two
religious Jews passing by – with the hat, and all the uniform they wear.

So Tibi goes immediately to the gate, and calls them in Hungarian, and says: 'Listen, we are Jews. Look at where they brought us! We want to get out of here'. So they promised that they would do something about it, and they did! Next day, they came and took us out: I don't know what arrangement they made with the French. They took us out but they said that we could not stay there, and that that night we were going to go with a particular gentleman. He would walk on one side and we on the other. And we were going to get on a train – they would get tickets for us, give us tickets – and we weren't to speak to anybody, in any language. Then, at one point before the border, the train was going to slow down; we would see a man jump off, and right after him we were both to jump, too. See: the religious Jews were smugglers of watches, gold, diamonds. Who knows? But that's what they were doing: smuggling contraband over the border!

But we were in good hands. Because we got taken down to the train, given tickets, and we jumped! But then we were stranded. We didn't know where we were. In a field, somewhere! I found out after that it was over the border in Switzerland. But at the time I didn't know where we were. Just in a field. And by the field was a little house, with a veranda. So we went there to find somewhere to sleep. But they had dogs, which began to bark, and the owner of the house came out on the veranda with a gun. So we ran! Back into Austria! With a lot of huffing and puffing.

We found we were in a little forest. But after a while we found a little canteen – like a mess hall, in the forest – with a wooden table. And we saw opened packages of jam, and crackers. And we were hungry! So we went in. And what we had found was the Bricha. Do you know what Bricha is? It was the Jewish consortium which carried people over the border: a Jewish organization for saving the Jews. This was one of their stations! But they came and kicked us out! They said we had not registered there, with them. And that only the people who were scheduled to go over the border that night could stay in the station.

So what to do? We made our own fire in the forest, Tibi and me, and went to sleep. But they came after us and said we weren't allowed to make fire there either. But it was cold in the night! And we were hungry. And we saw that the people who *were* going across that night had money: because they had bacon hanging up, from the trees, ready to take with them, and salami, and other goodies. And Tibi was really cut up about it. So I jumped up on his shoulders, got up where the meat was hanging, took it down, and we went and had our own feast in the forest! Ha ha. 'Let's eat!'.

So the Bricha realized they couldn't get rid of us: they had to incorporate us into the group of people. And who became the leader

of the group? Me! And why? Because I spoke a few words of Italian.
And the border we were now going to cross was from Austria into Italy:
Bergamo. I was told to shout: *Via via! Dai dai!* That means, 'Let's go.
Go!' Anyway, I was leading a crowd of immigrants who were carrying
all their belongings in bags on their backs: pots and pans. And all this
noise – everything! And I am the leader! But how can you go over the
border, over a mountain, when you know the police are there, and you
have a group of people like this? ... You know, you can cross any border
any time, even today. It's easy if you find the way and you know the
people. It's no problem. The problem is when you are *there*, not to be
caught! So we go, and sure enough the Italian police soon surround
us, and arrest us. 'Where are you going with all these people?' I don't
know how many we were: sixty, seventy, a hundred. So they take us
to this village, and put us in the charge of this local policeman. One
policeman! He cannot take care of all these people. So who do you
think is hired to manage them? It's me! I become the leader there,
of this group. But the people are starving; they have nothing to eat.
So, this friend of mine says: 'These Polish people have money: you
just have to tempt them with something and then you'll see how the
money appears!' So I went out into the village, looking for food. I get
into this house basement, like a cave, and I find a big wheel of cheese.
Hard, like a wheel. So I roll it back and ask people if they want to buy a
piece, and everyone began to come with their money. But they hadn't
eaten for a long time by now, and their stomachs were empty. And the
cheese constipated them! And they had cramps, crying and yelling!
Ha ha.

I don't know how many days we stayed there, but they finally made
an arrangement that a train would take the whole group to Milano.
There was a camp there already which provided for displaced people.

But I think I'll stop here for now. Can we stop? It's a long – it's
years! And it's a different feeling when you say it, to when you go
through it ... I can't believe now what I was capable of doing then.

Notes in the Margin 3

Rickey has been speaking for more than an hour now. We have had
tea, sitting at his dining table, with the dictaphone between us. His
fluency has been such that he has needed little from Andrew and
me besides our absorption. And this has been easy, and genuine. The
details have seemed to me both stupendous and unbelievable. I have
wanted to corroborate them where possible: Sidi Belabes, Bregenz,
his mother working in Bucharest's Galeries Lafayette (a detail I have
not mentioned), Liberty Ships (2,751 were built for cargo by the

Americans between 1941 and 1945), the Parabellum or Luger P08 pistol, and the Bricha (the Hebrew word for 'escape') which organized the extra-jurisdictional movement of Jews from Eastern Europe across the Occupied Zones (and ultimately to Palestine) by way of a clandestine network of way stations and escorts. (Between August 1945 and the end of June 1946, some 48,000 refugees left Poland in this way.)

Equally striking, however, has been the sense of Rickey 'skating' across this landscape, as it were. Amid the welter, the helter-skelter of detailed happenstance, it has seemed to me that Rickey has had a home in himself. I am reminded of an image of Ralph Waldo Emerson's: 'We live amid surfaces, and the true art of life is to skate well on them' (Emerson 1981: 275).

The image comes in an essay where Emerson discusses the relationship between what he calls 'society' and 'solitude'. His theme is that there is a 'vulgarity' to society which can be fatal to a proud independence, while on the other hand solitude is impracticable and society necessary: inevitable and possibly pleasurable. The skill, he concludes, is to 'keep the diagonal line': 'keep our heads in the one [solitude] and our hands in the other [society]; this way we 'keep our independence, yet do not lose our sympathy' (Emerson 1981: 394). Rickey would seem to me a paradigmatic exemplar of Emerson's 'diagonal line'. He skates across war-torn Europe, across national borders, among places he does not know the names of; he slips in and out of relationships, assuming and dropping roles and personae. The social is a surface and he shows himself adept at negotiating its demands while retaining an independence of self-consciousness. The social is necessary and often pleasurable – Rickey finds comradeship in his escaping from hard labour, on the Liberty Ship, with Tibi, and receives valuable help from the secret policeman, from prostitutes and captains, from orthodox Jews – but it is as if the social remains distinct from the proud project of Rickey ensuring his survival, as himself and on his own terms and conditions. The details bespeak a variegated mix of kindness, luck and cunning, of taking and making opportunity, but I want to agree with Emerson, when he concludes: 'Under the oldest mouldiest conventions a man of native force prospers just as well as in the newest world, and that by skill of handling and treatment' (Emerson 1981: 275). Rickey's 'native force', his force of character, affords an identity to the course of his life – amid social 'conventions' that are disadvantageous if not murderous – that I can appreciate as essentially his own.

Rickey's apartment looks out over downtown Montreal from high in a well-to-do block of condominiums. Rickey occupies it alone now, but it possesses the fullness of a lifetime's activity. There is a mixture

of furnishings (new North American and old European styles), there
are books (Rickey is at present enrolled in an extra-mural university
course in psychology), and there are paintings. The following week,
Andrew and I meet up with Rickey in his apartment again, to hear
more of his life story. As we settle ourselves again around the dining
table, Rickey notes that I have been scrutinizing his walls.

Act Four

Yes, these are my paintings. Sometimes I sign the work 'Rickey',
sometimes 'Rickey Hirsch' and sometimes just 'R'! I started with
'Rickey' and then someone said, 'Do your whole name'. This was an
art dealer and auctioneer: he said he would make me a name. 'Put
your full name and I will promote you. I'll make you a c.v.', and all
kinds of things like that. But I think it was mostly Jews he was talking
about selling to – not the Big Time. But that's why you see different
signatures.

I wasn't sure about H-*i*-r-s-c-h to begin with, because in German
pronunciation it's 'Heersh'. But in English you have to spell it with two
'e's instead of an 'i' to make that sound. So people call you 'Hirsch',
and you feel insulted, because it's not your name. But that's it: you're
stuck with it! Even 'Rickey' is not my name: my name is 'Rudi'. But
when I came here to Canada, my wife said I should call myself 'Rickey'
not to have the suffering again that comes along with the name – it's
a German name. And she even spelled it for me: 'R-i-c-k-e-y'. So I went
and legally changed the name. From 'Rudi' to 'Rickey'. Now most
people only know me by that name: 'Rickey'; 'Mr Rickey'. But a name
doesn't mean a thing, really. I don't know your full name, Nigel. But I
know your face: I feel your character. A name's not important to me.

So, my story: you want to hear more of my story. Well, I'll tell you –
I don't know if it will be the *second* part, but another part. And I know
we have been jumping from one part to another. And there are *many*
years' difference. When I was telling you that story about Constanza,
I needed also to tell you about my four years in elementary school,
and four years in high school. If you can understand all this, I think
that's thanks to your intelligence! Some people, I can talk to them, tell
them the same story and they'll make something totally different out
of it. I've not told my story to many people. Because if you tell them
your story, they always have another story to tell you, and so it goes
on – I want to forget all these things. At my age, I have a different
philosophy now, thinking about myself. I don't want to live with the
past, I just want to live in the moment. Because, who knows when the
time comes. So why? ... Every day I walk in the mountain: Mont Royal.

In the summer when you walk there you see lots of people, sitting on benches, contemplating, whatever. And you see them with long faces – like this ... and you wonder why. It's because they live with the past. Everything that they regret, it shows on their faces. Well, *I* don't want to be one of them. So I'm looking ahead. My past is a story of survival, mostly. I think I had the stamina, physically, just because I was young.

So: my story. Another part, 1945. I was in Italy, after it had been liberated. I had crossed the border with this group of displaced Jews. And the Italians were flabbergasted. Just one chief of police there, and one sergeant or somebody, to deal with the whole small village. And they put me in charge because I'd been to different countries and could speak to the group. I know my vocabulary is very poor, but I can speak enough to get across what I want to say. People understand me in most languages. (You only learn languages one way, you know? By force. You learn because you have no choice: if you want a glass of water, you have to communicate. And when you're young you absorb things very easily.) Okay, so I become the *Gruppenführer*. You understand what that is? I became the immigrants' *Gruppenführer*: help them move from one country to another and find themselves a niche so they can establish themselves and stay. They were like Gypsies, nomads, moving from one place to another. So, there we are in the camp, for displaced people. But we have an address. And mail comes every day, and they distribute the mail in the camp like you are a soldier in a regiment. And say they had a friend in France and he tells them in a letter: 'Come to France: in Italy there's nothing! Here, they give you this and this'. But now you need to travel there: you need somebody who knows the road. So that's what I did: found the road for them, spoke the language – I was their *Gruppenführer*. I escorted people from Ventimiglia across country borders. From Rome, Milano, Torino, to Genova; from Genova to Ventimiglia. In Ventimiglia we'd take a taxi. I knew where to tell the driver to stop, and then we'd walk through the mountains and across the border into France. After doing it once or twice, I found a connection who wanted people brought the other way too. Each individual would pay me the transportation costs plus a hundred dollars! And that was a lot of money, a hundred dollars. One night, I remember escorting two people, and one of the guys gave me a parcel wrapped in newspaper, I think, or brown paper, something like that, and he said: 'You keep this, and if we have to make a run for it in the mountains, I'll meet you later at the train station'. I said, 'Fine'. So it all went well, nothing happened, and we reached the train station together. We took the train, and then I asked him for some money, part of my payment, because I was hungry. So he took twenty US dollars from the packet and gave it to me. I went to the food car – I spoke the language – and I ordered something to eat, and I paid in the American money, which they took because they were hungry for the currency: gave me a good exchange rate. But next day I read in the newspaper that the police were searching for a guy in a light blue jacket and a white shirt and red tie and grey pants – and that described me completely! It was false money that he had given me! Counterfeit. I had paid the waiter in the train with false money. I didn't know that in that package there had been 100,000 false US dollars! Ha ha. Well, when I saw that description of me I was walking in the street, and there was a guy selling – I don't remember what – candy or peanuts or something, so I took off my blue jacket and I gave it to him! I was scared: I didn't know what to do. So I ran away to Rome, and I didn't go into the mountains any more. Ha ha.

You know, we laugh, but it wasn't funny while we were doing it. But I had the guts to do it! I can't believe it myself: me, this small little kid, skinny like this, with such experiences in my mind. It's hard to believe this myself when I relive these experiences now in my mind ... You know the other day, Nigel, you asked me if I liked to read? Afterwards, I told it to my son, and I said that you probably thought that what I was describing came from a book: that you didn't believe it was me who went through it all: 'Nigel probably thinks that I'm narrating something that I read in a book!' I said. Ha ha. And my son laughed.

Anyway, so now the year is about 1946. In '44 I left Romania, with the Russians. And I think '44 was the year the war ended ... All my struggles, just because of religion ... So now another episode: I go to Israel. And again an adventure.

I was a *machad*. Do you know what *machad* is? It's a volunteer. I was recruited in Italy, with four or five or six other boys, and we were to go to Israel. We were promised that they were going to give us a house, blankets, everything. We're going to have a farm, it was going to be all ours. But in the meantime I have another proposition from a guy who wants me to go with him to Libya. Why? Because I had lots of girlfriends and he was intending to open up a nightclub, and I was to bring all the girls there and we would make a business together. Well, that didn't inspire me much!

I was still living in a camp at that time, and the fiancée of the director of the camp fell in love with me. And so I was in danger of being kicked out of the camp, by the director. There was another young girl, too, a farmer, who fell in love with me. She would bring me chicken, roast chicken, leave it by the camp fence, and we would kiss and she would be happy. I don't know if I was happy! Because I just wanted to escape that camp. So: they were collecting volunteers to go to Israel. They had a kind of representative there who was looking for people to volunteer ... but how did I get to him? I remember I was in Lido. I remember I was in Rome ... But how? ... It needs deep, deep thinking to try to get these

memories that are already dead ... Somehow they put us on a ship,
and they sent us to Israel.

I don't know where we landed. I know we were downloaded into
inflatable boats and we were guided to a shore: there was a lot of sand.
Then they said to everybody: 'Stay here. Two trucks, two buses, will
come and pick you up and take you to the *machaneh* – how do you
say, 'training camp' – where the military instruction and everything
is done, and exercises, and you sleep there. So the buses came, they
took us to the *machaneh*, and in two days I was already a sergeant! Ha
ha. They taught me and then I was instructing the other people how
to utilize their arms. I had a good *kop*, a good head, and I learnt fast. I
spoke the language. They needed me. Because the immigrants didn't
speak Hebrew. They spoke Italian or Jewish or German, or French. So
you have to teach these people in their own language: you can't teach
them Hebrew when you need them quickly at the front with a rifle. So I
was a great asset to them – I didn't realize just how much they needed
me. But I have no idea where this camp was. I cannot even ... Pffft.

The English were still there, of course, at the time. That's the reason
we couldn't disembark in the harbour. Anyway, I stayed in Israel about
five years. Most of the time I was in the army. But when I had *chofesh*
– when I was out relaxing with the boys – I have no reminiscences
of that at all. I do remember not knowing what was going to happen
to the boys in the camp who I was teaching. Because we had rifles
from Czechoslovakia. And from England we had sten guns. And the
big problem we had was that the machine guns, the sten guns, were
heating up very fast. Then they could get blocked with a bullet, melting
in the barrel, and then you could do nothing to defend yourself. You
had to fire sporadically, and time it: even touch the barrel to find out
if it was too hot, and then stop and take another weapon. Because if
you used the sten gun when it was blocked you were dead. Another
problem was that the sten gun could discharge itself when you dived
for cover. That was not fun. A couple of boys died like that.

What I remember: there was a lieutenant there, a Sabra – an
Israeli-born kid – maybe eighteen years old. Smart! He knew the
field, knew the language – spoke Arabic, Hebrew and English. He was
fantastic, I trusted him completely, like a brother. And I went with
him into Syria on this *sayar* job. You go behind the enemy lines, make
your observations, then communicate back. We were eight of us, and
I was the telephone guy. I never even knew that I was in Syria, but
there were Yemeni people with us – you know they immigrated to
Israel – and they spoke Arabic, so it was easy. But still you never know
exactly where you are and you don't know what risk you take. So: the
lieutenant sent a Yemeni to reconnoitre, because we saw lights. He
went ahead and he saw a booth. So he put his head in the window to

see who was inside, and there were four Arabs drinking tea or coffee and talking. And when they saw him: Alarm! Alarm! So, he runs back down the hill, and we are coming halfway up the hill! Everybody runs, disappears, going this way and that, me with the telephone still – I was responsible for it – and I can't tell you what I went through! Ha ha. Eventually we find each other again, and the lieutenant guides us back. Ehhh!

But before the British left, no one suspected a war with the Arabs. The Druze were allies with the Israelis: they were both fighting to throw the English out. And only when England decided to go and they finished with Palestine, then the trouble began between the Arabs and Jews. Until then they were okay; after, they were separate.

I was very upset. I worked as a waiter in Israel for a time, and there was a guy, a barman, named Jewel, a very, very nice individual. An Arab. One day per week, when we were free, we used to go drinking together. He used to take me to Arab places – what they called *maza*. They give you a bottle of arak, and all kinds of little things, sour things and hummus, and you eat and drink, and you tell stories, and you sing: a happy time. But Jewel would express his sorrow, about his family, about the loss of their property – and not only the property, also about why the Arab leaders had scared other Arab people into running away. They said: 'If you stay here, the Israelis are going to kill you'. And it was not true. Because the Jews had other problems to deal with: enough problems. Like finding accommodation for their people. The Israeli leaders – Ben-Gurion, and then Golda Meir – they would probably have paid or asked the Arabs to support them and help them: to arrange the immigration.

I don't know if my Arab friend is still alive or what. But in 1952 I got married, and I also quit the country. My wife was Romanian: she came with the boat *Daltalena*, that had gotten returned from Haifa to Cyprus. She stayed in Cyprus two years before she could get to Haifa! Anyway, I decided to quit Israel because there was no way to make a living there. They didn't have any meat, they didn't have any eggs, they didn't have anything! And I was a working guy: I needed to eat. I can't just live on soup – like my wife's mother used to make. I used to go to the harbour and there were merchant-marine boats there that had been sailing to Europe, and the people working on them were Jewish, immigrants, some of them, and they knew that people in Israel were starving, so they sold you pork, ham, salami – all this – on the black market. You could buy slabs of bacon in the harbour, and you'd bring it home and hang it so that the fat dripped out of it, and then you'd eat it with garlic and bread. Ooh! ... Ha ha. But still, I had hardly any revenue, and I had to support myself. And now I have a wife, too. I have to buy a house. So: I decided to leave. I wanted more than this.

I had volunteered to come to Israel – a *machad* – and now I wanted to cash in on their promises.

I went to an office in Tel Aviv. When you were discharged from the army, they gave you a book, like a passport, and in the book was your picture and your name. So I stood in line, with my passbook, until it came [to] my turn. The guy behind the table opens the book, looks at it, and says: 'I'm sorry, but you were declared dead in Jerusalem'. I said: 'I wasn't ever in Jerusalem! Look at me: it's my picture!' 'No way', he says, 'We're going to investigate this and we'll call you. What is your address?' So I gave him my mother-in-law's address. And I left. And coming out, I thought: this is probably some kind of gimmick. Them wanting to wash their hands of me and not give me what they promised. And this made me more pissed off. Another reason to quit the place and go back to Europe.

There were ships going to Europe, and I knew that there were still camps for displaced persons in Germany, mostly for Jewish people. (There weren't any more in Austria, or Italy, just concentrated now in Germany, the last refuge; maybe there were two still available in France.) Anyway, we decided we were going to go to Germany, but on our Israeli passports it was stamped that we were allowed to go anywhere in Europe *except* for Germany. Because of relations between Israel and Germany – the Germans making the people suffer so. But we found a way to cross from Austria into Germany (and before that from Italy to Austria), illegally, and so we reached the camp. We had to sneak in because we had no acceptance papers to live there. One night we slept with some friends we knew; another night somewhere else; and you could also buy room space for a certain amount of money. But we didn't have access to other camp benefits. But you know, Jewish people are very smart. You know what they did there? Some of them that had money bought a little minibus, and went into business transporting people from the camp. 'You want to go to München? Come!' 'You want to go to Salzburg? Come!' They were making money – with no taxes, no government interference, no nothing. Ha ha.

But then somebody squealed on us, because we weren't registered there as displaced, and the police arrested us and put us in jail. My wife was still a minor, so they put her in a jail for minors, and I was with all the other criminals. For about three months. Until the Jewish National Fund found out about us and came and released us – on the condition that we would go back to Israel. But we didn't go back to Israel. Instead, we made an application for Brazil. Brazil was available. See, everybody was dreaming about the United States: 'America', 'America'. That was their dream. These displaced people, they could have gone back to Hungary, Poland, wherever, after the war, but it would have meant starting life there all over again. All they had before was destroyed. But then my wife got pregnant and they wouldn't let us go to Brazil. My son was born in the camp – we even gave him a Brazilian name so he would be at home – but they wouldn't let us in. Then, my wife's sister was married to a fellow whose mother was already in Canada – in Hamilton – and she made out papers for us to go there. I don't know for what: a restaurant was going to give me a job, and I was to go work there! This was 1953.

And so I came to Canada. And I have no regrets! You can't make comparisons with what might have happened elsewhere. You accommodate yourself. In your mind, anyway, is just how to make money. Work, make money, work. In order to have security. Because I had learned that we live in a world where if you do not have money, you do not live. With money you can buy life. Or whatever. You can buy land, gold. (If you plan on moving around, don't buy land, buy gold.) But you know, it's uppermost in your mind when you're displaced: security. How are you going to handle yourself? You have no family, you have nobody who's going to give you any advice. Your neighbour is going to take the blanket for himself, not you. In the war, you walk over dead bodies. You watch pilots parachuting from planes: sometimes they reach the ground safely: sometimes they die before they reach the ground. You're seeing them but you're doing nothing about it. What is more important for the individual is himself: taking care of his survival ... Maybe the first time you get a bit emotional about death, but after that ... I worried for nobody but myself. Not my sister, even.

I brought my mother here in the end, from Romania. She died here: she's here in that cemetery. But I could not ... I was too busy to take care of her more than... I thought that she was going to be a help taking care of the kids – I had a daughter by then, too. They were small, they were going to school. They needed someone when they came out of school. But my mother – God bless her soul – she was like a dictator. 'Da-da-da'. 'Da-da-da'. It was like that. So the kids began to dislike her; she was not a good grandmother. And then the kids want a dog, so I bought them a dog, but my mother didn't want to have a dog, and she was beating the dog. All kinds of things. And I was coming home late – 11 o'clock, 12 o'clock, after a day of work – and I didn't have ears for anything. I had no time to think. My wife, too. She was the backbone of my business. She was so scared that everybody was stealing from it that she would stay seventeen hours a day, to count the money.

What I had on *my* mind was what mistakes I had made today and what I was going to do tomorrow. That was probably why I did not give my children what they needed: parental guidance. I didn't have time for them. (I didn't have time for friends!) And it was not out of selfishness – because of what I wanted for myself – it was for them that

I was working. For my children. But they did not understand. So ... But I didn't have a childhood as a model to understand how to behave and what to do. I didn't have a family or anybody to guide me any better. So I did what I thought was best. I substituted attention with gifts and money. Which is wrong. But ... But my father: I never saw his face again.

My sister has photographs (she lives in Israel still). But I have nothing from those early years. The bundle I had with me when I went to the French Foreign Legion, to be a mercenary, they stole! And I had to start again. But I don't regret this. Because I don't want to see the past.

Figures 2–5. Rickey's narration

I had one experience: going back with my son to Romania. The port at Constanza. The gates. And I know how hard that was for me. So I don't want to go back there again. I don't want to live with the past. Just the now. What Hitler did to the Jews is over. I want to live for the moment. Now. I enjoy your company now: I am happy. It's hard: there are things you want to forget about, not to reveal them all the time. Because they're not nice events.

Notes in the Margin 4

It is striking, the change that comes over Rickey's demeanour when his narrative reaches the point that he begins to have responsibilities for people other than himself. I would say it is as if Rickey socializes himself.

In war, Rickey admits, you walk with death and your relations with the living are fleeting, momentary, uncertain. The constant is the concern with self; and the constant is a kind of pragmatic lack of sentiment. On his helter-skelter passage across Europe he did not even consider his sister. After mementoes of his past were stolen in the French Foreign Legion transit camp at Bregenz, he was unemcumbered even by these material connexions. But after the end of the Holocaust, and after the Israeli war of independence, a change comes about: he gets married and has a child. His energy remains, his resourcefulness and his independence, but now Rickey directs himself to making a living that is profitable enough for others too, and making a home in which a family might prosper. The risk and excitement of survival is also now tempered by a sense of uncertainty and guilt. Could he have been a better son, husband and father when he set up a home and a business in Montreal? We shall hear more of those postwar details below.

Besides change, however, there is continuity. The character of Rickey as the 'feral' war-urchin carries on into Rickey as the 'socialized' family man. Here is Anyone, the player of social roles, I might say, and Rickey is consummate in his skills at adaptation. He can play the husband, father and son just as he can the unemotional, lone survivor, and he can measure the distance and difference between the two: he can question his own performance in his social roles and wish he had had better role-models for the former. But he remains himself in both contexts, I find. Rickey is Anyone, I would say, exhibiting the capacity to pass in and out of different social settings, particular cultural classifications, with an abiding 'human' irony, an individual self-consciousness.

A postwar Rickey is no more anonymous or pliant an actor, then. Although anonymity is a key concept here. Being afforded a conventional name or marker by which others can identify you is not the essence of identity, Rickey insists. He has been called many things, while he does not know or cannot recall the names of many places and people in his life. But having and recognizing character is distinct from having a name, Rickey claims, and character is what is important. He may be anonymous in his passing through and between social settings and statuses, but he is far from being anonymous in the individual and human imprint he gives to his life. After the years of war, he returns with his new young wife to Germany, finding in its displaced persons camps 'a last refuge'. There is a sense of grievance that five years working for the State of Israel are not reciprocated. Nor will he abide by the conditions that the Jewish National Fund lays down on freeing him from German arrest (and return to Israel). He will press forward: on to Canada, if not to Brazil. Let us see what path Rickey now clears.

In introducing us to the next part of his story, Rickey begins by taking Andrew and me on a car journey around parts of Montreal, so that we could see and record parts of the city that became significant to him. His story was still one of movement.

Act Five

Get in, get in. We'll talk as I drive: I'm used to it! This Mercedes is now seventeen years old. And I had another one before that, a diesel. I paid 13,000 dollars for it. I drove it for five, six years and then I sold it for

Figure 6. In Rickey's car

22,000! I made money with the car because of the market for German marques.

So: back to my story, eh? Where were we? 1954 or 1955 we came to Canada, me, my wife and my son. My daughter was born two or three years later. I had no real goal: my ambition was just to make enough substance, money, that we could survive as a family, and not worry. Especially the children; not to go through what we went through. With four dollars in my pocket, and not really a profession, I had to make my way by myself. All the way through. I had no choice. I was cut off: no mother, no father, no home or family to protect me. I had no time to think, I just had to survive. I could not go back to school, I had to bring up the family. We were hungry to have everything, and they had an abundance here: furniture, television. And we had nothing. My grandmother used to say: 'You're poor not if you've got an empty pocket; you're poor if you've got an empty head'. Ha ha. You're poor not in your pocket but in your mind; if you're poor in your mind you can't provide yourself with what you need to survive.

The story of a life is created by the individual: you create. Some people give up. They don't try. But if a life ends up being good or being bad, it's because of the individual's own decisions. I took my chances and my decisions. I knew I was capable of doing it. I try. If you ask me to hire myself out in a whorehouse, I'll be in a whorehouse. So what? What's wrong with that? I survive. If I succeed, it's good for me.

What I saw, in my passage through life, was that the people who had money could save or prolong their life a day or an hour or a week more. Because they had something to purchase more time with. So that was what was in my head. In the end I became the president of the International Association of Driving Schools. I was powerful in the Quebec government. I appeared in a half-an-hour programme on CBC Television, with the presenter Barbara Smith (she's in Toronto now). So when somebody tells me they're poor, I question it: 'What do you mean?' Remember Alexander Dumas: When a guy asked him for money to buy bread he replied he would rather buy him a plough and give him seeds: 'Now you will have bread all your life'.

I did have a goal, as a matter of fact, a dream. I love Italy, and when I knew that we were going to Canada, I said to myself that I was going to make 10,000 dollars and then I was going to come back to Italy and live like a king! But then, when I really did make 10,000 dollars in Canada there was nothing to make me want to go back to Italy anymore! I had been young and to make 10,000 dollars was my first goal. Ha ha.

Well, here we are, Clark Street: my first apartment in Montreal. That one, upstairs.

It was convenient: we didn't pay rent because my wife was doing babysitting instead. I worked round the corner as a waiter. At Moishe's. We never got as far as Hamilton or my wife's relatives who had signed for us. We got off the train at Montreal. Someone I met on the ship said he had a brother-in-law in Montreal who was going to help me. So I go and I meet this guy, at The Balkan Restaurant: the brother-in-law. He invited me. So there we are, he orders his food, he eats it, and then at the end he asks me if I want a cup of coffee! Big help!

Figure 7. Outside Rickey's first apartment

But I did like the flavour of the city. Maybe a month or two later
– maybe six – when we finally visited Hamilton, and I saw the city, I
never regretted stopping at Montreal. At that time, Ontario was very
Catholic. All the stores closed on Sunday – Saturday afternoon and
Sunday – there was no liquor sold at all. All this made the place like a
mortician's! A dead city. I would have gotten bored like hell.

So I began work in Montreal as a waiter. Like I had in Italy, too,
Germany, Israel, on the ship, all over. I worked at Moishe's, and a short
time in a deli on Park, and then finally in Ruby Foo's, where I'm gonna
take you next. My wife got an old tuxedo and made it fit me, and the
lining she made into a bowtie. I don't know how I looked – believe you
me! – but I made it. Today I probably wouldn't put on something like
that. But when you're hungry, everything on the plate tastes good!
Two to two-and-half years I worked as a waiter in Ruby Foo's. Till I
felt I had some reserves of money in my pocket. Because if you have
reserves you can take chances, not like if you have to pay the rent
next day and you have no money. Ruby Foo's was a great place: a lot
of life, a lot of movement. Like a family. (Now it's different there – like
everywhere else. All about individuals.) Anyway: this is Ruby Foo's.

But it was fun. It was a free country, a free city in those days,
everybody laughing and enjoying themselves. And warm: it was an
open city, gambling all over the place. I know I did a lot of foolish things
before I set up the Montreal City Motor League. But I had guts: I never
had an education. But I never thought I was going to fail: I always
thought I was going to win. And by trying, you find out whether you

Figure 8. Outside Rickey's restaurant

fail or not, eh? And if you don't try how can you know? Life is about trying: if you don't try something, you'll never know. 'Don't say you've been unlucky in life if you've not played the Lotto!' Ha ha.

I'll jump to another episode. I was still living on Clark Street, and nearby, on the corner of St Lawrence and Mount Royal, was a bank: Royal Bank of Canada. And the director of the bank was Mr Smith. And people had told me that whatever money I had I should put it in a bank. But not all in one bank: a little bit here, a little bit there, a little bit there. Like this, the government wouldn't be able to follow you; and the police wouldn't follow you. Anyway, I'm a likeable person, and this guy Smith gets to like me, and one day he calls me in his office and he says, 'I have some good news for you!' He says, 'Is Rudi Hirsch your real name?' I say, 'Yeah'. He says, 'We have a wire, here, that says you have inherited a large amount of money from Poland! You were in Israel, yeah?' 'Yes, I was in Israel'. 'But then you left Israel, and the banks have traced your name here and found it corresponds to the name on the will'. But there was a difference: the guy they were looking for was born in Poland. I wasn't. But they were overlooking that, the banks were, and only looking at the names. But I still told them the truth. Then I came home and I told my wife, and she said: 'What a stupid idiot you are! Why didn't you just say it was you, and get all the money?' But I had been caught by surprise and I couldn't fabricate anything, so I told Mr Smith the truth. (This was the same person I was confused with in Israel, remember? Rudi Hirsch. When the army guy said I was dead and I'd been killed in Jerusalem.) So: a bit later I need a car. A Pontiac 1953 was what I wanted to buy, and it cost 900 dollars. But I didn't have any money. Now: you can get a bank loan, but for that you have to have seven signatures, seven people to guarantee you. But where are you going to get seven people? Everybody is going to say, 'If I do this for you, you gotta do that for me'. So I told this to Mr Smith and Mr Smith says: 'No problem: you got the 900 dollars. Go buy the car!' See what I gained? I gained so much confidence – in credit and esteem – because I was honest! And that's the way I built up the driving school. Through Mr Smith.

The first driving school was called Rickey's Driving School. I was the only school working 11 o'clock at night. At the end I operated forty cars, forty instructors. I sold it at the end to two of the instructors who wanted to become partners, with my son also having a third share; my wife wanted it for him, as a legacy. (He has a Ph.D. now, my son, but the hourly wages they pay him at the university, for services, are the same as I paid my employees thirty years ago!) I take courses at the university, now. You know? Psychology, mostly. For many years. I like the scepticism of it: 'Everything is changeable'; 'Accept a theory for the moment only. Play with it. If it works for you, use it'.

But what guts I had in those days! The Montreal mayor at the time I set up the driving schools' association, the Montreal City Motor League, was Monsieur Belon. So I asked Mayor Belon to become an honorary member of my association! Ha ha. Do you understand the magnitude of *chutzpah* to ask that! But I was so 'into' traffic safety, I was sick! I push, I push, I push, and nobody could contradict me!

They said I could have sold ice-cream to the Eskimos! I think you're the best salesman when you *believe* in your product. And nobody can take that away from you. So: I was an inventor, a creator. I used to go to the government and I'd say: 'How can you send an inspector, to inspect me, when the guy does not have half of my intelligence and my capacity to understand traffic safety?' So we ended up creating courses for government employees, so that they could have the authority to go and control driving schools and how they practised, and give them certification. But you have to have imagination: I was the only Jew they ever had as president of the Quebec Driving Schools' Association. With access to the legislature, and to open doors in Quebec City. Never!

But when I came here in the '50s, it was like that. You had freedom. You could do anything. Nobody said anything to you: you just kept on going.

But except for the freedom it was offering, I did not identify with... The so-called 'democracy' of the French Canadians you could see when they came to church each Sunday! In their furs and jewels. Interested only in who was looking at them and how they looked. The more time I have to think about it, I see that Montreal is now a sort of dictatorship. All you have is the right to speak. That's what they call 'liberty'. Because there are so many rules you have to follow now, you're not really free. And what are the rules for? I believe nobody can protect you but yourself.

Ah, look! Mont Royal! My mountain!

Every day, at 6, 6.30, in the morning, I'm up there. Other people living in Montreal don't understand. Don't see the treasure of the mountain existing in the middle of them. But I'm fanatical: me and a few other friends who meet there every day. You know: I say the mountain means my life! If I am not there I am not sure that I'm alive. I have to pinch myself, otherwise, to check I'm alive!

In the beginning, I would puff after just walking up a little incline. But I disciplined myself to get up every morning until it became a habit. So now, every day at 5 o'clock, I'm up. Even if I go to sleep at 1 o'clock in the morning, at 5 o'clock I'm up again. And I go up the mountain. It's my life: I have a family up there, lots of friends. And dogs, a lot of dogs: they all know me. Even after the dog goes to Florida with its owner and comes back three months later, the dog still comes and runs, like this! 'Look! It's Rickey!', the owner says. Ha

Figure 9. Rickey's mountain

ha. I don't know: I give him cookies. On the mountain I find myself in another world. I find people who take responsibility – because they are responsible for their animals – I find people who make sacrifices: going out there at a certain time every day. The people I meet there are another breed in our society. They are lawyers and judges, secretaries and plain people, ordinary people. And they are *responsible* people: that's what I like. We see each other, we say 'hello' to each other; from the start. We didn't know each other's names, but the faces radiated for all to see.

Before Christmas, there was a man, about seventy or something, who we didn't see for a while. Every time, someone would ask: 'Did you see Alex?' 'No, I didn't see Alex. What's happened to that guy?' 'I don't know'. We don't know his family name, we don't know his address, don't know where to look for him, but the inquietude of these people shows how related to each other we are. You walk, look at the view, the sunrise. This morning a family of four was there. She's a doctor and he's a ... I don't know what he is, Chinese. And when we see each other, we bow! That's the 'hello' we do. I don't know his name. Maybe he knows mine, but that's all. I hug him sometimes. I mean the people you meet all have their restrictions still: you can approach them to a degree, but not further. I mind my own business, I walk my own way. It's not so much intimacy, except in cases where somebody is really ill, or really has a problem, and you gain their trust and then they open up and talk to you about it; they talk to you about it because they know that you will not talk about it to others. That kind of intimacy exists on the mountain.

I'm blessed with this, because I like people and people like to be listened to. And if you can give them your shoulder, so that they can talk, and you listen, you did them the best medicine. That's all that they need. So ... that's my mountain!

I don't feel comfortable going later in the day, or in the afternoon, because all the people then are strangers. We are like a family there, we know each other. Even though we don't know names, we know faces. Sometimes I wear a hat with *España* marked on it. You saw it on me before? So they all know me by this. See, I was in Barcelona in 2004, and I met my cousin who lives in Germany. And he was wearing this cap that he had bought at a soccer game. And I said: 'Marcel, I like it!' and he said, 'You can have it', and he gave it to me! So I walk with it! Ha ha. I am fanatical!

And now I'll take you back to my apartment.

Act Six

Well, here we are in the warm. My apartment is warm ... It's amazing: when I think, Ruby Foo's, my restaurant, was the most elegant, the most sumptuous: the star of Montreal in the restaurant business when I worked there. But it's not the same now. You can't even recognize it, hardly ... Let me see if I have some old photos of these places to show you ... Here we are ... There are so many things ... I have about three more big albums like this ... This is when I got married in Israel: that's my wife, me, her father, her mother.

Nigel: It's a shame that you're obscured.

Rickey: Yeah, look here: this is my son when we arrived here.

Andrew: And where's this? What street is this?

Rickey: That's here in Montreal.

Nigel: When did your moustache go!

Rickey: Oh, when I erased it. Because I did it with a pencil! Ha ha.

Nigel: What? It wasn't a real moustache?

Rickey: No! I just had a few little blonde hairs here, so I put it on with a
          pencil! I wanted to have a moustache at the time. Ha ha! What do
          you want!?

Nigel: Is that your son?

Rickey: Yeah. And this is me when I was a little boy with my sister.

          – That's my sister in Israel.

– That's her husband who died.

– That's my wife's sister who died, and that's my wife's sister and her mother who died. Ahhhhh...

– That's my uncle and his wife who was a director of the National Theatre in Bucharest.

– That's my sister.

– That's Christos Stasinopoulos, the cousin of King Constantine of Greece. He was seven feet tall, and I had a Renault Dauphine – do you remember that little car? Stick shift – and I had to teach him how to drive. He was like a question mark in the car! But what a character, what class! So, we stayed friends. He died, poor guy. He invited us when we were in Greece, in Athens: we spent eleven days on his family yacht in the islands.

– This is Copacabana, in Brazil.

– Ah, this is in Germany, in the camp for displaced persons where I lived. Wolfrathausen. Where my son was born.

– And that's me, my mother and my sister.

Nigel: That must have been just before the war ...

Rickey: Oh yeah, I was ten or eleven here.

– This is still in the camp in Germany, teaching my son to play soccer.

– This is my aunt, died in Israel.

– This is the guy, Jewel, I told you about, Arab, who I worked with in the restaurant in Moshava Germanit, in Israel, who took me drinking.

Nigel: Did you ever think of living on a kibbutz?

Rickey: No! No, no. A free life! Adventure life ...

– Here I think it's me in school, in Romania. Look at me here, with the uniform!

Andrew: Do you know what happened to these people?

Rickey: I have no idea.

Andrew: Not a single one?

Rickey: I remember the name of the teacher: Madame Nicolau. But the director's name, I don't remember, even though he was very nice to me and gave me a bottle of milk every day.

Nigel: You didn't wear spectacles in those days?

Rickey: No. Spectacles is another story. I think I was 40, 45. I was in traffic
            instruction and education, and I had teachers from high school
            teaching the material, the theoretical part. And one of them, who
            worked for me for twenty years, Larry Chadowitz was his name,
            his brother-in-law was an ophthalmologist and made glasses.
            At the time, they used to have those American pilots' – aviator
            – glasses, so I said to Larry that I liked them, and he said to go to
            his brother-in-law and he would make me some. Nothing: just
            plain glass. So I went and got some, and as soon as I began to wear
            them, I begin to lose my vision for real! Now I needed glasses! Ha
            ha.

            – Here I think I was in Las Vegas with my wife: look at how I'm
              dressed!

            – I haven't looked at these in such a long time! Believe me.

            – Look, here I'm in New York with my grandmother: she died at
              the age of 104 ... Souvenirs, souvenirs.

            – This is my sister. When she went back to Romania, she went to
              the cemetery and took this picture and sent it to me. What do I
              want to see it for? I don't want to see it.

            – I don't even know who that is, here.

            – Oh, that's the sommelier of Ruby Foo's. And that's the roast-beef
              man of Ruby Foo's.

            – I have so many things here. I have two, three more albums like
              this.

            – Here's my daughter.

            – Here's Montreal City Motors. All these are my employees. I was a
              creator! I created here.

            – That's Alfredo in Rome. He's dead. Have you heard of Spaghetti
              Alfredo? Well, this is the man: Alfredo.

            – This is the day they nominated me as the President of the
              Driving Schools' Association of the Province of Quebec. So the
              Minister shook my hand and congratulated me.

            – That's at a conference, in Portugal. I took the microphone and
              amused people. And that's on a cruise. And who's standing next
              to the captain!

Andrew: Where was it going?

Rickey: To the Caribbean. *Cadalla Costa* was the ship's name. See? What
            a memory, eh? When I think of all the things I did in my life, I
            explode in laughter to myself. Ha!

– Uhhh ... but I don't find what I'm looking for. I wanted to but I don't. I'll find them when you've left ... That's Moishe's, where I worked.

Nigel: Do you feel nostalgic about any of these?

Rickey: No. That's the Tavern, and here, on top of it, I had the driving school. Have I told you what I did in Mexico? When I was an impresario? Have I told you that?

Andrew: No, not yet.

Rickey: Well, ha ha! In 1967, I was teaching a driving lesson on Sherbrooke Street. It was at the time when the first Datsuns arrived in Canada, in Quebec. And I was with a student in my Datsun, when a Cadillac smashed into us. At that time the cars were not so strong and the Datsun went like an accordion! So, I made a report to the police, explaining I had been hit from behind. The other driver was a car dealer from New York and he took all responsibility. But now I have no car to work in! So I said to my wife that I wanted to accomplish a dream of mine: I had no car for work so I'm going to go to Mexico for a vacation; and I'm going to grow a beard; and I'm going to walk barefoot in the sand; and I'm going to feel happy! And my wife allowed me to go. But when you go somewhere by yourself, you know, I took the first place I could get: the travel agency sent me to a rooming house in Mexico City. So, I arrived there at maybe 2.00 in the morning. The rooming house was dark, hot, no air conditioning, no television. So I came downstairs again and refused to stay there. I asked a taxi to take me to another hotel, with television and air conditioning. Well, it seems a new one had just opened up: the Casablanca. 'Okay: take me there!' So: I arrive – marble everything – I go in, it's 3.00 in the morning, now. First thing: put the television on, air conditioning on. But I still can't sleep, because I'm jet lagged. So what are you going to do? I go down to the bar. Twenty-four hours' music. 'What you want? Cerveza?' 'Yeah, give me a beer'. Now, if you want to know anything, in any country, you go to the concierge at a hotel; or you go to the barman. And they will tell you all the stories. So he asked me, the barman, what I was doing here. I said I was just visiting. He said: 'What is your profession?' And I said: 'I'm an impresario'. Ha ha. I don't know why I said that! But after that, you know: they were changing bands three times a night there! To impress me! Ha ha. I couldn't find anybody to laugh about it with, but by then I was afraid to tell them the truth! So: performers were performing in front of me; they brought me to meet their wives, families. For three days! Oh God! Ha ha. They made records for me, gave me records. (I gave them to my son: he has them now.) And they all wanted – the Montreal Place des Arts was about to be opened here – and they all wanted to come here to perform. And I found that they were really good bands and really

good singers! And what power I had down there! But what could I
do? Ha ha. I was afraid to tell them the truth ...

Coda

There is a superfluousness to my words, I find, next to Rickey's. There
is nothing that really needs to be added to his own full and nuanced
account of his life, and nor would that be appropriate. But I have
wanted to see in his story an account, also, of Anyone.

There is a way in which Rickey seems to wish to decentre himself
in his account, and I find this significant: he renders his character and
his actions less personal and less revealing than they might initially
appear. Far from a character trait that was centrally his, for instance,
'smartness' becomes simply a 'Jewish trait'. And exactly who was the
gutsy youth who practised such war-time derring-do? Rickey claims
barely to recognize him, hardly knows how to reconcile then and
now. Rickey speaks as if he is sometimes unsure whether the truth he
has to tell is his, or should be claimed as such. There have been many
occasions of misunderstanding in his past – others constructing
him as someone else, as versions of themselves, or using his own
revelations merely as means to tell their own stories – and he would
avoid such occasions in future. Can he tell the truth about himself?

Montreal and social responsibility change matters to an extent,
as I have mentioned. Now Rickey admits more to the ownership of
actions and traits, recognizing himself in his past, becoming both
more positive and more negative in his self-judgements. But even
here I feel uncertain of the extent to which Rickey's public persona
is a surface phenomenon that remains unconnected to the centre
of his self. Rickey does what he needs to to survive and succeed – 'I
took my chances and my decisions. I knew I was capable of doing it'
– but the truth behind the cheeky or powerful or fanatical front was
often something else besides. 'Rickey Hirsch' was not the same 'Rudi
Heersch' from Bucharest. There is the new Montreal businessman,
father, son and impresario, but the relationship Rickey has with these
identities – his creations – seems complex and often conflicted. He is
both proud of the roles he played and remorseful. In endeavouring to
provide for others and for himself did he always attend either to others
or to himself in the best way?

But it is precisely in this space between the public and the private
Rickeys, and in his self-consciousness concerning the distance involved
– his capacity to ironize the roles he played – that I would see evidence
for Anyone. Rickey's decentredness from any particular social setting
and cultural symbolization is at the same time his centricity as an

Figure 10. Rickey at the Middle Eastern café

individual human being. My own conceit, then, would be to see behind the various Rickeys ('Mr Rickey', 'R') to a kind of 'Rudi *Irgendjemand*': Rickey as Anyone, a version of the universal human actor. What is to be taken account of for this purpose is not so much the particular substance of Rickey's life, the historical circumstance, social roles and cultural forms – the feral Holocaust survivor, Jew and Montreal family man – as the capacity evidenced by Rickey to navigate historical socio-cultural landscapes while making his own sense and charting his own course.

By 'version' and 'Anyone' I hope for something that is more than further labelling: I do not foist more guises on Rickey. I would address him in analytic terms that are more truthful than the social roles he so adeptly skated across: terms that address an ontological state as against a merely symbolic one. Rickey is a version of Anyone, I say, at the same time he is his own person, gratuitously himself and beyond others' description. Indeed, Rickey is Anyone insofar as he is his own person. The relationship is complex but I do not see myself as taking anything away from Rickey by seeing him as a 'version' of the universal human actor. It is in his very individuality that his representativeness as Anyone lies. Rickey's life instantiates an individuality that is generalizable: Rickey embodies Anyone inasmuch as there is a human commonality to his individual uniqueness. I am reminded of Andrew Miller's observation, in reviewing a book of autobiographical account of lives caught up in twentieth-century fascism, that what we read in such individual stories is not a 'footnote' to history but history as such: 'one of the millions of private tales of evil and astonishing endurance that make up the awful whole' (Miller 2008: 25). The objectivity of human lives derives from their subjectivity.

I place my words about Rickey next to Rickey's own, then, through a wish to draw out the characteristics and nature of Anyone from the character and life story of one human being. There *is* a kind of typicality, here, a part–whole relationship that I would posit, but my analysis avoids designations of averages or common denominations that typify by reducing detail. It is in the fullness of an account of the substance of Rickey's life that his manifesting the capacities of Anyone emerges. In prefacing his book, *In the Land of Israel*, a collection of conversations that he conducted with individual residents of the country in the early 1980s, Amos Oz is careful to point out that 'representative pictures' and 'typical cross-sections' are misnomers when applied to human lives if one thereby implies that 'every man is [not] a world in himself' (Oz 1983: viii). One says that 'the individual is a world in himself or herself' – or 'Whoever destroys the life of a single human being – it is as if he had destroyed the entire world' (*Jerusalem Talmud*) – and so implies that a human life, Rickey's life, has a nature that is distinct from historical, social and cultural circumstance and should not be deemed or depicted as the cipher, puppet, embodiment or expression of such.

'Anyone' is not a simple figure and 'version' is a complex relation but they are central to my purpose. The cosmopolitanism of individuality entails the appreciation of the way in which a unique individual life partakes of the universally human and embodies a human singularity; the human exists in individual instances, yet each of those instances manifests the capacities and possibilities of the human whole. The analytical (and also moral) treatment of this relation is not a matter of subsuming the substance of Rickey's life or character into a human whole if by 'subsuming' we imagine an overcoming of the particular, an averaging, and an immersion or integration in the general as a common denomination. Rather than the general class of the human being treated as a monothetic phenomenon, it should be deemed polythetic; individual members form an aggregation not an integration. In an analytical account of Rickey's life I endeavour to identify capacities for making an individual life – self-consciousness, sense making, intentionality – whose instantiations are typically, universally human.

Certain stylistic features of Rickey's narrative stand out. He is remarkably fluent, given the decades that often intervene, the episodes being delivered with enormous clarity and detail. So vivid had it been that as a listener I had come to query its authenticity – with Rickey picking up on my uncertainty and joking with his son how his interviewers suspected him of purloining the account from a fiction he had read. Indeed, there was an unreality to the account, as escapade piled on escapade and chance upon chance, that partook, in my mind, of the fairy tale or Boy's Own adventure. The non-saluting soldier who inadvertently allowed the handcuffed teenagers to escape, the French Foreign Legion recruiting for Algeria in Austria, the mess hall and open jam pots of the Bricha on the Italian border; then Mayor Belon and the Driving Schools' Association, the impresario in Mexico City, multi-million dollar real-estate ventures in downtown Montreal... I have not included all the remarkable details, each of which seemed in a way to add to the distance between the world I imagine for the dapper octogenarian facing me and Andrew and the marginal, feral states of caprice, of social and moral attenuation, and survival, being suggested by Rickey's narrative. Rickey picked up on this too, of course, in his laughing aside that 'all these stories' of his are likely to make listeners 'bitter' about their own anodyne lives.

But it is also the case that Rickey is himself at a distance from the events which he recounts and also from their protagonist, as we have seen. This is particularly so concerning the war-torn years of his life in Europe and Israel, the adventures he effected and the serendipities, before he reaches Canada. 'The guts I had', is a repeated refrain. When he reaches Canada and Montreal the form of the narrative alters: less episodically discrete, more proud assertions ('I took my chances and my decisions'; 'I was an inventor: I was a creator') and more didactic proverbialism ('You're poor not in your pocket but in your mind'). His early life, Rickey says a number of times, is something he does not want to dwell on; perhaps he rushes through narrating it as part of a desire to live in and for the present. When he does once return to Romania and Constanza, on his son's urging, he reports that a black fug engulfed him and he found it hard to reconcile what he saw around him with his own past: Did he get through all this, get away with all this? That he should have had to have done all this...

The most fluent sections of the narrative, dealing with Rickey's early years – so fluent and breathless as to resemble a fictional adventure – are also those in which Rickey claims to recognize himself least. The clear-cut and striking episodes are perhaps now experienced by Rickey, too, as if a kind of story he has read or seen performed. Rickey openly struggles with his memory: with the order of events and with whole chunks of time (What did he do in Bucharest to survive before he and the undercover policeman went to meet the Russian advance? What did he do for recreation during his time in the army in Israel?), and where geographically he was or was going. Memory, as he admits at one point, attaches itself best to particular objects, occasions and people. It is also true that Rickey was not necessarily more knowledgeable when actually living through the times of his life – concerning where he was, where he was being taken, how things came about or when. Where was the soldier taking him to begin his twenty-five years of hard labour after his 'court martial'? Where did he land in what was then Palestine?

'My past is a story of survival, mostly', Rickey concludes. He admits to possessing the physical stamina of the young, but it is also clear that the drive, endurance and skill continued throughout his life, imbuing also his working years in Montreal: the move up the ranks of the restaurant business; the setting up of his own business; the dealing with government bureaucracy and policy; the investing in property. There is a Philip Larkin poem entitled 'Ignorance' (Larkin 1990: 107), in which Larkin marvels at the way in which his body clothes him 'with its own decisions' and wonders at his body's 'skill' at finding what it needs to survive. Larkin uses the poem to suggest a dichotomy between his body and his conscious awareness, and there is something of this distantiation in Rickey, too: him marvelling both at what his body performed in managing its physical survival in Europe and also the *chutzpah* in pursuing financial security in Montreal. But there is also more of a connection in Rickey: I find him to be more of a piece – body plus mind, physical stamina plus social aptitude – throughout his life. Rickey was alert to circumstance and opportunity mentally and physically. This leads me to read his distantiation from his past possibly as a kind of politeness or modesty, also as a convenience in the process of the continuing reinvention of his social self in very different sets of circumstances.

I have described Rickey's aptitude for skating over social surfaces in terms of 'passing'. Rickey *passed* through the discriminatory circumstances of Nazi-dominated Europe that could have proved fatal. He *passed* through the territories of a number of nation-states and their borders ('You know, you can cross any border any time'). He *passed* through the categorial expectations of a range of interlocutors, making friends and acquaintances, becoming useful and respected. He was the polio-victim's child mentor, the Liberty Ship steward, the spy in Vienna, the French legionnaire, the translator with the displaced persons, the Israeli *machad*, the Montreal waiter. He escaped the clutches of the French Foreign Legion by gabbling some words of Hungarian to passing Hassidic Jewish smugglers espied through a locked gate. He reached Canada when Brazil closed its doors by having himself, his wife and son sponsored by his wife's brother-in-law's mother in Ontario – before a man on a boat recommended Montreal.

The human figure who passes through physical environments, social situations, social structures, personal relationships, and yet still remains himself (or herself), and has a sense of himself *as* himself, is the one I identify as Anyone. Rickey evinces that figure. Even his name, he admits, the personal label by which others know him, is not ultimately coincident with himself. Names are irrelevant, even when known, for identifying who a person actually is; it is the face and body and its behaviours by which Anyone may adjudge and come to know anyone else.

Rickey's eighty-four years have been largely spent amid twentieth-century fascism, nationalism, ethnic fundamentalism, diaspora and postcolonialism. Yet, while 'caught up' in global events, forces and structures, Rickey has not been their cipher or pawn, product or plaything or dupe. Engaged with the world, his life was yet always and only his own.

Rickey has made his own way, I conclude: he has attended to what is before him in his own way; he has appropriated what is before him such that it takes the shape of his own intentionality. Emerson (1981: 95) described this existential capacity as the individual making his or her own circumstance: an alertness to events, forces and structures that translates into a creating of opportunity. There was a power of the person, an individual nature, an existential power – of self-reliance, self-examination, self-balance, self-sustenance, self-recovery, self-evolution – Emerson elaborated, which preceded and perdured, transcended, the proximal particularities of historical situations, social structures and cultural normativities:

> I make my circumstance. Let any thought or motive of mine be different from what they are, the difference will transform my condition and economy. I – this world which is called I – is the mould into which the world is poured like melted wax. The mould is invisible but the world betrays the shape of the mould. You call it the power of circumstance, but it is the power of me. (Emerson 1981: 95)

In the conversation Rickey has with himself, with his history, with the interlocutors who would know him, I have wanted to see an irony that also marks the distance and difference between Rickey as role player and as himself. The Rickey who adopts this ironic stance is Anyone. Rickey proclaims that 'the story of a life is created by the individual', and that: 'I was a creator. I created'; I hear him speaking in the voice of Anyone.

PART 3

How is the individuality of Anyone to be accommodated by an objective science and acknowledged by a democratic society?

ANYONE IN SCIENCE AND SOCIETY: EVIDENCING AND ENGAGING

Having observed Anyone as an empirical reality, the intention of this part of the book is to consider the problems that arise in locating Anyone in discourses whose humanistic ethos may seem to necessitate a kind of averaging. There is an issue of inscribing the particularity of Anyone in a human science intent upon the universality of the species; and there is an issue of recognizing the particularity of Anyone in a civil society intent upon proceeding equably and equally with all.

I first approach the question by way of subjectivity (3.1). If Anyone is capacitated to make worlds of his or her own interpretation then there is a subjectivity to the truths by which Anyone lives. To do justice to this is to develop notions of evidence whose criteria allow for the subjective and recognize its reality. I argue for a kind of human science prepared to explore ways in which Anyone's personal truths manifest themselves in individual ways in individual lives.

A problem lies in conceiving of the relationship between the uniqueness of individuality and the generality of the human without recourse to the reductiveness of stereotyping. I contend, next (3.2), that modelling of the one and the whole which retains the authenticity of the individual as a thing-in-itself is possible. An emphasis on capacities as distinct from the instances of their substantiation allows one to configure both a rational human science and a rationalizing liberal society.

A problem of social engagement exists alongside that of modelling: assuring the individual of space and of recognition within society-wide codes of civil exchange. Everyday interaction in stable social settings calls for a kind of routine formalism: conventional cultural symbologies mediate between public traditions and private consciousness. It is necessary to conceive of a kind of politeness, I suggest lastly (3.3), a code of manners, which anticipates a public place and space for Anyone while not presuming to know what

Anyone might hold true and dear. 'Cosmopolitan politesse' is the name I give to a species of civil ritual which operates not on the basis of categorial or stereotypical identities but of a human universality, and hence serves, too, as a medium of individual emancipation.

3.1

PERSONAL TRUTH, SUBJECTIVITY AS TRUTH

Introduction

What is the nature of evidence that a cosmopolitan anthropology should accept? More broadly, what is the nature of truth in human life? If experience, the *qualia* of consciousness, are individual to Anyone, and environments of the life-world come to be fashioned as part of his or her personal phenomenology, then how is this to be accommodated conceptually and discursively? If there is a kind of personal truth to individual life, something that Anyone embodies in a particular way, then how is a cosmopolitan social science to do justice to this?

I shall make an argument in terms of how Anyone performs his or her truth or lives it. The subjective phenomenology of human life may be evidenced insofar as it manifests itself in individual intentionalities – lifestyles and choices – and also in the body of Anyone. Consciousness, body and environment form an individual whole for each human being, and the truth of Anyone's interpretation and experiencing of the world(s) which they construe and inhabit may be accessible by way of subtle readings of bodily expressions as well as from Anyone's own introspective and autobiographical accounts (Rapport 2007, 2008).

My route into this argument, as well as the evidence of personal life on which I shall draw, is provided by the personal-cum-conceptual writings of Søren Kierkegaard (1813–1855) and Friedrich Nietzsche (1844–1900). These nineteenth-century names bear witness to the genealogy of cosmopolitan thought – as a commentary on Enlightenment advances in human knowledge – as well as demonstrating the longevity and broad relevance of an argument concerning the status of subjectivity in an objective universe. Doing justice to the ultimately embodied nature of human truth is an issue for science in general, not merely a cosmopolitan anthropology; it is, I would contend, highly pertinent to the practice of modern medicine, for instance.

My course is to begin with a philosophical excursus on Kierkegaardian themes. These are shown to be highly relevant in the context of the standardizing and massifying tendencies of versions of science and of social policy alike which pay insufficient attention to the individual case; again, modern medicine is a particularly pertinent arena. The argument ends with a discussion of the case of Nietzsche, as evidenced by autobiographical insights and biographical commentaries. Nietzsche's last years of sickness are examined as an example of the individual holism of consciousness, body and environment in a human life.

Kierkegaard's and Nietzsche's stories bear a lot of weight. My contention is that in them we can read of human sensibilities. In their subtle and complex self-examinations we can find versions of our own. In particular, it is against their detailed examinations of the metaphysics of self-consciousness that we might profitably juxtapose a merely physical or objective (biomedical, bureaucratic) construction of human embodiment, and find the latter wanting.

Evidence in the human sciences should encompass a kind of respect, of recognition. There is an ethical component to the act of regarding a phenomenon as evidence. The rise of scientific evidence as a universal form of objectivity accompanied an Enlightenment battle against intrinsic differences being claimed between human beings on a categorial basis: in terms of race, nationality, ethnicity, religiosity, class and gender. All of humanity possessed the same body with, for instance, the same capacities for health and susceptibilities for sickness. The contemporary 'regression' to communitarian identity politics aside, that battle has over the past 200 years of scientific advance largely been won. Human rights – the rights to a universally human condition of life – we have seen to be a global ideology. My claim is that a further, 'cosmopolitan' step is for us to afford respect for a more finely grained appreciation of 'the human', one that recognizes individual differences as the fundamental characteristic of the species. Human nature is individual nature. We should afford the cost (epistemological and practical) of a version of evidence which is sensitive to the truth of our universally individual human embodiment: we should take into account, for instance, the range of individual differences between healthy and sick human bodies. Each illness is unique, as Gilbert Lewis (2000) argues. It is evidence of an individual life that a cosmopolitan project in anthropology must properly hope to accommodate as truth.

A Kierkegaardian Excursus

[P]eople still consider it proud and haughty and presumptuous to talk about the individual when it is of course the really human attitude, namely, that everyone is an individual.

—Søren Kierkegaard, *Journals*

Kierkegaard's philosophy developed as a reaction to what he called an 'Hegelian' orthodoxy (Kierkegaard 1941). According to Hegel, world and self all partake of the same basic structures, all meet through Christ in God, all are part of an encompassing, spiritual, cosmic process: *Geist*. This meant for Hegel that individual knowledge and realization were impossible apart from a collective, spiritual realization. Contrariwise, Kierkegaard insisted that a human being was first and foremost an individual, not an organ of a larger body or process. To make the individual accidental or incidental to the human condition was to transform existence into something indifferent, almost incidental. There was nothing indifferent, however, about an individual's life to himself or herself, and any account at deciphering and inscribing the truth of the human must begin from this point.

More precisely, Kierkegaard was antipathetic to Hegelianism on three accounts: its abstraction, its systemicism, and its impersonalism. Under the influence of Hegel, Kierkegaard felt, contemporary thought and practice were preoccupied by illusions of objectivity which had the effect of smothering the vital core of human experience – subjectivity – beneath historicizing commentary, pseudo-scientific categorization and abstract theory. In point of fact, existence was a narrow, inward, personal adventure: each person by himself or herself in the face of others and of the infinite. Indeed, existence had infinite depth: it could not be reduced to or even assimilated by the purely surface and historical phenomena of conventional systems of ideas or shared practical norms. To know what it meant to exist was to appreciate 'what inwardness signifies' (Kierkegaard 1941: 223). How, for instance, was suffering to be translated into thought, ideation or language such as it could be accessed by another? Only living was like living; experience could be reduced to nothing else, it was a separate reality where 'passion [was] the culmination' (Kierkegaard 1941: 176). Or again, how was spontaneous feeling to be made sense of in terms of a systematic view of consciousness?

The major failing of systemicism (such as Hegelianism) was that it transformed actual states of affairs into abstract theoretical possibilities, removed from the world of concrete realization. It treated matters entailing personal choice as if they were topics of common, objective insight; it transmuted living issues into generalized curios thus doing violence to their nature. 'Causal regulation', as a notion describing either the contents of consciousness or the relation of the latter to an unfolding universe extraneous to it, failed to do justice to the vital inconsistencies and creativity of an existence which defied the limitations of timeless essences or teleological sequences.

To questions of personal fulfilment there could be no objective approach. One could attain to no impersonal, transcendent viewpoint on matters of ongoing, individual experience. Existence was 'precisely the opposite of [such systemic] finality' (Kierkegaard 1941: 107). It was not that the kinds of question raised by systemic philosophy did not have relevance but that they did so only when seen from the point of view and the life narrative of the existing individual. Live issues could only be faced in their appropriately living form. This meant a concentration on the world of inner experience, and gaining knowledge through reflecting on what the individual did, had done and might do.

Kierkegaard sought thus to affirm the integrity of subjectivity. Pure and passionate, subjectivity possessed an intransigence in the face of an objectivizing, universalizing or absolutizing mediation of reality which must be recognized. The subjectivity of experience had an all-encompassing breadth: it was behind and within all human things, including abstract systems such as logic or physics. Existence preceded all and could be reduced to nothing. The existing individual and his or her subjectivity had to remain the touchstone of any human accounting.

In positing existence over and against abstraction, and individual consciousness over and against systematization, Kierkegaard did entertain a form of methodological dualism. Two possible stances were construable with regard to human perception, he argued: the disengaged, contemplative, objectifying and objectivizing (what Kant called 'pure reason'), as against the engaged, participatory and agential (Kant's 'practical reason'). The former 'impersonalism' was fine for mathematics and science (for stars, flora and fauna), even for history, but it was out of place where Anyone was a particular centre of action, choice and self-consciousness. And the difference was absolute: only the qualitative could treat human existence. Far from aping the perceived objectivities of natural science, then, a human science ought to resist the pressure to transmute knowledge of experience into abstract generalizations, and individuality into typification. If it was to approach the truth about human existence, human science must eschew notions of category and treat live issues in their appropriately living form.

Kierkegaard based his notion of methodological dualism on two main insights, one concerning human ignorance and one knowledge. The limits of human reasoning were such that human beings could never take the place of God and his total vantage point and knowledge; only God could formulate an existential system of reality. All human judgement was made from a partial, subjective and limited standpoint. Furthermore, life was movement, and human beings could accede to no Archimedean resting place from which to view it askance. Put differently, life could never be properly understood in time because there was no stopping place. The human being who existed prior to analytical systems, in short (as all did), could not be turned into their object.

If this was the nature of human ignorance, then Kierkegaard also had something to say about the particular nature of human knowledge. What was true for and about human beings depended on the place of a state of affairs in the forward movement of an individual's life. The truth, its apprehension and its representation, could not be separated from individual being and could not be made abstract. Truth did not derive from an external system but was intrinsic, something encountered through individuals' own efforts and made part of their own nature. Truth was subjective: 'subjectivity [was] the truth' (Kierkegaard 1941: 118).

Let me elaborate on this point because it is central to my argument. The paradigmatic kind of individual knowledge or truth for Kierkegaard was faith. The essence of faith was passionate commitment by an individual to an inner, personal sense of what was most fundamental to existence: 'the idea for which I can live and die' (Kierkegaard 1958: 1835). This was a sense that could neither be rationally justified or proven nor even communicated to another. Even to himself, Kierkegaard's own Christian faith seemed unintelligible and absurd. It resulted for him in despair and guilt, fear and trembling. And yet nothing, he insisted, felt more real, more authentic or wise or true: 'The only reality that exists for an existing individual is his own ethical reality' (Kierkegaard 1958: 1835).

As well as faith, love: What is involved in someone claiming 'I love you'? A passionate intensity felt by one individual that another can never feel for himself or herself. Calls for objective proof in this context were, too, inappropriate. Logic could no more capture the uncommon peculiarities of individual existence – feelings, thoughts, dispositions, emotions – than could other individuals. The truth of the claim was, for Kierkegaard, determined by the manner and intensity of an individual's belief in it: their degree of commitment to their feelings and its manifestation in their life. All our most fundamental knowledge is of this kind, Kierkegaard concluded. Here are the commitments to unique self-knowledge of unique selves consequent upon a knowledge which is delivered by way of passion. Reason does not assist here (any more than can logic assist in uncovering the truth of another's feelings). The individual needs to know what to do, demands it of his or her interpretations, and in this project is alone with his or her passions – whose deliverances are beyond the scope of pure reason.

Individuals should act on the basis of what feels most true to them, Kierkegaard counselled, even while they are aware that the decision can find no support in purely rational principles: it is a category error even to posit such a recourse. The 'leap' to a way of life, to values and identities, must be based on commitment to passion. Indeed, it is this act that most defines us as human beings, as individual existents: '[I]t is not so much a question of choosing the right [any choice is equally unjustified and unjustifiable] as of the energy, the earnestness, the pathos with which one chooses' (Kierkegaard 1958: 1850). Discovering one's personal truth was of primary importance: the search, possibly desperate, for a way of being-in-the-world and behaving, all day and every day, that was subjectively authentic. This was the most dignified venture in which human beings could involve themselves. One accrued the moral integrity that accompanied one's physical integrity: 'eternally it is the task of every individual to become an entire man' (Kierkegaard 1941: 309).

Philosophical commentators have suggested that 'truth' may not be the correct term for Kierkegaard's notions of subjectivity; we should distinguish between the terminology we apply to science and mathematics and that to metaphysical commitments (Solomon 1978: 72). I would like to keep with the term, here, for the way in which it brings into sharp focus the issue to be addressed: the truth of an individual life that a human science, a cosmopolitan anthropology, might properly hope to entertain as 'evidence'. The choices on how to live and what to do that an individual might make – must make – Kierkegaard argues, derive from a unique embodiment, and feed further into that embodiment. An individual's truths are matters of passion and they give on to action.

This is not a negation of Enlightenment rationalism, I would insist, but a recognition of the fullness and diversity of individual consciousness: reason plus the politics of momentary sentiment (cosmos plus polis). Anyone's deepest realities are constituted by the truths he or she performs in the course of his or her life. Subjectivity is not only an individual's truth, then; 'subjectivity is [their] reality' (Kierkegaard 1941: 118).

Personal Truth as Political and Physiological

'Romanticism versus the Enlightenment' are the terms often chosen, nevertheless, to gloss Kierkegaard's kind of critique of Hegel. Romanticism represented a reaction, it is said, against the generalizing rationale of the Enlightenment: a wish to reinstate the individual case, with all its particularities and peculiarities against arid classifications and typification. But one need not introduce a counter-Enlightenment term here, for Enlightenment thought itself contained the paradox: it was internally conflicted regarding the individual case. In overturning the tyranny of the *ancien regime* – that which would insist on essential differences of moral quality, bodies and rights between patrician and plebian, man and woman, Frenchman and Briton, Christian and Jew – and claiming, instead, that all who respected the rule of law of the liberal-democratic state should be guaranteed equal treatment under the law, the Enlightenment inadvertently ushered in a potential 'tyranny of the majority', a standardizing rationality. How was one to inscribe equal rights for all, frame policies that hope for the greatest good for the greatest number, without facilitating an overlooking of individual difference, treating as secondary an individual's right to be different and tending towards an institutionalizing of the average and common-denominational? Bureaucratic rationalism tended, in the words we have heard from Michael Herzfeld, towards 'the production of indifference' (Herzfeld 1993).

The justice of equality and the freedom of difference have contested for liberal attention since the Enlightenment without resolution. '[W]hatever crushes individuality is despotism, no matter what name it is called', John Stuart Mill (1972: 121) propounded, and against the impersonal 'utilitarian' impulses of his father, James Mill, and of Jeremy Bentham, he sought ways to reconcile individual difference with the 'rationality', the universalizing project, of liberalism. The following quotations are taken from his essay *On Liberty*.

> The only freedom which deserves the name is that of pursuing our own good in our own way, so long as we do not attempt to deprive others of theirs, or impede their efforts to obtain it. Each is the proper guardian of his own health, whether bodily, or mental and spiritual. Mankind are greater gainers by suffering each other to live as seems good to themselves, than by compelling each to live as seems good to the rest. (Mill 1972: 75)

> If all mankind minus one were of one opinion, and only one person were of the contrary opinion, mankind would be no more justified in silencing that one person than he, if he had the power, would be justified in silencing mankind ... [T]he peculiar evil of silencing the expression of an opinion is, that it is robbing the human race; posterity as well as the existing

generation; those who dissent from the opinion, still more than those who hold it. If the opinion is right, they are deprived of the opportunity of exchanging error for truth: if wrong, they lose, what is almost as great a benefit, the clearer perception and livelier impression of truth, produced by its collision with error. (Mill 1972: 75)

To his own satisfaction Mill squared the circle between liberty and equality by making each individual responsible for their own notion of 'good' or 'right' – 'truth' in Kierkegaard's terms – and of health. He restricted the state to a role in ensuring that individuals do not deprive one another of their different truths, and do not make a nuisance of themselves in others' ongoing self-determinations.

But Mill does lay claim to a larger truth nevertheless, if not in terms of the state then of 'the human race'. The right of an individual to their opinion, to their version of healthiness and good, delivers the wider public good that humanity as a whole, now and in the future, might learn what is in fact true. Moreover, in his later years Mill became more comfortable with bringing together the notions of 'wider public' and 'human race' with that of 'the state'. The growth in human populations, their density, and the extent of their need might well justify organized social reform, even to the extent of a socialist economy in which might be 'unite[d] the greatest individual liberty of action, with a common ownership in the raw material of the globe, and an equal participation of all in the benefits of combined labour' (Mill 1957: 149).

Referring to Mill shows how the issue of personal truth and its accommodation within the rationalizing procedures of a state, albeit a state careful of the conditions of all its citizens and considering the legitimacy of policies it might universally exercise on their behalf, has been a thorny political issue as well as a philosophical and methodological one for at least the past 150 years. Let me bring the matter up to date, however, as well as introducing more specific questions of medical policy into the frame, with reference to a 2005 article by Allison James, 'The Standardized Child: Issues of Openness, Objectivity and Agency in Promoting Childhood Health'. James's argument is that medical science has been integral to the establishing of norms in health, such as child growth and development, which, while appearing to offer beneficial measures against which individuals can be judged, can also work to stigmatize difference as pathology. The standardization of norms operates as a kind of coercive strategy, even tyranny: 'health promotion' for all, regardless of the particularities of individual lives. There is stigma accorded to the individual case that chronically refuses to be standard (as if 'malingering').

James elaborates: nineteenth-century, utilitarian interest in the physiology of the changes undergone by the child's developing body fostered a view that such changes were fundamental to the health of children and that, therefore, in respect of any individual child, their bodily change was in need of measurement and monitoring. This interest in the objective charting and surveying of the child population gradually began to define certain limits of normality for children's bodies, culminating in the development and later widespread use of the height and weight growth chart as a regulatory device for ensuring the health of children. The chart, together with a number of other monitoring tools, has in turn had great political and social significance with respect to policy interventions. It has, for example, been instrumental in improving the health of 'working-class' children by enabling patterns of growth retardation to be detected and, consequently, ameliorative welfare measures to be put in place.

What has also developed, however, is a kind of 'surveillance medicine' no longer simply focused on the epidemiological mapping of disease or the monitoring of growth. Statistics on child ill-health, ostensibly part of the benign state regime of governance and legislative care, now manifest processes of regulation and control through which children's bodies and development are 'constituted' by adult carers (James 2005: 100–3). In one sense surveillance practices are highly democratic. The identification of risky behaviours within the population, the public dissemination of such knowledge through the publication of survey and research findings, and the drawing up of standards and norms against which individuals can assess their health status, all work to open up science to the public gaze. Ostensibly, people can choose – or not – to modify their behaviour accordingly. The real costs, however, are that individuals are identified as categories of persons. Information giving and seeking carries the seeds of standardization and essentialism, and coercion.

Furthermore, James fears that children's opportunities to take on responsibility for their own health and lifestyle become increasingly restricted. Effectively, children are distanced from taking an interest in their own health status by strategies of health promotion that rely on paternalistic techniques of persuasion or legislative process rather than encouraging self-awareness, self-management and the assumption of rights. We occupy an increasingly medicalized social world: medical experts assume roles as masters of lifestyle. Is the apparent widespread public concern for health focused on ensuring the better health of individuals, James wonders, or – regarding them collectively as 'the nation's life-blood' – are we seeing professional medicine acting as a kind of relay between political objectives and personal lives which deliver collectivist notions of the good life and public good?

So-called 'healthy' practices may be less rational and scientific than we might wish to claim them to be. Theories of child growth and development upon which the models of the standardized child and ideas of normalcy ultimately rest may, for instance, provide a perhaps spurious veneer of standardization on actually diverse childhood realities. The standardized child, it may be argued, rests on 'bad' science in not concentrating on the actual variations within the child population. Simply put: standardization is cheap, a quick fix. '[U]ntil medical science can be used to celebrate diversity', James concludes, 'to widen our visions of normalcy and to permit children more participation as social actors in respect of their own health status, those children whose bodies are conceived to differ still run the risk of being headlined for being deviant' (James 2005: 107). A 'liberal' welfarism, as Ronald Dworkin (1977) might have described it, is one whose fundamental commitment is less to uniformity of treatment than to uniqueness of person.

Personal Truth as Physical Environment

If this were simply a matter of ethics and politeness, of accommodating different perspectives on the body, health, disease and the life course into medical practice in the course of sensitive carer–patient communication, then one could point to the many reforms already in place. Issues of cultural and regional differences, of gender and faith, of class and age, are highly prominent in modern Western medicine's awareness of the fashion with which it delivers care to individual patients. In other words, biomedicine accommodates itself to the fact that an individual's world-view and social affiliations will impact upon how the doctor–patient interaction will be entered into and understood, and how illness, diagnosis and cure will be conceptualized.

I want, however, to argue something other than the case of perspectivism, and the dignity which is said to accompany 'other' cultural recognition. I want to explore the extent to which the personal truth which an individual patient might hold (including child patients) might effect the aetiology and process of disease – and hence the nature of what is scientifically evidential. Should one not speak of a physiology, a sensorium, a physical environment – of healthiness as well as disease – being brought about by what individuals hold to be true and the practices in which they partake? Does not Anyone's ongoing personal way of being and doing, the way he or she practises a life-project, translate into a particular embodiment? Anyone's performance of his or her personal truths gives rise to their own kind of physical truth – a truth which demands scientific recognition as evidence.

It is in partial recognition of this kind of argument that 'healthy lifestyles' are currently promoted by medical policy makers in the West. It has been increasingly recognized in statements of policy that an individual's personal history as a smoker, a drinker, a sunbather, a miner, an eater of red meat or olive oil or the brains of one's dead relatives will affect the course of their bodily health and morbidity. This recognition has still involved, however, a kind of essentialist differentiation, subject to profiling, to typifying and massifying. Medical experimentation and drug-trials render 'lifestyle', too, within the compass of statistical norms. No new concept of evidence is thought to be called for.

But should one, can one, demand more?

Kierkegaard, it is suggested (Solomon 1978: 80), saw no point in 'abstract' knowledge, and he defined this quite broadly to include all scientific enterprises. Knowing oneself – towards the aim of knowing what to do with one's life – should be, he felt, the end of all enquiry. Perhaps the state of medical and natural sciences in the early to mid nineteenth century could be said to justify the Kierkegaardian stance, at least in part: one might just as well have lived one's life according to personal truths for all that medicine could accurately prescribe pathways to bodily comfort and longevity. Almost 200 years on, however, such a stance seems reactionary, superstitious. How, then, might one begin to admit a place for Kierkegaardian notions concerning the centrality of personal truth in an individual's (bodily) existence – and hence, too, Mill's notions of an individual's right to live that truth, and James's notions of the bureaucratic need to shape policy around that truth – amid twenty-first-century scientific practice and notions of evidential truth?

Let me begin by considering the significant role of reflexivity in human experience. Our distinction between the natural and the human sciences is more than a convenience, Gregory Bateson (1980: 16–18) suggests, because it draws attention to the extent to which 'mentality' is immanent in the world of living creatures but absent from the world of 'non-living' galaxies, billiard balls, sticks and stones. In the latter, purely physicalist universe (Bateson borrows the term *pleroma* from Carl Jung) external and observable forces and impacts are the causes of events. Contrastively, among the metaphysical realities of living things (the *creatura*), a cause is better understood as an idea: a reaction to the perception of a difference to which the living thing attends. Consciousness is fundamental to behaviour, and behaviour is an extension into an environment with which living beings maintain a relationship of mutuality.

An idea is not a thing or an observable event, Bateson (1972: 426–32) elaborates, any more than is awareness of differences between things or states of affairs, and yet in the world of mental process, of information processing, which living creatures inhabit, such no-things are intrinsically consequential. They are, one could say, the ground of understanding and explaining living things: in human science, certainly, one ushers in a species of complexity and hierarchy absent from mere pleromic circumstance. Where does medicine reside in terms of this dichotomy? Perhaps along the fault line, but surely with a foot firmly planted among the *creatura*. It is appropriate for the neurophysiologist, say, to appreciate the physical determinism that eventuates in a fracture to the skull but also the conscious awareness that preceded and followed the physical circumstance – causative of the (otherwise indeterminate) human behaviour relative to the physical event. The course of the injury and recuperation, moreover, will be equally dependent on the interpretations of its situation which the brain makes.

It has long been a sociological truth that what is distinctive about the human actor is the role which world-view (theory, belief, the imagination, *poeisis*, desire) plays in decision making and action. There is a 'hermeneutic circle', a process of recursion whereby our assumptions are preconditions of our active encounters with reality, and further affected by the latter: 'If men define situations as real, they are real in their consequences' (Thomas and Thomas 1928: 572). There is, indeed, according to Anthony Giddens (1991), something particularly contemporary about the extent to which human actors are able to lead 'reflexive' lives: to engender a 'direct feedback from knowledge to action'. It is increasingly the case, for Giddens, that the physical worlds in which human beings live are reflections of the assumptions with which they approach the world and reactions to what their assumptions effect. Both our technology and our liberality make of our world-views self-fulfilling prophecies.

What is distinctive and attractive about Bateson's work is his 'cybernetic' or recursive instinct to see clear connexions between the sociological and the biological. The world of *creatura* – of all living things, including human beings as species of organisms – is reflexive to the extent that the processing of information is responsible not only for ideational change but physical change too. The physiology of the human organism, of any organism in any environment, is a matter of feedback (manifested as transfers of energy) between purposive actions and judgmental reactions to their effects.

The claim which I began was that an individual's interpretation of, and intentions towards, the world – as an ongoing personal history – gave rise to the phenomenon of individual-plus-environment as a kind of thing-in-itself. The individual in its environment was a distinct and discrete organism to which cosmopolitanism, as science and as morality, had to do justice. Anyone came to occupy his or her own environment, which was at once cognitive, affective and physical, and born out of a lifetime of attending, in a distinctive way, to what the senses relayed concerning the body's circumstance and activity. Anyone comes habitually to engage with what is beyond itself in a particular way and so structure a distinctive, personal life-world.

In elaborating this argument elsewhere (Rapport 2003), I have drawn upon Scott Turner's (2000) work on animal physiology and what he describes as animals' capacity to act as 'architects and engineers' of their own living conditions. In furtherance of a physiological homeostasis that is conducive to their longevity, security and adaptability, Scott explains, animals often can be seen to 'choose' to expend their energies on changing their immediate environments to suit their needs rather than (slowly) adapting their own physiologies. What they do, in effect, is to extend themselves – their intentions, needs, metabolisms – beyond the integument of their skins and so make their environments into kinds of external organs – such as kidneys or lungs existing outside their bodies.

Earthworms, for instance, have, over the past 650 to 700 million years, constructed soil burrows which co-opt the soil so that it serves as an accessory kidney, ensuring the worms' survival in otherwise uninhabitable environs. Earthworms evolved to be primarily freshwater creatures. Their problem in living on land is keeping the right balance of water and salts in their bodies: maintaining a differential between the condition of the liquids inside their bodies and out, and offsetting a thermodynamic flux which would naturally tend towards equalization. If earthworms were animals simply adapted to their environments (and not vice versa) then they would be severely limited regarding the soils they might inhabit. Soil particles tend to weather and to decrease in size, becoming clay-like and soggy – a kind of liquidity earthworms cannot survive. Earthworms' practice, therefore, is to aggregate particles of soil together. They do this by secreting mucus from their body surfaces, by passing soil through their bodies so that mucus adheres to it, and by defecating calcite. These three processes act against soil erosion, keeping burrows open, and enabling the soil to absorb sufficient water but also to hold it weakly enough for earthworms to gain access to it. The result is vastly to expand the soil horizon where worms can live and to affect soil qualities at a scale many times larger than the generating organisms themselves. Earthworms, one can say, possess the energy and exercise the agency to change soil ecosystems, and to maintain them in the face of entropy.

Animal-built structures are ubiquitous, Turner explains, whether ephemeral in their construction and duration or more lasting. (Turner also instantiates how termites' mounds transform wind energy, how crickets' burrows modulate, amplify and direct sound, and how spiders' webs work as organs of respiratory gas exchange underwater.) May it not be appropriate, he concludes, to consider these environmental mouldings as parts of the animals themselves, as much organs of their particular physiologies as what we are accustomed to thinking of as their 'internal' bodily workings? Do 'their bodily workings' not extend beyond them, into the environments they fashion? Here are fashionings which affect the flow of matter, energy and information to and through the organism, and between it and its surroundings. What makes an organism distinctive, individual, is not the existence of its boundary or integument per se but the nature of what its boundary does. The boundary around a distinct living creature is a process whereby certain internal conditions of life are maintained despite external conditions or variations. Structurally modifying their environments, organisms extend the range of homeostatic conditions necessary for their form of life from inside their 'bodies' to outside, adapting their environments to themselves (as themselves). They confer a degree of (their own) livingness to what is seemingly inanimate: 'the environment can [come to] have physiology' (Turner 2000: 7).

It is important to stress that this environmental modification is individually controlled: fuelled, initiated and maintained by the animal's metabolic processes (metabolism being the process whereby animals engineer the controlled combustion of fuel, usually glucose). Channelling energy through their bodies, individual animals can be said to be producing 'order' in the world. (Turner would describe physiology itself as the study of 'how animals use energy to do order-producing work', 2000: 24.) 'Order' may be understood in abstract terms as worldly conditions that require less information to describe them (than 'disorderly' ones): order is an organization, a homogenization, a harmonization of the world from a particular point of view, for a particular purpose. If a large number of simple molecules are, for instance, reduced to a smaller number of more complex molecules, then the world has become more orderly. Less abstractly put, environmental order means conditions that possess a stability, an organization and a predictability relative to an organism's ongoing needs: assembling a complex protein, say, from simpler amino acids. Through the metabolic process, animals use energy to produce homeostatic conditions, or the potential for these: an environment they have ordered into a known and usable space relative to their own intents and purposes. Causing physiological functions to operate far beyond themselves, animals' individual lives and projects ramify in time and space.

What kind of connection should we be willing to make between an animal-physiological and thermodynamic proposition and human science, between the world of the earthworm and the worlds of human being? I am encouraged by significant resonances between Turner's thesis and recent work on human development, phylogenetic and ontogenetic, such as Gerald Edelman's individual approach to consciousness. According to Edelman (1992), it is through activity-in-the-world from before birth onwards that the brain comes not only to structure itself, but also to structure, to know and to form, its bodily 'hexis' in a particular, personal way. Habitual bodily dispositions and habitual personal environment are shaped together by way of individual histories of physical-interpretative engagement with the world. '[E]ach individual person [comes to be] like no other', for each is motivated by their own historical system of physiological 'values', of what has worked successfully for them in the past (Edelman 1992: 171). Brain-plus-body-plus-environment, we are to understand, amount to one phenomenal unit: that individual's 'consciousness'.

This is resonant, too, with Karl Popper and John Eccles's (1977) argument that it is the decision regarding which behaviours to put forward into the world as means to interact with environments which makes the world into a certain sort of place. Indeed, since human beings have a larger repertoire of behaviours at their disposal even than other higher organisms, among which their choice is more conscious, it is true to say that our active subjectivity and cogitation alter our natural-selective chances and affect our evolution. Natural selection takes the form of an evolving relationship between external forces and human products and purposes, human consciousness. One may describe human beings as active creators of their environments and their contents, indeed, creating by way of action. Furthermore, this is something that each human being, as an individual organism, is responsible for doing (well or badly) for itself: '[by way of] individual action, the organism may "choose", as it were, its environment ... Thus the activity, preferences, skill, and the idiosyncrasies of the individual animal may directly influence the selection pressures to which it is exposed, and with it, the outcome of natural selection' (Popper and Eccles 1977: 12). In the terms of my argument, I say that the personal truths which Anyone construes and endeavours to effect are crucial to the ways in which an individual attends to what is around him or her; and in this attention, this interaction, identity and environment are formed alike. Anyone's world-views – insofar as these lead to particular ways of being and acting in the world, to life-projects – give rise to a kind of environmental architecture, conditioning a personal environment to which Anyone possesses a bodily adaptation, including a certain kind of healthiness.

More precisely, personal truths may affect the choice of relationships, human and non-human, in which Anyone engages and the way he or she conducts these. Personal truths may affect the speed of an individual life, the individual's patience and haste, the discipline imposed on himself or herself, his or her engagement with time and space. Personal truths may lead to specific reactions to events – to a recognition of certain things in the individual's environment as 'events' – and personal truths may lead to the recognition of certain things as resources towards effecting one's goals. In short, personal truths amount to forms of intentioned undertaking: ways of being active, ways of attending to the world which have certain significant consequences for their individual executors. In his or her impassioned commitment to certain ways of making sense of life, Anyone creates and recreates meaningful physical environments (within and beyond the integuments of their skin) in which he or she lives and dies. These personal environments will abut against others'. Indeed, Anyone's personal environment is likely to overlap with others' and to contain within it shared elements – from oxygen to the cultural symbologies of language and behavioural norms. However, the argument is that these environments are, in a crucial sense, manifestations of the creative intelligence and the physiological natures and needs of the individual human beings who occupy their centres and direct them as extensions of themselves. A social milieu is an aggregation of personal phenomenologies, of individual bodies-plus-environments. To understand Anyone, and to do justice to the complexity and individuality of his or her life, is to apprehend the personal environment that is his or her habitual, healthy (homeostatic) way of being. Human consciousness, embodiment and environmental inhabitation form a whole that is specific to Anyone.

Nietzsche's 'Night-time'

Let me introduce as a case-study the well-known conundrum surrounding the physical and mental demise of the philosopher Friedrich Nietzsche. In 1889 Nietzsche suffered a physical breakdown in Turin, possibly a syphilitic paralysis. He caused a public commotion when he embraced a beaten carthorse, and had to be escorted back to a university clinic at Basel, thence to a university sanatorium at

Jena, and thence to his mother's house at Naumburg. He was nursed there by mother and sister until his mother died in 1897, when his sister assumed sole responsibility; she removed him to Weimar where he died in 1900.

The years between 1889 and 1900 have come to be known as Nietzsche's 'night-time' (*Umnachtung*): eleven years in which he seemed to relinquish control of his physical life. What was his state of mind? In particular, what connexions should be made between the philosophical-metaphysical edifice which he construed and the physical-personal truths he lived?

Famously, Nietzsche had described philosophy as a species of memoir: 'ultimately', he wrote, 'one reaps nothing but one's own biography' (Nietzsche 1994: 238), for at the core of an individual's mental endeavours lay 'physiological demands for the preservation of a certain species of life' (Nietzsche 1979a: §3). In other words, Nietzsche had sought to root intellectual projects, including his own, in Anyone's personal embodiment: the metaphysical was a version of the personal and in particular the physiological. Nietzsche's night-time offers a case-study of the ways and extents to which an individual can be seen to inhabit a personal sensorium, his environment a summation of particular body and particular life-project.

Nietzsche's years of breakdown followed a lifetime of physical accidents and incidences of ill-health. His father had died when he was five, the cause of death being recorded as encephalomalacia or 'softening of the brain'. By the time Nietzsche entered his teens, he had himself begun to suffer from headaches and eye pain, as well as colic and stomach cramps; these were never to leave him.

Notwithstanding these disabilities, Nietzsche was a very physical man by nature, enjoying exertion and sport. He was also keen to experiment with his body and diet in order to ascertain the conditions of best performance. Food, sex, music, walking, and 'brainwork' were all tested similarly, and the results recorded in diary form: the body's economy translated into a mental project (Chamberlain 1996). But then, having begun accompanying university friends to Leipzig's brothels (aged 21), Nietzsche possibly contracted syphilis in 1867 – a wasting disease, at the time incurable. To this he added diphtheria and dysentery during the Franco–Prussian war, in 1870. For much of his life Nietzsche was extremely focused on his bodily states but unable, seemingly, to allay a gradual deterioration. Finally he suffered his breakdown in Turin in late 1889, and, although he lived on for another eleven years, throughout this time he was reported as being gentle and childlike, incapable of coherent thought.

While sickliness may be described as an existential constant in Nietzsche's life, complemented in adulthood by poverty, loneliness and obscurity, he also demonstrated a strong will concerning what he should do with his talents and his time. Having in his adolescence taken up writing in a concerted fashion, this remained a favoured practice: a grace and also a deliverance. In this writing Nietzsche sought to transform his experience: to overcome himself. In his writing he becomes pugnacious, ferocious, overtly masculine, even contemptuous and malicious. It was a kind of compensation, sometimes seeming as if was the work of another person entirely: 'I am one thing, my writings are another' (Nietzsche 1979b: 69).

However, Nietzsche also wanted his writing to embody the tensions he felt, so that it might possess integrity, and aspire to wholeness, be subtle and metaphoric, its meaning manifold and open-ended: 'I am a nuance', as he also wrote (Nietzsche 1979b: 124). Above all Nietzsche wanted to capture in print the complexity of his knowledge and its rootedness in himself. Individual realization of the world not only emanated from bodily (including mental) states, Nietzsche contended, but was also lived and experienced by way of bodily states. And yet this was something that philosophical science traditionally ignored. All of Western philosophy to date was based on a misunderstanding of the body and of the role of desire, of sentiment and will, in knowledge.

More precisely, Nietzsche was determined to do justice to the way in which individual being-in-the-world and the knowledge it gave on to amounted to a complex of emotion, will and experience. These were distinct bodily forces, none of which explained or caused another, but all proceeded contemporaneously, sometimes in alignment, sometimes in contest. A body was like a community, or a state of struggling forces, and only a name – 'Friedrich Wilhelm Nietzsche' – gave the impression (and maintained the illusion) of singularity or stasis in character. The body's forces struggled with one another, and with the world beyond the body, while all the time the bodily entity itself changed (ingested, grew, moved, became diseased, died), giving rise to different mental and physical states, and different knowledges.

Doing justice, in writing, to the shifting and contingent nature of an individual's bodily knowing, however, Nietzsche also recognized to be a kind of overcoming. His experience showed him that when he wrote – giving vent to his loneliness, his shyness, also his ambition and morbidity, his sense of tragedy, of melodrama, his impatience – he gained an overview upon the shifting complex of his bodily forces and experiences, and a narrative sense of the processes of their becoming. It became possible, therefore, not only to have knowledge but for the individual also to gain insight into the processes of his or her knowing. This allowed for a possible controlling perspective on body and life. To write was to experience experiencing, and hence go beyond: to overcome the body, its sickness and shifting demands, also to see through the illusions of conceptual categories, of forms and names imposed on life (at least to see them as illusions), and hence to re-evaluate, to 'transvalue', an individual human existence as such.

In his prophetic vision of the Overman (*das Übermensch*) Nietzsche depicted all that he felt human individuals could, notwithstanding their corporeality, aspire to and wish to achieve. Chief among these ambitions was that individuals should recognize their lives as their works of art: theirs to experience, continually evaluate and recreate. It was within Anyone's capacity to be 'the poet of [their] lives' (Nietzsche 1974: 240), and for Nietzsche this was the ultimate expression of their humanity. The Overman set a continual overcoming of contingency as life's goal. To transform the struggle of embodiment into an expression of will. It was a superhuman goal but at the same time it dignified the name of humanity. Yet another illusion, perhaps, but a powerful one, as Nietzsche felt his own experience demonstrated. A constant accompaniment to his own life, his writings made him not only a 'nuance', but a philosopher 'with a hammer' (Nietzsche 1979c: 21), and a 'destiny' (Nietzsche 1979b: 126). To what kind of human future of overcoming might not his writings pave the way?

My own question here is a more proximate one: Can Nietzsche's writings be seen to impact directly on his own body and life? For the years preceding his breakdown Nietzsche criss-crossed national borders, living in boarding houses, his homelessness deepening his sense of being simply 'European'. All the while he wrote his philosophy. He had resigned his professorship in philology at the University of Basel in 1879 – despairing of combining the intellectual with the institutional – and now wandered, monitored his bodily and mental states, reflected and wrote. There might be no eternal answer to questions of truth, Nietzsche considered, just as there was no release in life from bodily pain, but still one could aspire to a strength that enabled one to convert what appeared to be the necessity, even tragedy, of circumstance into a reflection of one's will. During his nineteen, migrant years Nietzsche can be said to have taken control of his body insofar as he brought it under the conscious sway of his experimentation and observation and writings. If 'man is the animal whose nature has not yet been fixed' (Nietzsche 1979a: §62), then in his own case, Nietzsche would fix this by his creative writing of himself.

But then? An apparent physical and mental breakdown due to constitutional decay: the *dementia paralytica* of the terminal stages of syphilis. It has been suggested, alternatively, that Nietzsche was overwhelmed by the life-project that he had set himself, by all he wanted intellectually and physically to accomplish. His breakdown was, then, a sign of his realization of mental and bodily limitations, and a return to a feminine domestic space as a child. Or again, that the contradictions inherent in his life and his philosophy became too much to bear. He held that only independence and solitude generated first-rate thought, but at the same time his loneliness, his publishing failures, brought Nietzsche unbearable anguish. He was in possession of truths that needed to be revealed to a deserving audience, yet how was he to teach the Overman to the vulgar crowd? How to celebrate art and theory, metaphysics – contribute to them – and still know them to be illusory? How to prescribe the Overman's individual becoming as a kind of universal pragmatic? More nearly, how to be 'Friedrich Nietzsche' when human embodiment was polymorphously perverse? And how did 'one' overcome polymorphous perversity?

If contradiction was key to Nietzsche's breakdown in this way, then was his night-time even another chapter in his self-intense journey of discovery? Further immersion in the conscious body, exploring the fragmentary nature of personal identity: a further kind of writing? J.P. Stern, one of Nietzsche's biographers, offers a suggestive version of this reading when he notes that while many Nietzsche commentators have called attention to diagnoses of tertiary syphilis not all of Nietzsche's contemporaries were so convinced (Stern 1981: 33). Franz Overbeck, for instance, a friend of Nietzsche's for twenty years, concluded that he 'could not entirely resist the thought that Nietzsche's illness was simulated – an impression derived from my long-standing experience of Nietzsche's habit of taking on many different masks'. Critical of his own inability to master an increasingly unmanageable set of writing plans, tormented by what he might not achieve yet finding it impossible not to care, or to compromise on his passionate engagement, Nietzsche takes the radical step of turning clown, invalid and child (Stern 1981: 34).

Significantly, an archive of memoirs exists where such an analysis – concerning a kind of direct relationship between Nietzsche's intellectual project, his exploration of personal, embodied truth, and the particular trajectory of his own embodied health – can be taken a step further. I refer to *Conversations with Nietzsche: A Life in the Words of his Contemporaries*, edited by Sander Gilman (1987). One of the key themes that emerges from this text is the general uncertainty regarding Nietzsche's health during his night-time years, his kind and rate of decay. There was, indeed, a widespread contemporary interest in the question. (The year 1902 saw the publication of neurologist P.J. Moebius's *On the Pathological in Nietzsche*, and 1904 its republication.) Had Nietzsche truly contracted syphilis, either as a university student or as a medical orderly, which then manifested itself in his retinal infections (and deformation of the iris) and progressive paralysis and insanity?

At the least, Gilman's collection throws doubt on this. 'I began to doubt it more and more as time went on'; more likely it was a 'luetic infection of the brain' (Dr S. Simchowitz, in Gilman 1987: 225). It was a stroke brought on by the large doses of 'choral hydrate' which Nietzsche had administered himself over the years to cope with his insomnia, neuralgia and migraines: his nervous system gradually deteriorated, causing impaired consciousness and sight, limb failure and loss of language (Philo vom Walde, in Gilman 1987: 244). Certainly, with no medical regimen after 1899 besides clean air, a largely vegetarian diet and regular bathing and massage, the process of Nietzsche's 'disease' was found to be 'almost uniquely' slowed, while his 'good appearance' and general constitution remained 'astounding': there is no proof, Health Commissioner Vulpius concluded, that Nietzsche ever even consummated sexual relations (cited in Gilman 1987: 258). Perhaps a metasyphilitic toxin could have entered Nietzsche's system via the cigars he smoked while working for the military ambulance – manifesting itself in the jaw infection then diagnosed as diphtheria – but no acquaintance or doctor reported any externally perceptible luetic symptoms on skin, mucous, bone or gland.

What of Nietzsche's behaviour after his breakdown? While given to occasional, sudden and unpredictable states of excitement and agitation, his usual state was placidity: a 'harmonious silence' and 'deep inner calm'; 'brooding' and 'withdrawn', 'sealed off in a world of his own', eyes focused on the middle distance, 'sightless' or 'looking inward'. This extended to a lack of interest or awareness concerning who was near him and what was enacted. Only music would be sure to rouse him. Then, 'blissful rapture transfigured his features, his whole body quivered with feverish excitement – and behold new life flowed through his transparent, lame hands' (Izabella von Ungern-Sternberg, in Gilman 1987: 260); alternatively, the 'ecstasy' eventuated in 'ugly, unarticulated sounds, a dull, horrible groaning' (Ernst Horneffer, in Gilman 1987: 255). Besides, he displayed an interest in toys and dolls, a babyish reaching for shiny objects to put in his mouth, and a fascination with movement: locomotives coming and going, a beaten drum. What might this signify? An unreceptive vegetative state due to the extinguishment of consciousness? Apathetic immobility? A self-chosen solitude and distraction? '[S]ilent and indifferent, hour by hour, week by week, year by year ... occasionally muttering indistinct sounds under his mustache, which grew to fabulous size' (Gabriele Reuter, in Gilman 1987: 242): an 'impenetrable mask' which 'bore the seal of human helplessness' (Resa von Schirnhofer, in Gilman 1987: 238).

Amid the 'horrible mystery' of Nietzsche's night-time, certain things are clear. For nineteen years Nietzsche had led an anonymous peripatetic existence around southern and central Europe. His itinerary included: Lugano, Naumburg, Leipzig, Klingenbrunn, Bex, Genoa, Naples, Sorrento, Ragaz, Schloss Bremgarten, Zurich, St Moritz, Naumburg, Riva, Naumburg, Bolzano, Venice, Marienbad, Frankfurt, Heidelberg, Locarno, Basel, Stresa, Genoa, Recoaro, Riva, St Moritz, Sils Maria, Genoa, Messina, Rome, Tautenburg, Naumburg, Leipzig, Basel, Rapallo, Genoa, Rome, Sils Maria, Naumburg, Nice, Venice, Sils Maria, Zurich, Nice, Naumburg, Leipzig, Sils Maria, Genoa, Nice, Sils Maria, Venice, Nice, Genoa, Turin, Sils Maria and Turin. During this time he had written continuously, seeking in vain an audience for his discoveries. For an ensuing eleven years he remained immobile and uncaring in a 'mattress-grave' in Naumberg and then Weimar. Now, ironically, his fame grew and visitors came to play court at the 'prophet's' and 'genius's' bedside and Nietzsche Archive. His public 'career' as a notable philosopher and social critic began, indeed, precisely as his private mobility ended (Kaufmann 1976: 14).

The irony did not escape contemporary notice. 'The man whose mind had encompassed the whole world is restricted physically to two rooms on the second floor of this little house' (Sophus, in Gilman 1987: 232). The imagery that contemporaries employed is equally telling: 'Those are Zarathustra's eyes which now rest on me. They have seen into the deepest abysses of life, and into the sunniest heights of creative happiness – that is why they are lost in dreams' (Philo vom Walde, in Gilman 1987: 246); 'eyes which had looked deeper into the abysses of the human heart and higher up to the icy peaks of his longing than those of any other living person' (Fritz Schumacher, in Gilman 1987: 246).

A manic quality, of feverish effort and mood swings, seems to have been characteristic of Nietzsche's temperament as a peripatetic. Between 1870 and 1889 he published (privately) some twenty monographs and followed a punishing physical schedule of writing and exercise. This was heightened even further in 1889, when four manuscripts were completed and the notes for a fifth. In that year, too, he suffered from a serious case of influenza and increasing insomnia. In the final few months, 'his handwriting also changed completely. He suddenly uses the most incredible abbreviations, leaving out letters and syllables and finally writing almost only the consonants' (Ernst Horneffer, in Gilman 1987: 256). It was as if 'Nietzsche resembled a man who must suddenly begin a great journey and now hastens through the house hiding all valuables, locking old locks, taking care of old duties' (Karl Strecker, in Gilman 1987: 216).

A diagnosis of nervous and physical breakdown consequent upon 'ascetic over-exertions' is not difficult to suppose, then, for a manic (even Freudian hysteric) Nietzsche. However, let me draw attention to a fundamental tenet of Nietzsche's later philosophy: the 'will to power' (Nietzsche 1968). Here, every living thing possessed a drive for free expression of itself, Nietzsche supposed: a desire to grow, expand and develop. Every specific body, he wrote, acts as a 'centre of force' (Nietzsche 1968: §636), in constant struggle with others, seeking to increase its power at others' expense. The world could be said to consist of a vast aggregation of individual wills to power: a plurality of discrete and separate 'dynamic quanta', expanding or contracting depending on their overcoming or being overcome by other such quanta (Nietzsche 1968: §635). What Nietzsche included in his conception of 'living thing' or 'specific body', moreover, was 'everything' that the world contained, both organic and inorganic. Everything was alive in the sense of being constituted out of the fundamental active drive to increase its power. Crystals 'encompassed' molecular particles in order to be; liquids 'compassed' the energy of gases; acids 'attacked' metals, 'assimilated' their constituents and so 'grew'. Animals 'assimilated' vegetable matter and one another; bacteria 'broke down' animal matter. Humans 'domesticated' animals, and also one another; they 'employed' scientific, poetic and moral knowledge in order to further their earthly interests. The only real differentiation between things-in-the-world, Nietzsche concluded, was in the quantity of their power: in things' ability to assimilate and overpower and control other things, other power-quanta. If inert and live things could be said to be different, then this was merely in terms of the one and same criterion of the quantity of their power: weaker as opposed to stronger.

Since the world consisted solely of competing power-quanta, continuously struggling with one another for hegemony, strategically aligning and realigning to increase their chances, there was no place for fixed or permanent 'things'. Nothing remained the same between moments of struggle besides the mass of struggling power-quanta. There were no consistent objects, no self-identical cases, no stable facts, no overriding or underlying order; continual transition forbade one to consider 'individual things', and even 'number' was in flux (Nietzsche 1968: §520–21). Rather than things-in-themselves, then, single substances or unities, the higher organisms in the world should be conceived of as federations of separate and ultimately antagonistic forces which temporarily exploited their mutual alliance.

A human 'individual', for instance, far from being a homogeneous and unified entity should be seen to be a power constellation. In the individual human body there resided an aggregation of different drives and instincts, affects and urges, orchestrated with more or less longevity and success by such forces as intellect, reason and conscience. These domineering forces or ruling passions – whether drives for sex, athletics, learning, drink or a combination of such – caused the different power-quanta within the constellation to direct their energies efficaciously, and not against one another, thus keeping the personality and the body intact. But then 'ego', 'will', 'thought', 'reason' and 'consciousness' were themselves emanations of aggregations of wills to power – turbulent, multiple, ephemeral – that provided no actual consciousness or control over 'the whole'. At the best of times it would be appropriate to describe human behaviour not as the activity of a 'unified mind' so much as the outcome of tensions and struggles between different power-quanta. Fragmentation and disruption could occur at any time. It could be short-lived, chronic or fatal. It might go by the names, 'neurosis', 'disease' or 'death'. It might be interpreted as an extraordinary occurrence but it was in fact ordinary. Breakdown sooner or later was inevitable. The death of the individual occurred and the constellation of power-quanta 'returned' to its component parts. The self-identity of any higher organism was thus of a tenuous and provisional kind: the temporary outcome of a tense relationship between power-quanta at a particular moment of its evolution (Nietzsche 1968: §488–92).

With the will to power as the motive force in the world (and underlying all phenomena), and with there being an immanent contrariety between different power-quanta, tension and antagonism give on to a grand and monumental worldly chaos. The currency of concepts such as 'order', 'structure' and 'form', 'beauty' and 'wisdom', 'identity', 'being' and 'things-in-themselves' were simply efficacious strategies by particular power-quanta for the further increase of their power. Such concepts were kept with purely because of their practical usefulness. The notion of an individual human being having a fixed and substantial centre of intellectual and spiritual gravity, a perduring 'I', had been of considerable use to human development, for instance, playing a major role in the evolution and hegemony of religious, philosophical, legal, artistic and scientific discourses. 'Individuality' gave a common name to an alliance between power-quanta whose integrity proved a good strategy for all in a particular agonistic context. But in reality there were no such objects. For different wills to power, the world was a differently constructed place, with different pleasures and pains, different orders of things, and as power-quanta changed, increasing or decreasing their influence and alliances, so did the world they regarded, and the objects, subjects and circumstances they constructed.

In short, will became the only principle to which Nietzsche's final writings afforded any sustained character. But ultimately, even the notion of 'will to power' was to be seen to be an illusion, a metaphor, a piece of written fiction. In proposing it Nietzsche hoped to offer a more powerful and pragmatic 'truth' by which now to take humankind forward (more useful than earlier philosophical and religious cosmological constructions). Its usefulness was its flexibility and fluidity: its sensitivity to the constantly shifting balance between the drives and urges that, for a time, comprised the individual human body; also its accuracy in describing the breakdowns (in 'quanta' and 'alliances') that, to greater or lesser degrees, were constant. Finally, then, comes one of Nietzsche's utterances during his night-time as reported by his mother:

> I loved [my doctor] very much. Health. I am no longer a child. I loved someone very much, myself. I have lived in many places in the world ... where. I did not love Friedrich Nietzsche at all. I lived in many good places. I liked very much to be in one place, née Oehler. I read very much. I liked to live in a house it was really a good house. I liked to go out of house. I didn't love anyone not even one person. (cited in Gilman 1987: 235)

Names and substantives, houses and places, biographical facts and preferences, affirmations and negations, memories and solecisms. Perhaps one reads in the confused tangle the practice of nominalism giving way to a view of truth – and a bodily performance of truth – as fluid to the point of chaos. Perhaps the speaker had overcome the desire to be 'Friedrich Nietzsche'.

The evidence concerning Nietzsche's demise, given the number of intervening years and the state of medical understanding at the time, remains partial. Maybe this is appropriate. Evidence of another life is always going to involve interpretation, and traces of radical difference, of the gratuitousness and mystery of individuality, should remain. The evidence that does exist, however, allows at least the possibility of surmising that the outward physical display of Nietzsche's symptomology bore a homology with the personal truths that comprised his philosophical world-view. In other words, to endeavour to know Nietzsche's demise and death it is appropriate to interrogate the truths by which he conducted his life and the environment he secured for himself.

Moreover, while the extent of Nietzsche's self-intensity and introspection – his determination to occupy his metaphysical world-view with complete integrity – might have been special, the capacity for Anyone's embodiment to reflect his or her purposive awareness is, I would contend, a universal human facility. While the demise of Nietzsche's body lies at a historical distance, its intense documentation, through self-examination and a public commentary that has not ceased, I suggest that his individual story can serve as a metonym of a human one, elucidating the embodied capacities of Anyone.

Conclusion: The Pragmatism of Personal Truth

'We commonly think of the external "physical world" as somehow separate from an internal "mental world"', Gregory Bateson (1972: 429) observed. It would be truer to say, Bateson concludes, that '[t]he mental world – the mind, the world of information processing – is not limited by the skin' and that there is a 'mental determinism' immanent in the universe of living creatures (Bateson 1972: 441). I have argued for a reappraizal of the notion of evidence in human science so that one recognizes the extent to which human physical reality may be an extension of Anyone's consciousness of that reality, and his or her purposive action and judgmental reaction in regard to it. If Anyone is capacitated to make worlds, then to do justice to that subjective phenomenology is to furnish human science with criteria sensitive to these realities. Nietzsche's ambiguous case history has carried the weight of my seeking to exemplify what Kierkegaard defined as the personal nature of significant knowledge and its objectivity in our physical experience. Anyone carries personal truths in his or her body and performs those truths in their lifestyles and projects.

Let me be clear: I do not talk about a 'politically correct' human science: a multiculturalist medicine or anthropology that accommodates itself to a diversity of notions of bodily purity and pollution, of honour and metaphysical integrity. This would be a category error, still. Cultural differences are aesthetic matters, of rhetoric, of symbolic classification and labelling. Cultural communities occupy different worlds of tastefulness and public normativity. But cultures and communities do not experience: membership of different cultural communities does not entail different embodiment; only individuals occupy different bodily life-worlds of sensation and interpretation, being and knowing (Amit and Rapport 2002).

George Steiner (2003: 143) was blunt when he accused political correctness of engendering not responsible scholarship but witch hunts and ghettoes ('African-American History' and 'Islamist Philosophy' to accompany these purported essentialisms of collective identity). Yet, the 'penitential masochism' that flourishes in the humanities and the 'politics of cowardice' can have no equivalent folly or bluff in science, he claims. Grains of ideology, socio-historical conditioning and value judgement may yet lodge in the purest of abstractions, but mathematics and natural science rightfully aspire to truths beyond conceptualization: '[t]here are neither capitalist nor socialist solutions to nonlinear equations' (Steiner 2003: 164). The ideal of disinterested progress, of knowledge of the human which transcends merely conventional, commonsensical or communitarian wisdom, makes of scientific discovery, Steiner concludes, 'the most mature construct of human freedom' (Steiner 2003: 164).

I share Steiner's impatience with identity politics, and I also contend that the difficult, subjective knowledge and experience whose evidencing are so central and so important to human science are more than merely matters of ideology, rhetoric and differences of cultural taste. One retains the aspiration towards scientific objectivity but recognizes, too, the objectivity of subjectivity: that for Anyone there is an individuality to their embodied being-in-the-world which renders the truth about their lives personal. The highest aim of science must be to give testimony to this difficult species of truth.

Towards what he calls a 'pragmatic' version of scientific truth, Patrick Baert (2005: 192) has suggested a differentiating between the logics of inquiry that guide different sciences. There is, he contends, not merely one scientific method (save for definition at a level of abstraction as to be meaningless). In particular the nature of the subject matter of the human sciences sets them apart from the determinate and law-governed structurings of the purely physical or logical. 'Biological complexity surpasses our computational and cognitive capabilities so that a complete account cannot be accomplished' (Baert 2005: 192). The biologist, the medic, the anthropologist, must alike be as pragmatic and instrumental as they are systematic. Numerical issues of critical mass, of how many is significant – even whether one is a number – are not the point, and difficulties concerning verification, repeatability, should not be allowed to detract from the significance of the truths to be evidenced.

Reducing the truth of human life, and evidence of it, to impersonal pattern, to the common denomination of standardized substance, is an insufficient response (Rapport 2012b). Despite the complexity of human embodiment – due to its very complexity – a cosmopolitan anthropology must aspire to recognize the entailments of those bodies in individual lives, and thus apprehend the realities in whose terms Anyone lives. How this is to be done, without losing sight of the objectivity of subjectivity, the generality of the human, is what I turn to next.

GENERALITY, DISTORTION AND GRATUITOUSNESS

Introduction

I find that the singular has often been sacrificed to the general in the human sciences and that, more often than not, this has resulted in a distorting simplification of the human condition; in a failure fully to appreciate its ambiguous nature and the ambivalence it generates; in an implicit, if not explicit, emphasis on determinism; in an indifference to human creativity, transgressive possibility and imaginative play; and in a failure to address the question of human freedom.

—Vincent Crapanzano, *Imaginative Horizons*

I begin with this passage from Crapanzano (2003: 6) because it neatly encapsulates my own concern: modelling the relationship between (individual) part and (human) whole while avoiding the distortion, indifference and unfreedom that are consequent upon a misuse of generalization.

The issue has a venerable history. It takes us back, for instance, to the seminal essays of Georg Simmel from 1908: 'How is Society Possible?' and 'The Problem of Sociology'. Generalization was, Simmel felt, the necessary idiom, in whose terms both human society might function justly and human science might function rightly. My interest here is similarly two-fold: I want to re-examine the issue of applying generalization both in the field of a rational human science and in the field of just, liberal statecraft. The examinations are really treatments of the same question: Is it possible to conceive of the relationship between the uniqueness of individuality and the generality of the human (species and society) without reduction or corruption? Can generalization be made moral – eschewing deployment of stereotypes in society – and can it be made authentic – enacting a human science which treats the individual as a thing-in-itself? The issue is both methodological and political.

Generality, in human (humane) science and in (liberal) society alike, incorporates according to universalist grounds which yet sustain individuality. Anyone is recognized as a member of the human whole in and through his or her unique individual embodiment. In generalization that is authentic and also moral one lays the foundation for a modelling of both science and society as cosmopolitan enterprises that emancipate at the same time as they include. D.H. Lawrence wrote: 'I know that I am the English nation – that I am the European race ... L'Etat c'est moi. It is a great saying, and should be true of every man' (cited in Furbank 1999: 36). The issue is to democratize such claims as statements that might be made of and by Anyone. One traverses a dialectic between individual and human which is inclusive of all, and for all, and yet where each one – a known quantity – remains an unknown quality.

Simmel's Distortions

Let me begin by rehearsing some of the points of Simmel's exposition and his conclusions. 'Society exists where a number of individuals enter into interaction', Simmel (1971: 23) begins, and its unity rests in the interaction of these individual elements. This means, moreover, that societies are structures inexorably composed of unequal elements, since the individual members are differentiated according to their natures, their life-contents and their destinies. A society may amount to a cosmos but it is nevertheless 'a web of qualitatively differentiated phenomena' (Simmel 1971: 19). A liberal society must therefore endeavour to engender a democratic equality by dealing with a reasoned equivalence between people or functions or positions.

However, Simmel continues, any society must yet function on the basis of certain distortions which it determines and which operate as 'a priori, operative categories' (Simmel 1971: 12). Only by means of these distorting categories is it possible to move from individuals to societal members. For individuality is, by definition, incomprehensible: one can neither understand that of another nor incorporate it by extraneous measures. '*Perfect* cognition presupposes perfect identity' (Simmel 1971: 9), and we can neither know nor represent an individuality that is not our own. For the construct that is society, therefore, certain distortions must be brought to bear upon individual reality: 'we see the other person generalized, in some measure' (Simmel 1971: 9).

Three main kinds of distortion can be identified, Simmel elaborates. They might be termed the 'human', the 'personal', and the 'social'. In the first, we conceive of each human being as being a representative of a certain human type such as is suggested (to us) by his or her individuality: the individual thus becomes for us 'a general human being'. In the second, we conceive of each human being as being an ideal or full or perfect representative of himself or herself: we idealize or exaggerate his or her personality (such as we perceive it) so as to make him or her into 'a general version of himself or herself'. In the third, we conceive of each human being as representing his or her social placement or membership or role: the individual becomes 'a general group functionary'. Society is possible, Simmel concludes, by virtue of these generalizations which operate as so many a priori veils which at once detract from individuality and substitute for it.

The problem of sociology meanwhile, indeed of all science of the human, is that whereas the explanation of human facts most frequently entails 'an exercise of psychological knowledge', it is the case that 'the scientific treatment of psychic data is not thereby automatically psychological' (Simmel 1971: 32). The science of human social life is a study of certain structures, symbols and classes that derive from psychic creativity and are imbued with psychological meaning and yet which attain an objective reality which possesses its own formal properties: patterning, compatibilities, development. One may say that the forms of social life operate as kinds of formalized veil behind which the psychic contents live. It is impossible to accede to generality in any other way, whether as members of society or scientists of society.

It was the human tragedy, Simmel concluded, that individual things-in-the-world could not be known in themselves but only in terms of extraneous forms. These were approximations, typifications, idealizations which nonetheless came to assume an objectivity in human social life and exchange which veiled and distorted. Hope lay in a kind of dialectical method by which one zigzagged between forms and contents – between forms and the meanings and intentions that animated them at specific moments – and thereby came to an understanding of how one influenced the other and so both gained a mutual state of co-presence. But even here one dealt with representation: with what one took to be, and could describe as being, the content within the form. It inexorably entailed a zigzag between one kind of distortion and another.

It becomes clear the extent to which Simmel's sociology subscribed to Kantian notions of phenomena as against numina: the extent to which the world becomes an object of contemplation and intention only by way of categories of human perception. There may be 'always one reality' and only one reality, he admits (Simmel 1971: 33), but we cannot grasp it in its immediacy and wholeness. Simmel did not agree with Kant, however, that these categories were 'transcendent', or independent of historico-social process. For Simmel, categories achieved objectivity as a result of the ongoing process of social interaction; they emerged from the flux of life and derived from experience in such a way that they stood formally over and against the noumenal as kinds of practical bulwark. Nonetheless, they were categories or classes, types; the transition from individual to human society and from individual to human species was in each case effected by a process of generalization which transformed the unknowable thing-in-itself into idealized and ideal-typical forms. The forms acted as kinds of necessary approximation and equivalence, with their own histories and relations; one's hope was that the 'tragedy' of the veils surrounding truth might be ameliorated by distortions which were, at least, 'reasonable'.

Beyond Simmel

Simmel was not entirely happy with his conclusions, and I am not either. This becomes clear in other observations of his, in *Schopenhauer and Nietzsche* (Simmel 1991). Let me elaborate briefly.

It was Kant's formulation that everything observed and known – observable and knowable – is a phenomenon: something delineated by human powers of cognition, by its being incorporated into a human symbolic scheme. Human cognition transforms things-in-themselves into symbols with homes in conceptual frameworks; beyond this, reality is left as it is. Human existence thus gives rise to a certain plurality. Things do not remain only things: as well as being parts of a natural order beyond knowledge and definition, things come to be rendered as part of any number of symbolic orders. The things of the world become symbolic forms for us human beings, as well as maintaining their status as real objects beyond any forms and any relations to us, untouched, in and for themselves.

But this also smacks of relativism or else of theism. Phenomena, the forms of life, are linked to numina by mere convention or else by a supernatural intervention and ordination. Simmel wished for more: a means to reground symbolic form in the real and to make human a prioris more authentic to Being. The solutions he preferred came from Nietzsche and from Schopenhauer. For Nietzsche, according to Simmel (1991: 142–48), there are fundamental aspects of the human condition which are independent of social formation even though they might of necessity be expressed in social forms. The individual, for instance, is a final element of being – there is nothing greater in human experience than his or her organicism – and it is this individuality which human action inevitably expresses. This is because humanity, which also exists as a fundamental aspect of reality independent of social formation, exhibits itself in individuals. 'Humanity follows a *single* line to oneself', as Nietzsche (1979c: 86) summarizes. Even if individuals only appear in society, and even if there is an impossible dichotomy here, such that social forms are never able to subsume the individual, still there is a sense in which there is a continuous, real, evolutionary line between the human species and the particular form of life which the individual human being embodies. Individuality and humanity have a conjoined reality against which that of social forms, norms, concepts and categories are recognizable as contingencies. There are real, transcendent human values and there are real individual natures.

It is real individual nature to be unequal, for instance, Nietzsche contends. Differences and distances between individuals are natural facts, and these differences are the hope of evolution: humanity proceeds forward not as an assemblage but through its particular, successful individual expressions. Humanity cannot be defined apart from individuals, while the latter possess ultimate value because of their embodiment of states or moments of the former. Personality, for Nietzsche, becomes the ultimate value of existence: a full and mature individual personality possesses a value that is absolute and transcendent.

Even though there can be no social comprehension of individual being and its worth, Nietzsche concluded, still individuals, as things-in-themselves, possess a recognizable objectivity and meaning. Each individual embodies the evolutionary culmination of the human species. Individuals' general meaning is their uniqueness, their difference and distance from everything else: here is enshrined the future of the species as a whole.

Morally, Simmel was fearful of identifying with Nietzsche too completely, however. How might one ward off extreme self-centredness and selfishness, and solipsism? He was happy to turn to Schopenhauer, therefore, to complement the Nietzschean picture with an emphasis on social obligation and identification. The objectivity of social forms was a means to inculcate a sentiment of belonging and an ethic of duty. One could be at once individual *and* recognize a duty to a humanity which manifested itself in a current social whole, an ambient society. Through social forms, the individual could find meaning beyond himself or herself; there could still be social unity and mobilization towards common ends in a disenchanted world.

Rather than Simmel's conclusions as such – my sympathies would remain with the Nietzschean interpretation (Rapport 2003) – I am interested in the way in which his search for a rational basis to the issue of generality, both in human society and in human science, led Simmel from a relativist or idealist position which concluded that the general was inevitably a distortion (with its roots in local classifications and in effecting certain practical ends) to a more realist position which would seek to ground the relation between individual human beings in empirical reality and not merely in a socially constructed phenomenalism.

I would wish to posit generality as real and not merely as a construct: not only a means to label and stereotype, define and process, an otherwise unknowable individuality. I would wish such contingencies of the socio-cultural to be overcome, and for generality to be both a route to genuine knowledge of the way in which the individual instantiates the human as well as a route to genuine democracy in which the individual and the liberal state share a relation of mutual identification (the individual sees himself or herself in the state, the state sees itself as an aggregation of individuals).

In what follows I attempt to mark out both such routes: towards the generality of a rational human science, and towards the generality of a liberal human society. The individual is unique and yet scientifically accommodated as an exemplar of the species; the individual is unique and yet the subject of statal policies of universal recognition and attention.

Generality and a Route to Human Science

The issue of generality in human science is, to repeat, how to know the unique human being – Anyone – in a general way without thereby traducing or reducing that individuality. How is the human to be seen manifesting itself in the individual in a fashion that does not obviate regarding the latter as at the same time *sui generis*?

Two ways to resolve the issue may be, first, in terms of specific models of the one and the whole that retain the uniqueness of the one, and second, in terms of characteristics of human embodiment that may speak to individuality and generality at the same time.

Modelling the One and the Whole

I am wary of certain arithmetic procedures for averaging-out difference, such as the 'mean', the 'median' and the 'mode', since they would have one figure stand for all as a common denominator:

one averages or generalizes in such a way that one figure replaces and gives on to the many. This average figure claims to possess a metonymic relation to the original, different instantiations. But I do not believe that individual human beings *can* be averaged in this way: their relationship towards one another is more metaphoric than metonymic.

The move from individual to human should not be modelled in terms of replacement or integration (denomination), I would say, but in terms of aggregation or juxtaposition. Three viable alternative models suggest themselves to me, which I shall call 'the flower', 'the family', and 'the spectrum'.

'The flower' is a way of naming Nietzsche's idea that the individual human being is the culmination or the florescence of the evolution of humanity. The line of the species ends, at present, with the individual who is as responsible as any other for how it continues into the future. He or she is an absolute or paradigmatic exemplar of the human: its current expression. As the florescence of the human species, the individual carries within himself or herself the entire human phylogeny and yet amounts to a unique expression, embodying the random mutation of one procreation. The individual heritage and parentage is clear, his or her placement in an evolutionary history is generally assured, and yet his or her nature is unique and non-predictable, and that of his or her progeny equally so. As a flower or flowering, the individual human being is both generalizable and unique.

Nietzsche's writings themselves serve as an analogy: they possess a German linguistic form and are imbued with stylistic expressions of a literary heritage, and yet they represent a flowering of his unique individual creativity. No one else wrote Nietzsche's oeuvre; until he had done so, its progeny was impossible; even after he had done so, its progeny remained unforeseeable. 'The flower', as a model, combines a common heritage with unique current expression.

'The family' is a borrowing of Wittgenstein's (1978) conception of the polythetic category. At its simplest this can be given the shape: (ABC, CDE, EFG, GHI, ...). In slightly more complex form: (ABC, BZG, YHF, JKL, AGL, ...). In more complex form again: (Abc, A11, 1c@, b@3, 3£@, ...). Key to the polythetic category is the notion that members of the category need share no single feature in common. Rather there is a set of features, a bundle of traits, shared randomly among them. There is no necessary limit or closure to these traits (no alphabet) and their particular possession and also their ordering is unique to each member, making each individual. It is, in Wittgenstein's parlance, as if each individual shared a 'family resemblance' to others in the category – the family nose here and here, the family eyes here and here

– but there being no one family trait shared by all; in combination, too, each individual amounts to a unique assemblage. The individual is both generalizable as a family member and yet also uniquely himself or herself. 'The family', as a model, combines a common set of characteristics with a unique combination of these.

'The spectrum' or sliding scale images a range of possibilities within which individual members find themselves while each occupies a unique position on the scale. Human beings may, then, need a certain daily calorific intake to survive: too little or too much proves fatal. Certain substances, moreover, may be absolutely excluded from supplying this total – those that are too stony, say, or too prickly or otherwise toxic to the human constitution. Within this range, however, individuals may be unique regarding their optimum calorific intake and their favourite dietary items and meals. Anyone is recognizably human in terms of the spectrum between whose poles life is sustainable, and yet irreducibly themselves in the expression which human life achieves in them. 'The spectrum', as a model, combines a common range of possibilities with unique actual location.

Each of these, I would argue – flower, family, spectrum – allows one to model a universal relationship between individual and human totality. I can rationally apply them to real situations while still being assured that the generalities they deliver do not negate my providing testimony to the uniqueness of the individual case. The models also work together, as should become clear when I consider one expression of the human in more detail: the body.

Bodily Characteristics as Individual and General

There is a universality to human embodiment. One can say that the capacities of the individual body, its capabilities and liabilities – in a word, its nature – exhibit a universal generality.

One can assert, then, that all human bodies possess a *distinct materiality* as living organisms. All have individual boundaries and componential clusters of cells. The constituents of one body cannot be at the same time those of another (though they might be over time). During its lifetime each body functions (develops, maintains itself, reproduces, dies) as a whole and develops its own recursive patterns. Yet, this characteristic of organic differentiation is at the same time shared. There is a human generality to our individual materiality: the relationship is a family one, and also a flowering, each body being the culmination of the one history of the species.

Then again, all individual human bodies, as material things, possess a *distinct spatiality*. The space that is occupied by one cannot at the same time be occupied by another. And this property is common, reciprocal: we are alike as human beings in needing to occupy a space, at any one time, that is uniquely our own. If I have short legs, a large belly, a protuberant nose, then the space I occupy may not be the same as yours; indeed, the dimensions of one's own personal bodily space will be unique to each of us. Nevertheless, there is a human generality to be found in the fact that the living, sustainable individual organism requires an irreducible space of its own. (The formulation claims that there is an essential integrity of human bodies in their own space which may not be supervened if life is to be sustained. The child leaves its mother's womb, then, at that point where its individuality is a separately sustainable condition. Thereafter, throughout life, when two human bodies come closely together – when they engage in sexual intercourse, or when one places a hand in another's mouth, a finger in another's ear – the challenging of bodily integrity is special for the very unusualness of the event: momentarily there is a close mutual accommodation of physical spaces – albeit effected by way of anatomical 'spaces', gaps or holes. Even here, moreover, an essential integrity cannot be supervened: as birth is necessary for both the child's life and the mother's to be sustainable, so later acts of physical congress soon meet those physical limits whose supervention harms the lives of one or all participants.) If birth is a new flowering, then the life of an individual human being – sustaining its own unique spatiality – manifests a family relationship, and also a spectral one, to the species whole: the spatiality of each individual organism possesses common elements – cells, skin, noses, sexual organs – whose particular expression is unique within a human range.

Related to this is the fact that all individual human bodies, as independent organisms, possess a *distinct temporality*. The time and the timing of no two lives is identical – the developmental processes, the longevity – and each must occupy its own temporal dimension and no other. At any one moment, moreover, each individual will posses a unique temporal signature: coming from a particular past, en route to a particular future. But again this is something that we share: the uniqueness of an individual time of life is general among all human beings. There is no stopping, no reversing, no repeating, no doubling for Anyone. The relationship is a flowering, an individual's temporality being derived from a species history, and also spectral, within a human range.

The materiality, spatiality and temporality of the individual human life are accompanied also by an *environmental range*, a spectral relationship as such, which characterizes their possible bodily workings. No human beings can operate with too little or too much oxygen, water, food. There are environmental conditions suited evolutionarily to the possible life chances of the species. Should gravity, sunlight, rainfall alter beyond a certain range of gradations, no member of the species would survive. Within this range, however, it is not possible to generalize upon optimal positionings. The unique materiality of each body, its unique experience of attending to environmental conditions, mean that the individual finds his or her own habituality and equilibrium. And the range of possibility is large: from tall to short, and fat to thin; from long-sightedness to short-sightedness to colour blindness to blindness; from high blood pressure to low, with variegated figures for cholesterol, iron, insulin; from nut intolerance to alcohol tolerance. In short, the range of possibilities concerning bodily functioning in environments bespeaks both a general delimitation and an individual location.

Lastly, there are *capacities* of the human body that identify it as a general phenomenon. These operate as universal potentialities, albeit that in their usage or deployment or expression – in the *substantiation* of general human capabilities – the universal is transformed into the individual. There is, for instance, a general human capacity to construe a life-project: it is an individual substantiation of this capacity to write the plays of Shakespeare, the philosophy of Nietzsche, or to join a kibbutz. There is a general human capacity to feel pain or find something laughable; also, a general human capacity to sense, perceive, conceive, ideate, imagine, interpret, define, intend, wish, hope, know, recall. The human being can express himself or herself, and interpret the expressions of others. The human being can be self-conscious, reflexive, introspective, ironic; he or she can effect changes on his or her own body and the world that lies beyond the borders of that body. The human being creates world-views, provides personal contexts to his or her life, and he or she can imagine a life course: the trajectory that his or her life should or might or will take within that world and among the others that it contains.

None of this talk of capacity, however, reduces the individuality of substance that a life does actually contain. A range of factors, furthermore, may supervene upon these capacities and affect their realization: from individual intentionality to circumstantial (social, cultural, historical) structuration to accidental or random intervention – the marital norms, the car crash, the famine that subverts the capacity to reproduce. Notwithstanding, the human might be known by the general capacities which it encompasses; while the individual is known by the unique fashion in which those capacities manifest themselves in a life. The relationship between capacity and substance is a flowering, from phylogeny to ontogeny, and also something familial, the substance of no two lives being the same however much history, society and culture may colour the set of elements – purdah, space travel, rugby football – of which they are composed.

'Symbolic modelling' and 'bodily characterization' I would offer as two routes along which one can significantly advance towards establishing and representing general truths about the human condition – authentic knowledge – while at the same time not detracting from or threatening the integrity of the individuality in whose terms the human everywhere expresses itself in and as life.

Let me now turn to the social practice upon which these general truths might be consequential.

Generality and the Route to Liberal Society

In formulating a 'cosmopolitan' version of justice, a civil treatment of all human beings in all times and places, we have seen how Kant isolated what he termed 'The Formula of Humanity as an End in Itself' (Kant 1993: 36): 'Act in such a way that you always treat humanity, whether in your own person or in the person of any other, never simply as a means to an end, but always as an end in itself'. This remains an ideal, but it may be approached by conceptualizing a liberal society as that which would recognize individual members as things-in-themselves – the ends of whose existence is for themselves to define – and not as means by which other, typical ends are made manifest.

The 'problem' of society, as Simmel discussed, is recognition. Is it possible for a state to know its members and for its members to know one another – except by way of the kind of distortion that he outlined? Can the generality necessary for social organization and exchange accommodate individuality except by way of stereotypification and labelling: turning individuals into types of human being, types of person, types of role-player? The problem is also one of regulation: society may be conceived of as a state of regulation. The liberal society would enact laws to ensure that the lives of individual members are ends not means: it must intervene in a rationalized fashion so as to maintain a Kantian 'kingdom of ends'. But how may individuality be legislated for?

A solution derives, perhaps, from an identification of capacities, or potentialities, as distinct from substances or substantiation. Liberal society recognizes individuals on the basis of universal capacities of human embodiment and consciousness. The liberal state intervenes in efforts to guarantee that individuals' capacities for creating the substance of their lives, for determining their own ends, is afforded as much opportunity for fulfilment as possible.

Iris Murdoch (1970) has suggested an understanding of 'goodness' as a social virtue in terms of refraining from visiting one's desires upon others. The 'good society' is less one where one 'does good to others' than where one 'refrains from doing others harm': goodness resides in a kind of space in which individuals can 'come into their own'. One cannot foresee and does not attempt to prescribe what this latter might entail in terms of the substance of a life, but one hopes to afford each an optimum of opportunity for its expression, and to treat that expression as a right. The problem of society – to institute arrangements which balance individual space against general regulation – is managed by way of guarantees that individuals' capacities may fulfil themselves.

The limitations of social planning and the risks inherent in statal intervention on behalf of the individual are the subject of myriad counsels. 'It is the common mistake of theorists to suppose a perfect scheme of government may be fitted over the poor imperfect face of humanity!' William Golding (1988: 11) concluded, and preference might therefore be given to the traditional forms of belonging that have survived in time (however opaque and irregular), albeit that they represent 'imperfections of a contradictory and cumbrous system'.

Some risks, however, are necessary. There must be social interaction; there is an individual human nature deserving of fulfilment; there are capabilities and liabilities that a post-Enlightenment human science elucidates and that a humanism sets itself the task of addressing with goodness. Allowing opportunity for the expression of universal human capacities that manifest themselves in individual 'creativity, transgression and imagination' (Crapanzano 2003) offers a way forward, albeit that risk and complexity are not overcome.

Children provide perhaps the paradigmatic case. To take seriously Kant's ideal of a kingdom of ends is, as Nicholas Humphrey (1997: 12) has recognized, to afford particular space to children at risk of becoming a 'means to another's ends' – which might entail a diversity of conditions from fulfilling a parent's ambitions to preserving community values or traditions, to pleasing a purportedly divine dictum. Kant (1974) deemed children to be endowed with a personal freedom. They possessed rights, congenital and hereditary, to be reared by the care of their parents till they were capable of maintaining themselves, but parents could not regard their children as if they were their own property, nor as mere things of their own making: parents have 'brought a being into the world who becomes in fact a citizen of the world' (Kant 1974: 115). Humphrey's discussion occurs in the context of his presenting a public lecture sponsored by Amnesty International which he entitled 'What Shall We Tell the Children?' He argues for special kinds of social recognition and regulation of parent–child relations, demonstrating both the complexities involved and also the necessity of formulating a general answer.

No human being has rights over another, Humphrey begins, rights to control, use or direct another's life. Even the relationship between parents and children does not enjoy a special privilege whereby children are somehow deprived of the rights to their individual personhood: children are not a part of their parents. Humphrey (1997: 13) cites a ruling of the US Supreme Court from 1986: the 'moral fact [is] that a person belongs to himself and not others nor to society as a whole'. Parents' time and love and investment produce mitigating circumstances, perhaps, but not rights. Children have a human right not to have their minds narrowed by exposure only to certain words and ideas or their environments deprived, Humphreys elaborates, even if the prescriptions reflect those of their parents. His particular target is religious faith. Parents do not have the right to enculturate their children in any way they choose: to close off horizons or to inculcate certain dogmatic ideology. It is, indeed, a duty of society to protect children from nescience and also to see that they are succoured by the best scientific and philosophical understandings of the natural world. One must neither admit to the relativist fashion that science is one version of truth among a number, nor to the special pleading that truth is not the thing that people in all circumstances need to hear. The only morally defensible inculcation of a child into a belief system is the case where, later in life, when the child comes to know alternatives, he or she would in all likelihood still chose the specific ideology for themselves. Insofar as this is uncertain, parents cannot choose (badly) for their children. Religious parents, Humphrey claims, threaten to deliver their children into an intellectual and cultural dungeon.

Humphrey's argument is that science can and should have a unique claim on our hearts and heads because it is an ideology that any reasonable person would choose for themselves. It is, perhaps, the only such ideology: all people will choose science if given the choice. It is a civil duty, therefore, to ensure a scientific education for all: all members of a society have the right to insist and the duty to ensure that science forms an asymmetrically weighted part of children's education. Nor should this be deemed 'big government' (or Big Brother): an overweening state removing the child's socialization from its parents' care. Rather, it is the apparatus of a liberal society affording the individual child the space to exercise his or her own capacities for critical reasoning. Part of our human liability is to suffer others' constructions of us – their labels and categories – and of our environments. The openness of a scientific education – the distinction guaranteed between scientific method and rationalization, and the substance of what is held to be true until further determination – uniquely corresponds, however, to those intrinsic and universal human capacities for learning from observation, experiment and critique, and determining the substance of a life as a result of conscious deliberation.

Humphrey's argument illuminates, as I say, both the complexity of the issue – 'the problem of society' – and its pressing nature. I find him convincing but I can imagine many who do not – 'Why not laud religion as that ideology which uniquely corresponds to intrinsic and universal human capacities, for reverence, selflessness and communion?' – and I am aware of the intractable issues of social intervention and regulation that could ensue. How is one to distinguish between those expressions of parental love and attention that are and are not injurious of a child's development of capacities to come into its own? How can one presume to know an individual's preferred ('scientific') ideological home? If science is itself the ideology of openness, then how can one prescribe only certain pedagogic discourses as being scientific when the fulfilment of openness in a human future is itself impossible now to envision? Moreover, it need not be seen that religious ideology per se is injurious, but rather those forms of dogmatism and intolerance, of 'inadmissible theology', as Karl Popper (1997: 9; 1998: 47) formulated it, which threaten the imagination of new structures of experimentation and critique. Towards the latter open and imaginative end, every source of inspiration is to be admitted, so long as none is afforded an authority that is immune from criticism (Popper 1980: 378).

I am also reminded, however, of arguments that correspond to Humphrey's: Ernest Gellner's (1995a: 6) identification of science – and the technological, military and economic power that its inculcation brings – as that ideology human beings everywhere would appear desirous of embracing if given the opportunity. Also Richard Rorty's (1992: 67–68, 80) prognosis that educational opportunities promoting 'free and open encounter' between members of a society who engaged in 'domination-free communication' would eventuate in individuals not abiding by concepts which ultimately caused self-harm. Individuals might be expected to insist on making the 'best selves' for themselves that they could, Rorty suggested, and not allow this potential to be curtailed by any cultural, religious or social norms (whether this curtailment was self-inflicted or imposed), and to grant others the space to do likewise. It is the case, Amitai Etzioni (2002: 8–9) has concluded, that in an era of cultural and religious fundamentalism, the liberal society must prepare to take a moral stance: to pursue a project of public virtue which engages with the private issues of parenting, neighbouring and community belonging. Secularism has after all been a fêted part of public educational policy in such liberal states as France and the USA for some time.

Let me return to the particular aspect of this issue with which I am here most concerned, however: How is the liberal state to know its members and to intervene in individual lives in such a way as to recognize and to assist (and not direct or obstruct) the fulfilment of their individuality? How does one treat that aspect of a unique temporality that is the individual only gradually approaching the mature human capacity to create self and world? How does one envisage 'the space to come into one's own' when the unique materiality that is an individual life is born of others (that of parents) and remains surrounded by others (family, friends, community) which would wish from it a special allegiance and sympathy? How does one know others rationally, in terms of universal aspects of their individual human embodiment, when they might insist on knowing themselves (and others) in terms of non-rational ideologies and particularistic essentialisms that would subvert a universalistic conception of Anyone? The key is, I believe, *potentiality*. The liberal society recognizes the way in which the individual embodies the human capacity to interpret truth, to determine identity, and always to become anew. The state is, most importantly, the guarantor of the individual right to exercise the capacity to reflect and to become: to become other than it is at present; to become other than any existing expression of the human condition; to become other than that which even it itself knew it might. Again, one treats capacities not substance: the state is not interested in *what* is created and chosen, only *that* it is chosen, and might be unchosen, recreated. If the child is that immature human being for whom choices are inevitably made by others, then the state is the guarantor of the immature individual's right to unchoose, to exit from parental choices and ideologies, at the point of maturity. The role of the state is further to ensure that no parental influence makes an unchoosing later overwhelming: the ideal is to conceptualize every moment as a possibly radical becoming, and every choice as free from extraneous impulsion. Given the unique temporality of an individual life, the ontogenetic consequence of each of us inhabiting only one, continuous biography, such free choice opening up at every moment of our lives will remain an ideal. But the criterion of state intervention can be nevertheless based on this: Is this a circumstance in this individual's life whereby an unchoosing, a future exit strategy and a wholly new rechoosing, becomes less than likely given the necessary range of conditions within which human consciousness might flourish?

In a striking passage from his *Essay on Liberty*, John Stuart Mill takes this principle to its extreme. It is the role of the state in a liberal society, he claims, to intervene to preserve the liberty of the individual even when he or she would choose freely to give it up; the principle of freedom does not extend to an individual having the power to sell himself or herself into slavery. 'It is not freedom, to be allowed to alienate his freedom' (Mill 1963: 227). I am not certain one can go this far in being able to justify statal interventions in individual life or to claim statal recognition of the substance of individual consciousness. Does Mill's 'alienation' extend to suicide? But children represent a difficult enough case. The individual child occupies a temporality, a materiality, a spatiality, that is his or her own: a property of his or her unique embodiment. The liberal society treats this nature as a right. A child is its own flowering of the human species. What a child will make of itself, now and in its maturing self-consciousness, is also its own right to determine. The state guarantees a child's capacity to find its own equilibria amid the range of human possibility, and to find them in its own way and in its own time. The materiality of the individual life, the integrity of individual embodiment, is treated as sacrosanct: able to come into its own determinations of world-view and life-project, a child is ideally afforded the space to do so free from conditioning.

Liberal sociation, however rational its arrangements, will never represent an exact science. Can a society know its individual members sufficiently to recognize them as ends in themselves and to regulate their lives such that its interventions occur on the basis of their individuality and not a kind of typicality? I say 'yes', where the state knows the individual as a potentiality and legislates on behalf of its members on the basis of such potentiality. The deliverances of science concerning human individual capabilities and liabilities – the materiality, temporality, spatiality and range of individual human lives – are translated into rational policy. The individual is approached not as he or she is in terms of particular present or past substance – or the substance of any relational affiliation (family, community, ethnicity, church) – but as that being possessing the capacity always to exist beyond current identifications (Rapport 2010c). The liberal procedures of the state attempt to do justice to that capacity to go beyond by affording the space in which individual creativity of self and world may find expression.

Conclusion: Distortion Revisited

When your life is most real, to me you are mad.

—Olive Schreiner, *The Story of an African Farm*

I have been concerned with ways that might give onto a rational appreciation of the generality of human individuality which is non-reductive, both for the purposes of a human science and of a liberal society. I have earlier made the argument that 'the human' to which the anthropologist was able to give testimony by virtue of fieldwork was founded upon a complementary proclivity for introspection in his or her informants (Rapport 2007). Introspection, a general human capacity, was something which the anthropologist practised alongside informants who did likewise. The closeness of the emergent relationship with informants, together with the exaggerated self-consciousness and sensitivity to others which fieldwork spawned, enabled the anthropologist at least to sense the subtleties and varieties of individual consciousness within and behind the classificatory frameworks of social structure and cultural convention. The anthropologist recognized other human beings by virtue of an appreciation of commensurate individual capacities for introspection.

This was not the same as saying that the anthropologist was able to empathize with informants, that immersion in the routine habitus of others' forms of life enabled one to know the substance of other individual subjectivities. Rather, the introspecting anthropologist acceded to a recognition of the role that individual self-consciousness mutually played in human life: the 'oscillation' that universally takes place between introspection and projection out into the world, between self-consciousness and action (Rapport 2005). By virtue of his or her own self-consciousness – the human being amid a particular, intentional life course in particular historical, social and cultural settings – the anthropologist intuits the human consciousness of his or her fellows: self-knowledge delivered a kind of general knowledge. Joseph Conrad phrased the notion more lyrically, in connexion with the novelist's art, in his preface to *The Nigger of the Narcissus*: through introspection, he suggested, the human observer lays claim to a knowledge beyond the distortions of separation: 'the subtle but invincible conviction of solidarity that knits together the loneliness of innumerable hearts' (Conrad 1925: xii).

I do not intend anything mystical. My project remains rational. But I am concerned to incorporate the different ways in which one might do justice to the paradoxical relation between the individual and the human. In our individuality we are at the same time most distant from one another (most 'mad', as Olive Schreiner put it) and most the same. The relation is termed 'mysterious but real' by the literary critic Philip Furbank (1999: 29). That which links individuals to the human species is a 'monadic' phenomenon, he avers, whereby 'the entire potentiality of the species is reproduced in every individual' (Furbank 1999: 34). We are in many respects the exact replica of every other human being, and as new generations of humanity come into being every second, we can speak, by virtue of the individual, of the eternal present of the species.

The implications of this are moral-cum-political as well as methodological, Furbank feels. The monadic idea which sees a homology between individual and species is an opposite philosophy to 'the politics of difference' which would assert we are all one kind of different thing: woman, gay, Black, Muslim. 'Monadism' insists that in its singular potentiality, the human psyche cannot be split into different kinds and it is in its capacities rather than in any substantive difference that its essential quality resides. One can expect and attempt to know the other not on the basis of constructed difference – the substance of momentary or contingent or traditional identifications and affiliations – but by virtue of true generalities of capacity. The claims of a Conrad (or a fieldworking anthropologist) to a human knowledge through introspection usher in a more humane, and true, generalism than the collectivisms of identity politics. In the objectivity of our subjective phenomenologies we can claim the universality of human individuality.

I shall end by reconsidering distortion, the theme with which this section began. But rather than the distortions which Simmel felt were pragmatically and morally necessary in order for society and sociology to function, I approach distortion as evidence of the attempt authentically to represent the individuality of another. Distortion may arise from being true to the 'gratuitousness', the radical otherness (Schreiner's 'madness'), of another human psyche as it seems from the perspective of one's own (Rapport 2008). One cannot know that other as it is in itself and for itself. However, it remains the duty of a human science and a human morality (and a human art) to make the attempt, as part of that process of according just recognition to this perfect (and unique) instantiation of the human. One reasserts that only through the individual can one hope the better to know the species, its capabilities and liabilities, and better to provide for its fulfilment. Approaching the generality of the human through the particularity of the individual, and accepting the distortion as inevitable evidence of the paradox of that relationship, becomes moral as well as scientific practice.

My approach to distortion is motivated by the work of the great twentieth-century British artist, Stanley Spencer (1891–1959), in particular a set of paintings which he named The Beatitudes of Love (1937/1938) (see Rapport 2004). Spencer professed that these eight paintings were the ones he was the most loath to part with: 'I can do without all my paintings except these' (cited in Collis 1962: 142). The series was 'more genuine' than anything else he had completed. Here is Contemplation.

Figure 11. Stanley Spencer, *The Beatitudes of Love: Contemplation* (1938), oil on canvas. Stanley Spencer Gallery, Cookham, Berkshire. © The Estate of Stanley Spencer, 2009. All rights reserved DACS.

What Spencer felt he had achieved in *The Beatitudes of Love* series was to gain a true appreciation of the individual at the same time as the composition displayed a singularity and human unity. 'I have never seen any paintings that more truly reveal the individual', he wrote shortly after their completion, while yet 'each of the pictures shows the twined and unified soul of two persons' (cited in Collis 1962: 141–42). Spencer often wrote long commentaries in accompaniment of his paintings, words and paint complementing the project of self-expression. Of *Contemplation*, he writes that: 'it is of people making themselves endlessly acquainted with each other through passion and desire' (cited in Pople 1991: 387); 'the figures are engaged in contemplation of each other, as is expressed by their rapt gaze, as though they would never stop looking' (cited in Collis 1962: 141).

I cannot draw more deeply here on the philosophy behind Spencer's statements (see Rapport 2003: 179–211), but I would address the issue of his painterly style. The series was not well received by Spencer's British audience. Why the arresting and grotesque figuration, the apparent ugliness and deformity, and all but denuded of background? Even friends and erstwhile admirers found them 'terrible' to contemplate, and refused to find that people were really like that (Bell 2001: 147). Spencer himself admitted to some 'consternation' when he first realized, on their completion, how he had departed from people's 'normal appearances' and dimensions; for it was not a deliberate affectation or the outcome of a preconceived plan. He stuck with the distortion, however, and defended it. Distortion could be seen to be intrinsic to the composition: 'in the distortion is the meaning of the picture' (Spencer 2001: 187). The distortion, he explained, manifested strength of emotion and desire, imaginative integrity and 'spiritual intensity', and purity and clarity of vision, as the artist attempted to express two things: his intuitive knowledge of other human beings, and his knowledge of the relation that these others had to one another. 'Distortion arises from the effort to see something in a way that will enable [the artist] to love it', Spencer elaborated in the language of his own 'metaphysic of love': the 'loving' artist is able to begin lifting 'the barrier' to mutual comprehension whereby individuals may 'reveal themselves meaningfully' to one another (Spencer 2001: 165).

Imagine how individual passers-by in the street would appear, Spencer recommended to a radio interviewer, if they were stripped of their fashionable accoutrements, the stays of their status and position. His art revealed them in their reality, he claimed, his representation animated by an inner awareness of identity and relationality. Imagine the colours of desire and of pain (cf. Irving 2009).

In the terms of my argument, here is the distortion that derives from wishing to see others for who and what they are. What the artist sees is a distortion of what might be taken as normal, ordinary, conventional, because what is being espied is the irreducible specificity of others' individual identity and relationality. But the artist, as self-conscious human being, is capable, indeed duty bound, to make the attempt. Distortion thereby expresses the 'drama' of a human composition: sameness and difference in paradoxical relation. In effecting this drama, the artist gives the world an insight into the 'reality' of human unity. Certainly Spencer found the composition of individuality and totality which his paintings revealed to him 'remarkable' (cited in Collis 1962: 141).

Spencer was unable to reconcile the public to these paintings: he even hid some of them from view for fear of prosecution on grounds of pornography. He felt lonely but he did not recant: the compositions were new and unique and were revealing of a 'hoard of significant meanings to life' (Spencer, cited in Collis 1962: 142). Spencer's only regret, he attested (Spencer 2001: 230), was that the limitations of human anatomy meant he could not 'swallow' the world whole: some 'misshaping' had to occur when an individual brought the world within his or her personal representational schema, but the attempt was necessary and worthwhile in itself. The 'failure' of distortion was itself testament to the impossibility of occupying a position other than an individual's own, and the artistic effort represented that truth. Existing laws and norms may be serious threats but the 'ghastly vulgarity' of these could not touch 'the fullest extent of inspirational powers at the time of the conception of the idea'; nor the insights such 'inwardness' afforded concerning the human condition (Spencer, cited in Bell 2001: 153).

This work of Stanley Spencer may also seem an odd place to conclude. The mysterious artistry of distorted representations may appear a distance from the will to account rationally for the individual among the totality of his or her human fellows. But I recall Karl Popper's encouragement that no source of knowledge should be ruled out of the scientific canon at face value, and I recall the problematic with which Simmel launched his scientific study of society: How is it possible to know the individual other except as a type? In my estimation this corresponds to Stanley Spencer's project, wishing to portray the human individual, uniquely and in juxtaposition, as an authentic irreduction. His kind of distortion is preferable to Simmel's, however, because it is a general composition derived not from stereotypification but from a commitment to recognizing and to treating radical individual otherness as a thing-in-itself.

One accedes to a moral realization: seeking to represent the *substance* of another individual human other in its own terms results in a worthy distortion; seeking to accommodate rationally the *capacities* of the individual human other in general terms is a route to human science and free society.

PUBLIC AND PRIVATE: CIVILITY AS POLITESSE

Introduction: 'Politesse'

Chambers' Twentieth Century English Dictionary (1966) defines 'politesse' as a French import into English meaning 'superficial politeness'. The intent of this last section of the book is to raise politesse to the position of a virtue. The superficial polite engagement with an other is, I shall suggest, a means to interact with Anyone, the universal individual actor, at a respectful distance. One does not presume to know or to encompass the other, one recognizes Anyone as an actor, or group of actors, entrained on a life course, amid a life-project of his or her or their own devising. And yet one would afford the other the space to fulfil that life-project, to the extent that it does not prejudice the potential fulfillment of Anyone.

I would describe politesse as that virtuous social state where Anyone is recognized as an end in themselves – the end of his or her own life – and where norms of social interaction are in place such that a balance is achieved between space and care. One cares sufficiently about fellow individuals to ensure that they are afforded the space to come into their own and not become mere means to others' individual or collective ends; but one does not presume to know in any detail, or seek to influence in any substantial way, what another's 'coming into their own' might entail.

The key relationship implicated in politesse and the figure of Anyone alike is still that between the individual and the human, between the single case and the universal whole. Politesse is that global form of virtuous engagement whereby Anyone is envisaged as potentially meeting anyone else on their diverse individual paths to possible self-fulfilment. Politesse describes an interactional systemic which concerns any particular interlocutors as exemplars of humanity. My aim here is to identify a cosmopolitan ethos in everyday interaction so that local sociation is everywhere imbued with a global liberality. In politesse is a mechanism for mediating between Anyone, cultural community and global society.

The argument is in three main parts. The first explores politeness as it appears in ethnographic accounts of existing social milieux and how its significance has to date been anthropologically appreciated. The second explores issues concerning our abilities and our duties to legislate for a quality of civil society whose scale is increasingly global. And the third considers what cosmopolitan politesse might entail as a set of everyday interactional norms.

Politesse as Naturally Occurring

Anthropology and Interactional Routine

Anthropology has long recognized the significant role played by routine in social interaction. Interactional norms are both everyday means by which social groups maintain themselves as domains of exchange, and manifestations of fundamental cultural notions of identity and value (Josephides 1999: 139–42).

To advert, albeit briefly, to this anthropological tradition, Esther Goody begins her edited collection, *Questions and Politeness: Strategies in Social Interaction*, by noting that a common set of rules on how to proceed in social interaction is necessary for any social living and for achieving individual goals in these contexts (Goody 1978: 3–6). These rules, she suggests, are as much anchored in human nature as in a social structure. In other words, there are certain basic norms universally inherent to the nature of human social interaction. There are similarities in verbal style and strategy cross-culturally – the meaning of a highly pitched voice, say, or a hesitant one – showing common underlying elements in humanity's social nature prior to cultural learning. There exists a human strategic repertoire.

While politeness phenomena may be based on universal principles, Brown and Levinson (1978) elaborate, each cultural milieu may be described as practising its own predominant interactional styles, and possessing an interactional ethos related to social structure. Everyday, interacting individuals replicate tightly and systematically structured patterns of social exchange, leading to interactional routines of pan-cultural expectability. In the terms suggested by John Gumperz (1970), individual interactants are found within 'speech communities': groups characterized by routine interaction over a significant period of time which share a 'verbal repertoire', a totality of linguistic forms regularly used in socially significant interaction.

Particularly relevant for my purposes here is the widespread anthropological recognition of two fundamental types of interactional systemics. They might be glossed 'public' and 'private' or 'formal' and 'informal', or, as Gumperz (1970) has preferred, the more specific 'transactional' and 'personal'. In the first, Gumperz explains, speakers suspend their strategies for individual expression in order to enact relevant rights and duties and to achieve limited, socially defined goals. 'Transactional' exchange is status-oriented and predictable: a purchase of groceries, a church service, a job interview. By contrast, 'personal' (private and informal) exchange is less rule-bound, speakers acting out their preferred individual selves. In his conceptualization, Gumperz is looking back to Erving Goffman's celebrated distinction between 'front-stage' and 'back-stage' aspects of social life (Goffman 1978). Social life is everywhere a performance concerning 'front' or 'face', Goffman claimed, and politeness hides the dirty work of backstage efforts at impression management.

Equally, in his conceptualization Gumperz looks back to Basil Bernstein (1964), and his identification of two universal interactional 'codes', which he variously called 'public language' as against 'formal language', and 'restricted' as against 'elaborate'. The first is characterized by highly coded utterances: the attachment of ready-made terms and phrases to designate a common referent, using widely known catchphrases of a language community with implicit meanings, rigid syntax and predictable, restricted sentence constructions. Use of such 'public language' produces social and normative not idiosyncratic meanings and experiences, which are expressive of concrete and global relationships. Public language facilitates mechanical solidarity and group loyalty, and maintains the status quo. By contrast, 'formal language' is characterized by 'now-coding' utterances referring to particular referents. Here are individualized speech acts, less predictable, fostering analytical thought processes, independent reflection and fine gradations. The two codes, Bernstein concludes, are functions of forms of social relationship, or qualities of social structure: role-oriented ('restricted') versus person-oriented ('elaborate') occasions. The concern to maintain 'face', as Neil Thin (2001) has more recently suggested, is associated with a social-structural ethos that privileges social distance, status, orderliness and hierarchy, while informality, even rudeness, is associated with an equality of social closeness which can compass the anarchic.

Gumperz, Bernstein and others recognize that the above distinctions (transactional/personal, restricted/elaborate) are ideal types. In practice, contexts, roles, persons and strategies will be characterized by a mixture of interactional styles or codes. Nevertheless, the distinctions are important to recognize – both practically and morally – as I shall demonstrate. The politesse which I would identify might be described as a kind of public or transactional routine whereby a front of universal, human recognition and rights is instituted in the face of all manner of possible private (backstage) disagreements, dislikes, even disrespects, concerning the substance of different individual and collective lives. 'People agree in the language they use: this is agreement in form of life not opinions', Wittgenstein wrote (1978: §241). What is important for politesse – that which makes its superficialism into a virtue – is the instituting and valuing of a form of life, a surface of mannered routine exchange, beneath which all manner of individual and idiosyncratic opinion – on identity, on religiosity, on fashion, on football – might flourish. One anticipates that such diversity will be present and ongoing, but one does not claim or need or even endeavour to discern what diversity of opinion exists. Politesse is a universal surface of humane interaction: it vouchsafes private substance to be a matter of individual and personal construction, taste and predilection. The distinction between the form of exchange and its substance is crucial. This is something to which anthropology has also long paid attention.

Anthropology and Communication

One of the more provocative insights is Edward Sapir's (1956) concerning the 'friendly ambiguities' of language. There is a routine 'economy' to interpersonal relations such that members of a speech community can, he suggests, construe worlds as significantly different as if they were members of different cultures. Differences in world-view need not become apparent or appear significant in the mundane round of exchange, however, because they remain beneath the verbal and behavioural surface. On the surface, the common forms of members' social life together 'conspires' to reinterpret for each the behaviour they observe in terms of 'those meanings which are relevant to his own life' (Sapir 1956: 153). That is, individual world-views tend to operate as self-fulfilling prophecies, and those in a relationship will interpret as they expect or hope to see. The language of routine exchange, one might conclude, serves at once as a route to making social relations uniform, and as a most potent medium of individuality.

Sapir's recognition of the natural ambiguity of language – indeed, of any public, symbolic system of exchange, verbal or other – has a number of very significant implications. As Dell Hymes elaborated, what counts as a 'communicative event' of predictable content is not something that can be easily or superficially identified, for its status 'is entirely a question of [its] construal by a receiver' (Hymes 1973: 22). To identify a 'successful' exchange – even to identify what passes for 'interaction' or 'communication' – is a subjective judgement, a matter of what Peter Winch (1970: 107) has called 'internal relations', *within* a world-view. In short, it would be rash to extrapolate from the seemingly orderly nature of an interaction between individuals, and the verbal or behavioural routine in which they partake, to the character and extent of a shared set of meanings to which they subscribe. A second implication is that social interactions are not things-in-themselves. They possess the significance that individual participants diversely bring to them. They continue to take place because of the individual purposes they serve. However regular and routine, social interactions are effected by the regular work of individual management and interpretation. The verbal or behavioural routines are maintained because they continue to be worked by – and work for – the individuals involved. The routines, structures and institutions of social milieux do not work themselves.

It is important to emphasize this point. Interactional routines do not possess or assume an independent power, logic or life force. It is better to conceive of the routines as inert moulds or masks in which, and behind which, individual meanings are made and interests pursued. The interaction does different jobs for different participants, and while it may be incumbent upon each participant to know and employ certain routine, even standardized, linguistic forms in order to enter into the exchange, these will serve a diversity of ends. A shared language provides a fund of forms and cases which individuals adapt to their communicational purposes (Rapport 1993).

The tension between the common (routine, public) surface of public exchange and the possible privacy of meaning that operates within and beneath it has been anthropologically addressed in a number of interesting ways. Considering the psychical process whereby common interactional forms serve the interests of a diversity of individual users, George Devereux (1978) coins the term 'ego-syntonism'. '[B]oth organised and spontaneous social movements and processes are possible', he explains, 'not because all individuals participating in them are identically (and sociologistically) motivated, but because a variety of authentically subjective motives may seek and find an ego-syntonic outlet in the same type of collective activity' (Devereux 1978: 126). Ego-syntonism is a process whereby a number of discrete consciousnesses come routinely to interact one with another, either on an ad hoc or an ongoing basis.

A great advance in the appreciation of the processes of participation in social milieux by way of cultural forms, Devereux elaborated, would be to recognize that the collective or joint act (the family meal, the clan ritual, the regional market, the international war) should not be construed in terms of either a homogeneous set of individual experiences or a single massive, social one. Instead, the collective act represents the embodiment of an institutional medium, a channel and occasion, 'provided' by the society or culture, through which is achieved the public actualization, ratification and gratification (in different ways and to different extents) of any number of individual meanings and motivations (Devereux 1978: 127–28). The institutional medium may be regularly repeated (weekly church going) or represent a single event (the 1956 Hungarian uprising), and it may be revolutionary or conservative in consequence, but what is characteristic is that differently motivated individuals can come to perceive in that certain socio-cultural moment or event a suitable outlet for their various gratifications.

There is a fundamental tension, then, for Devereux, between collective action and the 'conglomerate' of individual motives underlying it: between public behaviour and its personal meaning. '*Si bis faciunt idem, non est idem*' ('If two people do the same thing, it is not the same thing'), Devereux (1978: 125) sums up, citing a Classical aphorism. The result is that any number of actors can come together in a group and form a public collectivity, and at precisely the same time remain apart, maintaining their discrete and diverse individualities. Indeed, for Devereux, the two processes are dialectically conjoined: the maintenance of collectivity and the development of individuality arise mutually through one and the same constitutive tension. Joint social events need not be singularly interpreted in order to be maintained, and need not eventuate in singularity either. Individuals need not be in agreement when they begin to interact, and constant interaction need bring them no closer to a joint or standardized world-view, or an overcoming of their idiosyncrasies: a great deal of their interaction can even go on in a situation of misperception or misinterpretation of one another's meanings and motivations.

The key to Devereux's portrayal – as it was to Sapir's – is the ambiguity of socio-cultural forms. The latter serve as significant synthesizing instruments by which the threads of different individuals' lives come to be routinely interwoven because they possess a basic indeterminacy. Vague and superficial, they can be inherited intact by different generations and adapted to a variety of settings; they are ready-made formulae always capable of being substantiated and revived by new motivations and moods (Propp 1968: 116). Their usefulness and prevalence issue both from their inertia or conservativeness and their malleability in use. It is the 'friendliness' of interactional routines (Sapir) that they accommodate diversity – even unbeknown, consciously, to those whose friendship (or indifference or animosity, even) is routinely effected through them.

Sapir and Devereux shift anthropological focus from an assumption that cultures or societies comprise common world-views to an exploration of how a diversity of world-views can co-exist within 'single' socio-cultural settings (cf. Goodenough 1963; Szwed 1966; Schwartz 1978). Important work in this regard is also that of Anthony Wallace (1961, 1962, 1964). One should not presume a replication of psychological or cultural uniformity within a social group, in personalities sharing a homogeneous 'cultural' character, Wallace begins (1964: 24). The situation is more accurately described as an 'organization of diversity'. Individuals in any one society need not be found 'threaded like beads on a string of common motives'; they can still interact in a stable and mutually rewarding fashion, and organize themselves culturally into orderly, expanding, changing societies in spite of their having radically different interests, habits, personalities, customs, and despite there being no one cognitive map that members share. Indeed, the 'mazeway' of each individual – that cognitive map of values, plans, techniques, people and things; that organized totality of meanings which each maintains at a given time and which is regularly evoked by perceived or remembered stimuli – will be unique (Wallace 1961: 131). In this way, all human societies can be described as plural and all cultural traditions hybrids.

Wallace describes the orderly relationships which constitute stable socio-cultural systems as 'equivalence structures': sets of equivalent behavioural expectancies (Wallace 1964: 24). Individuals can regularly engage in routine interactions with one another not because of a cognitive or motivational commonality but because they have developed a capacity for mutual prediction whereby the specific behaviour of one is highly likely to eventuate in the specific response of another, and so on. That is, individual behaviours come to form routine joint systems by learning that under certain circumstances others' behaviour is predictable and can be confidently interrelated with actions of their own. This system of organizing relations, Wallace suggests, fits interactions of different levels and types: between Native Americans and Whites, for instance, trading and fighting for years without mutual comprehension; between different social classes who may operate with distinct ideologies concerning their economic relations; and between different role players, such as bus drivers and passengers, whose interests in avoiding traffic jams may be commensurate but very different.

Nonetheless, what the bus driver and passengers (Native Americans and Whites, and so on) do share is something very precise. Their interests in keeping to timetables overlap, their motives in riding the bus are complementary, and they possess detailed, mutual behavioural expectancies. Moreover, the relations are standardized between any driver and any passenger within the urban or regional or national system. Wallace describes this as a 'contract': something where the equivalent roles are specified and available for implementation to any parties whose motives make their adoption promising. He also calls it a 'meta-calculus': something which is the sum of at least two parties' particular 'calculi', or recipes of behaviour (Wallace 1962: 356). And he goes on to say that a society may be described as a 'family of meta-calculi': an array of standardized models of contractual relationships; a system of interlinking equivalence structures.

In my ethnographic monograph, *Diverse World-views in an English Village* (Rapport 1993), I charted the relations between two long-standing neighbours in the English village of Wanet: farmer Doris Harvey and builder Sid Askrig. Doris and Sid partake in interaction which is regular and routine, and which both regard as appropriate and legitimate. Members of a speech community, they share notions of conversational propriety: turn-taking, politeness formulae, the use of space, and so on. Their interaction can be described as a regular sequence of mutual interpretings: there is a habitual 'talking relationship' which they maintain between themselves (Rapport 1987). At the same time, however, the contours of reality which their interactions maintain and develop are found to be far from shared or even compatible. That is, Doris and Sid write themselves into often very different worlds: they use the conventional devices of expression in different ways. The behaviours they share and exchange prove ambiguous enough for each to impart to them their own meanings, and for each to house them in very different cognitive contexts or world-views. More generally, for the village of Wanet as a whole, while there were many forms of behaviour which people routinely employed – even regarded as special to them in the locale – there were no standard definitions of what these forms meant. Rather, usage was individual, connected to particular talking relationships and expressive of particular world-views. The forms of interaction that many locals agreed upon as common and proper to Wanet – forms which manifested an identity of what it was to be a member of Wanet as a community – came to be mediated in use by a diversity of individual ends and were the means for achieving satisfaction of a variety of kinds and amounts.

In short, the interactional routines through which social relations were effected and by which memberships were emblemized functioned without necessitating or entailing substantive agreement on the meanings of the symbolic forms that were exchanged.

To sum up what we have been saying, anthropological appreciation of routines of interaction as necessary, naturally occurring features of socio-cultural milieux has produced subtle insights. Regular exchanges between people should not be conflated with common understandings or a coming together of individuals on anything but a formal, superficial level. A speech community amounts to a collection of individual 'talking partners' who may be described as meeting on the surface of their selves. Through the routine exchange of common cultural forms, individual members of a society are able to build one another into expectable characters in any number of different worlds. Meanwhile, 'talking partners' can be seen to influence one another in all manner of indirect, incidental, contingent, contradictory and changeable ways. Interaction need not equate to direct communication, or indeed any meaningful communication at all.

Socio-cultural milieux can be described as collections of individual world-views which are expressed in a range of common forms. By virtue of these forms, Anyone can be conceived of as a member of communities and living in individual worlds at one and the same time. Indeed, the two states may be inextricably related: Anyone develops and manifests an individual consciousness by way of the symbolic forms they routinely deploy in social interaction; and routine exchanges continue – Wallace's behavioural contracts – by way of the continuing individualities expressed through them. To consider the behavioural forms existing as things-in-themselves is to assign the forms a misleading metaphysic and reality. To represent the forms as an objective grammar, abstracted from individual usage, is to do violence to distinct situations of exchange. In social milieux a 'fund' (or funds) of symbolic forms is routinely exchanged. The exchange amounts to the continuation (development, evolution, revolution) of cultural tradition(s) and the expression of individual world-views, the realization of individual life-projects.

My reason for rehearsing these anthropological insights is the better to conceive of a kind of politesse that might be encouraged, universally, in an emerging global society, and as part of an anthropologically informed policy. I imagine a routine social state where Anyone can potentially figure as the 'talking partner' of anyone else. Anyone is accorded the same recognition and respect, a potential member of the same speech community since he or she is an individual manifestation of the human whole. In this conception of politesse, the distance, the tension, between public form and private meaning will provide crucial leverage, as we shall see.

A partial analogy can be drawn with Freudian psychoanalysis in which consciousness figures primarily as a kind of buffer or filter whereby the unconscious and the deeper parts of identity are protected. It might appear, argued Freud (1997), that the conscious person is aware of all, but actually consciousness is highly selective, as are memory and recall. More akin to a sleepwalker, the conscious person lives the unconscious dream. I do not agree with a Freudian depiction of consciousness and unconsciousness, but his imagery does speak to the layering of polite society. There is a 'conscious surface' to social life – the public, routine forms of everyday interaction – which can be said to act as a kind of buffer or filter for the privacy and individuality of Anyone's life. Politesse, in this depiction, is a form of myopia or forgetfulness. It is vital that a society possesses common interactional routines; it is vital that Anyone has equal access to the routines and may partake in them as an equal member. A democratic and egalitarian society, moreover, would be one where the roles which individuals play in the interactional routines are, potentially at least, interchangeable. In Wallace's terms, the person who plays the bus driver or the bourgeois or the White should also be able to play the passenger, the worker and the Native American. But the interactional routines should not be seen as providing insight or purchase upon – a right to know or actual knowledge of – the individual lives led in their terms. 'Democratic manners', as Jacques Barzun (1959: 64) named them, safeguard equality and facilitate social relations by ensuring the privacy of individual identifications and preventing these being evaluated, compared or disparaged in the name of a common and collective good. Anyone is given an equal place as a partner to public interaction on the basis of a democratic view of membership, and the truth surrounding individual world-views – how Anyone is interpreting self and world – as well as the distaste this diversity is likely to occasion, are kept from 'conscious' public concern.

Politesse as Political Policy

Anthropology and Global Society

Conceptualizing a moral discourse beyond culture was, for Ernest Gellner (1995a: 8), a vital aspect of anthropology's mapping out of global social options. This moral discourse would sit alongside the global reach of scientific knowledge and the global spread of the marketplace. What kind of claim can be made for cosmopolitan politesse as a possibly deliberately instituted policy? Can politesse serve as a methodology for configuring social integration and human rights globally?

Gellner's own work offers interesting leads here. I refer to his deliberation on the proper place of traditional systems of symbolic classification in a rational, liberal and democratic society (cf. Amit and Rapport 2002: 75–77). How does one accommodate human rights in regard to personal identity and movement alongside structures of justice and of belonging? Gellner (1993a) framed his discussion in terms of the necessary relationship between science and culture. Science represents a form of knowledge, a cognitive style and an understanding of nature which reaches beyond any one culture so as to transform totally the terms of reference in which all human societies operate. However, science has also proved insufficient in providing people with emotional, sentimental and spiritual support. Hence the need to underwrite civil society with trappings of community: with the ritual and symbolism of a 'constitutional religion' in the manner of a constitutional monarchy (Gellner 1993a: 91), a 'constitutional patriotism' (*Verfassungspatriotismus*) and 'constitutional faith' (Hann and Dunn 1996).

Gellner depicted the liberal societies of the West as 'well-matured political system[s], in which absolutist symbols, shorn of too much power, coexist amicably with pragmatic, effective powers shorn of too much symbolic potency' (Gellner 1995c: 9). ('Liberalism', here, did not equate with laissez-faire capitalism, moreover, nor any particular economic system: an argument on behalf of Western, liberal democracy should not be confused with an advocation of a global market economy. And critique of global capitalism need not be seen to negate – as so often was the case: e.g., Esteva and Prakash 1998 – an advocating of liberalism as a politico-legal philosophy.) In the contemporary West, Gellner continued, science sits alongside moral discourses, often couched in the form of religion or of cultural relativism, courtesy of an uneasy relationship of ambiguity or avoidance. A balance is achieved between the moral 'thinness' of science on the one hand and the moral rigidity of religion and the tolerance of relativism on the other hand by no one having to declare their loyalties clearly or finally. But such a relationship is unstable. There are threats to such 'free, individualistic choice of identity' (Gellner 1993b: 3). (Do not be so sure that we do not face a new 'Dark Age' of fundamentalism and fascism (Barry 2001: 32).) Culture per se, insofar as it translated in practice into closed communities – communities that called for unity and loyalty and 'continuity of faith', for commitment to convictions however absurd (Gellner 1995a: 6) – represented a possible threat. Hence, anthropology must 'not make a fetish of culture' (Gellner 1995c: 26). People ought not to be frozen in cultural categories.

The modern world of global diffusion offered better prospects of 'mobility, equality and free choice of identity' than humankind has before enjoyed, Gellner (1993b: 3) concluded. But to stabilize the relationship between the deliverances of science and the belonging of cultural community was to posit a form of 'moral decency' that existed 'beyond culture' (Gellner 1973: 72; 1993a: 54). Key here was the conceiving of an appropriate social order. Culture must be accommodated to society. The social is envisaged to be a domain of human knowledge, human policy and human practice – moral and scientific both – beyond the narrowly cultural, communitarian and symbolic. The critique of relativism and the identity politics pursuant upon a fetishization of cultural 'truths' mitigates against taking seriously symbolic classifications of people that detract from their universal humanity.

In the terms of my argument, cosmopolitan politesse is conceived of as a moral means to engage with Anyone on a potentially global scale: a medium of social interaction whose symbolic form accommodates itself to scientific knowledge concerning the human and shares in its rationality. As a universal form of routine interaction between Anyone, politesse embodies what Rorty (1992: 89–90) termed 'an ironic appreciation' of different cultures and communities. Ideologies of unity, loyalty and continuity, idioms of cultural sovereignty and absolute distinction – these may serve as convenient flags and badges of belonging, and may be instrumental as currencies of internal exchange, but liberal society does not admit them to an ontological reality or afford them moral primacy. To the extent that cultures claim absolute legitimacy based on, say, a revelatory tradition, and to the extent that communities lay absolute claim to individual members' loyalty and identity, these claims can only be taken ironically. Such claims pertain to the 'theatre' of culture (Gellner 1993a: 91), and this must be kept distinct from the morality of a social space where individuals have the right potentially to fulfil the capacities for self-development of Anyone. The variable nature of cultural ideologies of personhood must not occasion confusion concerning individuality as a human universal.

Politesse as Ethos of Global Becoming

We have seen that there is a dualism intrinsic to the cosmopolitan conceptualization of Anyone who is recognized as an actually existing individual and also as an instantiation of human being. Anyone is the person leading an actual life of social relations, affiliations and community memberships, the person with a particular biography, and Anyone is the person who could lead any life: possessed of the capacity to be member of any community, party to any relationship; capable of following any tradition and none, of inventing a life-way of his or her own. Cosmopolitanism recognizes that this duality continues to characterize any living human individual. Human beings at one and the same time lead one life and could be leading any other life. There is a contingent, provisional, quality to the life actually led: there is a continuing potentiality to become someone else, anyone else.

Cosmopolitan politesse also endeavours to be a mechanism whereby the duality of Anyone can be kept current, both as an actual and practical possibility and as a moral imperative. The ambiguity of politesse seeks to allow for an engagement with Anyone both as they are now and as the other they can be anticipated to become. Politesse is a transitional medium. It is a conduit between different identities that Anyone might assume.

After Wallace we have imagined politesse as a kind of 'equivalence structure', mediating between the distinct lives of different individuals, a means and mode of conversation. Politesse translates formally (superficially) between them, enabling individuals immersed in different life-ways, social relations and cultural communities routinely to interact. Politesse effects an 'organization of diversity', aggregating individuals and their communities, traditions, localities, professions and occupations into a social whole. Politesse also mediates between members of particular communities and Anyone as a member of none – as outsider and stranger and singleton, individual-for-himself or -herself, and as-himself or -herself. Politesse recognizes Anyone as general human being.

But politesse is a conduit, a transitional and translational medium, in another way again. It mediates between the current lives that are individually led and the potential lives that might humanly be led. It anticipates that Anyone will pass from one kind of life – one stage or moment or aspect of their life, one community membership, one enculturation – to others of their choosing or creating. I have said that this imbues politesse with a moral character but I might go further and say that this charges politesse with a moral role. Politesse becomes a kind of informal regulatory vehicle, chartered with sanctioning that free passage of individuals between public identities, so that no particular, contemporary attachments need be experienced as permanent and involuntary. Anticipating Anyone's futurity, politesse allows for Anyone to become anyone else. No particular identity can be imprisoning, or site of irremovable discrimination, for Anyone as universal human being undercuts any momentary manifestation.

The ethos underlying cosmopolitan politesse is that Anyone is to be incorporated into social milieux, social relations and social institutionality, on the basis not of who they present themselves as being or have presented themselves, but on the basis of what they are in themselves: the bearers of their own futures. Anyone has the capacity, at any and every moment of his or her life, to create and recreate their identities, to fulfil themselves in all manner of ways. Politesse would address this capacity and potential, intending always to ensure individuals the space to become, to be other than themselves, other than the world (up to the limit that this does not

co-opt Anyone, or treat the human being as less than an end-in-itself).
Politesse does not concern itself with the substance of human lives –
with what individuals do and say – except insofar as this continues to
be freely chosen and is thus an expression of their becoming. If the
ambiguities of language have a 'friendliness' to them, as we have seen
Sapir conclude, then they also carry a moral weight, I have suggested,
and they effect a significant regulation. Politesse is a kind of space
within which Anyone's individual substantiation of meaning and
value can flourish and find fulfillment; politesse embodies Anyone's
rights to their own world-views and life-projects, accommodating a
diversity of ways of being 'good' – of following personal, including
cultural or religious or occupational, dictates. Anyone has a right to
his or her particular version(s) of the worthwhile.

But such accommodation and regulation is of itself moral and
'good'. Politesse as a social procedure needs to be assured of global
recognition and respect: it is in itself a general good. Not only may one
particular world-view or life-project not be allowed to impose itself
on or colonize others, but the procedure of politesse itself must be
accorded a kind of moral priority. As a system of exchange, it is located
above the substantive differences it is responsible for arbitrating and
regulating. If there is a proportional character to politesse, balancing
between being considerate to Anyone and being intimate or intrusive,
then this proportionality also extends to the particular goodness of
a particular way of life (individual or collective) having to accord
with the general goodness of the system. The recognition accorded to
Anyone is balanced against the recognition accorded to humanity: to
society as a global aggregative of Anyone.

In short, politesse ensures not only the right of Anyone to their
world-views and life-projects against Anyone and against existing
collective traditions, but also must ensure the stability and continuity
of such rights as a system. Or to phrase this better, in a way that does
not reify politesse, Anyone must abide by two dimensions or levels
of goodness: his or her own and also a public or social goodness that
guarantees the right of Anyone to their own evaluation of goodness
(worthiness). At the same time as Anyone maintains his or her own
personally (possibly collectively) authentic moral worlds, Anyone
must also maintain the system of interaction that ensures his or her
rights to their own space and their own future becoming. Politesse
must be generally respected as that arbitrational process through
whose good offices diversity is organized and conflict is reduced, and
society comes to assume an aggregative holism.

Access to knowledge of the universal human condition is,
according to Gellner (1993a: 54), '*the* fact of our lives' in the post-
Enlightenment. At the same time, anthropology is wont to inscribe

global diversity and, increasingly perhaps, agonistic 'compression'
of constructions of meaning and value (Paine 1992). Cosmopolitan
politesse endeavours to mediate the inevitable coming together of this
diversity in such a way that the rights of Anyone to continue to tread
a voluntary path among a contrary array are secured. It must be seen
to be necessary – 'good' – to interact by way of cosmopolitan politesse:
the realization of a societal-cum-moral sphere above the sway of
cultural difference. The place of Anyone, and a space for Anyone, in
society-wide forms of exchange is always assured whatever may be
their particular positions in cultural systems of symbolic classification.
At the same time, the 'procedural' goodness of the cosmopolitan
society supervenes upon the 'substantive' goodnesses of its individual
expressions and collective memberships.

Cosmopolitan politesse amounts to a moral informal social system
in its own right. It arbitrates and regulates justly between substantive
world-views, individual and communitarian, while remaining itself
non-substantive, acultural and impersonal.

It has been objected that such a dichotomy between the social (and
procedural) and the cultural is a chimera: there is no acultural or
supra-cultural level or dimension and cannot be. Cosmopolitan
politesse is simply the institutionalization of a particular liberal
version of the human condition, of human society, its constitution,
its optimal working and its moral membership. The very notion of the
acultural privileges 'the provincial universalism of Anglo-American
ethical theory' (Avelar 2004: 63).

This is the position adopted by Richard Rorty (1998) in furtherance
of the critique of Kant's claim that 'justice' possesses an abstract
purity that absolutely distinguishes it from 'loyalty'. For Rorty, far
from a rational imposition of impartial systems of moral obligation
and a recognition of human universals, justice implies simply another
version of sentimental attachment to one's group, its historical
consensus and its arbitrary symbolic distinctions. And while Jürgen
Habermas remains a committed contemporary advocate of the
Kantian position, and of the procedures of 'public reason', the weight
of considered opinion is against him, Rorty decides. According to
Charles Taylor (1992), for instance, we do not possess a true Kantian
self that could obey the call of reason against sentimental attachment
and see 'humanity' before itself. Our moral vision is determined by
the group(s) into which we are enculturated and to which we remain
loyal. Seeming moral dilemmas between 'loyalty' and 'justice' simply
result from contrasts between different community discourses to
which we belong. Similarly for Annette Baier (1995), morality entails
a relation of reciprocal trust among members of a close-knit group: to

behave morally is to do what becomes second nature in one's dealing with fellow members of one's family, neighbourhood or nation. To envisage a 'global morality', then, is to imagine an enlarging of the group: one is 'loyal' now to the species. But it will never be a matter of a reasoned approach to an abstraction like 'human dignity'; the story one will be able to construct around a 'thin' or abstract notion such as 'the human' will never commit or sustain one in the way of the 'thick', concrete story one tells of oneself as a local community member (Walzer 1994). A global morality in any concrete, substantive sense will only be possible as a consequence of the practice of global community.

Rorty agrees with these critiques. Universal moral obligations to act justly will not be discovered and instituted through reason, he claims. There is no essential, true self that may respond to the call of reason by virtue of its humanity, and that may recognize fellow human beings as Anyone. Were the West able and willing to export its moral vision – liberal, cosmopolitan – to the Rest – and it may still justifiably do so, Rorty feels – then the conceptual foundation of this is pragmatic not rational: exporting a cosmopolitan vision of global rights to participate in liberal society is appropriate (even if not initially moral) because it is the source of the social and material success of the most successful – well-to-do, free – societies in history.

While I would agree with Rorty that it is appropriate for a liberal-cosmopolitan vision to be globally diffused, I do not believe it to be immoral or amoral (or unjust). Nor I do not believe that the fate of Anyone and of cosmopolitan politesse can or need be left to the caprices of practical judgements of 'success'. The anthropologist knows that cultural belonging entails the continuing production or invention of difference (Rapport 2010b). Culture is a rhetoric of difference: communities maintaining themselves by way of agonistic and contrastive practice. In James Boon's (1982) phrasing, to assert a cultural belonging is to 'play the vis-à-vis': to define and defend one's community in the face of otherness. 'We are who we are *because* our traditions of practice are different on these matters'. Global agreement is unlikely to be reached on the substance of 'success' in human social life – especially, perhaps, in regard to anything to do with 'the West'. Which is why Gellner's formulation is so pressing, and necessary: a morality beyond culture.

This is precisely the point of cosmopolitan politesse: that it is to be considered a form of routine mundane interaction and recognition based on universal capacities – the capacities of Anyone to author individual world-views and life-projects – as distinct from the diverse substantiations of meanings and values that Anyone will effect (as an individual and as a member of a diversity of cultural communities).

Politesse exists at the same distance from loyalty and belonging as science does from culture.

Politesse as Lived Practice

Case-studies of Complex Society

In a prescient essay, 'Custom, Law and Terrorist Violence', Edmund Leach (1977) examined the nature of a complex society. It involved a triangulation of relations, he suggested, between 'customary' world-views, a 'legal' apparatus and 'human beings'. What was 'legal' did not extend only to criminality but also covered normative arrangements such as rules of language (grammar, vocabulary and usage) and of economic exchange, of political competition and family life. The legal-cum-normative apparatus effected an overall regularity in a civil sphere: an orderliness to public behaviours and exchange. It also gave an appearance of consensus. Notwithstanding, all modern societies were culturally pluralistic, to the extent that customary interpretations of the same behaviour, within communities and private spaces, could veer from 'divine' to 'criminal', 'heroic' to 'crazy', 'legitimate' to 'terroristic'. A diversity of substantive meanings and values remained in play while it was the function of 'legal' offices – judiciaries, police forces, courts of law, but also polite, everyday public exchanges – to maintain a surface of unity and a formal stability above the contrarious complex of cultural difference.

A further complexity, however, was that the boundaries between communities of cultural members, while purporting to be clear-cut and continuous, were actually fuzzy and porous. Individuals were always in the process of crossing between: between locales, classes, churches and ethnicities. When one observed how individuals actually behaved as opposed to how cultural systems of symbolic classification supposed them to behave, categorial distinctions tending towards an orderly array of discrete community identities all but disappeared. 'The very essence of being a human being' was to work creatively against the dominion of present structures and systems, Leach (1977: 19) determined, 'part of our very nature' being to resent having others structure our lives.

The picture which Leach painted was a layered one. Cultures were contained by societies, where a contrariety of customary judgements and rhetorics was to be expected, pertaining to different world-views. At the same time, there were laws and norms of interaction across society as a whole which upheld routine and legislated on limits to 'civil' behaviour. And then, independent of both the cultural (customary) and the social (legal) were individual lives, moving with alacrity and facility between cultural worlds and across social spaces, in the creative, idiosyncratic, even rebellious pursuit of their own identities. Considering the fluidity of which individual lives were substantively comprised, Leach concluded, it might be truer to say that modern complex societies were home to 'almost as many distinguishable "systems of customary rules and conventions" as there are individuals' (Leach 1977: 28). Individuals amounted to their own hybrid cultural worlds and communities.

By 'modern' and 'complex' it would be wrong to assume that Leach was either idealizing some contemporary milieux over others or being exclusivist. 'Modern' and 'complex' were contemporary designations as such. Indeed, the ethnographic record offers interesting corroborations of Leach's portrayal. There are, in particular, provocative insights into the complexity with which public apparatuses of sociation and regulation are experienced and lived. The interactional routines that everywhere operate in social life serve as transitional devices, buffers and filters, between polite public exchanges and private diversities.

It is in this way that Michael Gilsenan (1976) describes the Lebanese code of status and honour. The code purports to stand for a kind of normative social order. Notwithstanding, the publicity of politics, prestige and rank is lived on an everyday basis by way of behavioural ambiguities, secrecy and deceit. While appearing to abide by strict public norms, Lebanese effect realms of personal privacy. Codes of public exchange – in this case pertaining to the proprieties of hierarchy and honourable essences – are inhabited in such a way as to give the lie to classificatory fixity and public surveillance. Lying is a complex social act, Gilsenan (1976: 191) concludes. It involves the purposive (and aesthetic) fashioning of a social personality, to be placed 'out there' for public contemplation. The individual makes an object out of his or her own subjecthood, thus exercising a lissome self-consciousness.

Sophistry and deception figure equally prominently in the social lives of the Mehinacu of Brazil, according to Robert Murphy (1972). Here are the rhetorical means by which people maintain regular relations in very close proximity with one another without the stock of knowledge that Anyone might otherwise gain on anyone else becoming suffocating and stultifying. To effect 'neighbourliness' as an ongoing code of moral behaviour it is necessary to practice means by which Anyone is kept in a certain degree of ignorance concerning anyone else. Ignorance is an egalitarian leveler and common denomination. Such 'indirection', Joy Hendry and Bill Watson (2001) conclude, can be regarded not only as a human commonplace but a kind of necessity. Indirect communication plays on the inherent

ambiguity of symbolic forms of exchange; employing a range of
devices from verbal expression through behavioural cues to pregnant
silences, incorporating a range of motivations from shyness through
deceit to diplomacy, 'indirection' effects social relations and distance
at one and the same time.

What is particularly useful about Felicia Hughes-Freeland's (2001)
account of what she calls 'dissimulation' in Indonesia is the description
she gives of its historical coming into being. She traces a development
of forms of politeness that evolved from local royal courts to national
ideology and state policy. Politeness at the Sultan's Javanese court,
she elaborates, took the form of certain bodily disciplines and
comportment (chief among which was dancing) which acted to
obscure personal fact, feeling and intention in public interaction.
A close connection developed between 'movement, manners and
identity, which serve[d] to articulate ideas about order and coherence'
(Hughes-Freeland 2001: 151). At the same time, participation in the
forms of politeness evidenced an able-bodied, competent and mature
individual who belonged to Java as a whole.

At independence from colonial powers and the formation of
Indonesia as a nation-state, the historically specific system of bodily
skills, techniques and disciplines – the politesse local to Java – became
a central plank in ideologies of nationwide identity and were developed
as state policy. Post-independence Indonesian cultural politics
concerning interactional routines of modesty and dissimulation
became fundamental to a development of a national social identity,
Hughes-Freeland explains. However, while Indonesia is a highly
centralized state, and forms of politesse are state-sanctioned, this still
does not mean that the politenesses of bodily comportment are lived
in the everyday as determinist and monolithic. Performance does not
reduce individuality. Certainly, limits are observed and confrontation
is avoided as political expediency as well as politesse, but individuals
go through the motions of doing what the state endorses for their own
reasons. '[W]hereas politeness may appear to be the effect of external
control ... politeness is also a way of doing and being, between the rules,
before the rules, and after the rules' (Hughes-Freeland 2001: 160).
As a social and cultural milieu, Indonesia is made by the continuing
intentionalities of individual actors who are neither pawns nor
prisoners: a perfect public formalism can be experienced as anarchic
at a level beneath the collective effect. Between the rules, individuals
engage with 'the extra-social, the transcendental' (Hughes-Freeland
2008: 241).

Idioms of politeness are 'top-down policies' in Indonesia (Hughes-
Freeland 2001: 156), which represents no ideal vision of democratic

freedom. Nor is it the case that 'indirection', the commonplace techniques of dissimulation, evasion and deceit used in social life, necessarily portends towards the securing of a personal preserve that is Anyone's haven. Such privacy can also embody a ghetto, a prison: the facility to secure a private space within public codes of civility also translates as the facility to disguise maltreatment of Anyone. The ethnographic record is heartening to the extent that it displays how politesse can appear as statal policy, also how even in an autocratic context the individual finds ways in which to live the system on his or her own terms, and how public surveillance can be managed for private relief. But what of public surveillance as a good: the protections that politesse promises to Anyone in the face of cultural tradition, communitarian closure, the system of existing symbolic classes – in a word, category-thinking?

And then, indirection and deceit. 'Collectively', Kant wrote, 'the more civilized people are, the more they are actors'. The norms of social interaction are a 'play of pretences', of politenesses: to be civilized is to 'want to put on a show' and, Kant concluded, it is 'a good thing that this is so in this world' (Kant 1996: 37; cf. Cohen 2008). But then how does one ensure that the fabrication of public identities serves equitable and not exploitative ends? How might one prescribe a way in which politesse becomes both state programme and a virtuous personal project for individual citizens in a liberal democracy? ('L'Etat c'est moi', to recall Lawrence.) This is Gellner's question in another guise. How does a scientific world-view come to be extended so as to include the universal treatment of human beings in a rational, just, egalitarian way? How does a liberal morality come to have the global range of scientific knowledge?

Invitation to Politesse

My answer takes the form of a kind of appeal to Anyone, an invitation.

Politesse can be construed as a variety of 'perfectionism' (Hurka 1993). It locates virtue ultimately not in what Anyone does for or to anyone else but in what Anyone does for and to himself or herself. Perfectionism represents a submerged line of moral argument with a long and continuous history, Thomas Hurka explains, which gives a central place to self-regarding duties. The foundational insight of perfectionism is that there exists a potential in human nature for self-fulfilment and that it is moral that each human being should develop their nature, their own talents and capabilities; it is immoral to hinder others from fulfilling their potential just as it is to squander one's own. What 'individuals developing their nature' precisely entails has been variously delineated. While Aristotle emphasized rationality, Rousseau emphasized character and Kant a good will; Kierkegaard looked to the passion of commitment and Nietzsche to self-artistry. But such variety is conducive to the philosophy. While perfectionism argues for the virtue of individuals making the best of themselves, and would describe the realization of this as freedom – 'the maximum power for all members of human society alike to make the best of themselves' (T.H. Green, cited in Hurka 1993: 23) – it cannot detail what this might entail as a general prescription. Perfectionism hopes for those social conditions where individuals might focus on self-development, and that normative environment where individuals are at liberty to fulfil themselves to the extent that they do not infringe on others. Given the innate variety intrinsic to individuality, moreover, such development and fulfilment need not be a zero-sum game: the self-perfecting of Anyone need not preclude that of anyone else.

Politesse invites Anyone to fulfil himself or herself. It locates in self-intensity and self-care a form of equitability and an inherent moral respectability. For in the endorsement of Anyone's rights to a prospective and purposive agency – to developing his or her potentialities and satisfying his or her desires free from arbitrary restriction – is also the endorsement of anyone else's (Gewirth 1998). The invitation to self-fulfilment, in other words, is a 'thickly' inclusive one, inviting Anyone to see in his individuality and free potential for self-development a membership in a global human family. Politesse invites Anyone to self-fulfilment and thereby to commit to universal standards: to the Kantian categorical imperative; to recognizing the potential fulfilment of anyone else anywhere on the globe.

My answer as to why Anyone might be encouraged to 'contract into' politesse (after Wallace) – recognizing it to be an overarching organization of difference; accepting its status as universal arbiter; being convinced that its judgments instantiate a form of acultural morality and speak to and for a human whole – is that in it Anyone recognizes himself or herself. 'Why do I accept as good the procedures of politesse that appear to supervene upon, even conflict with, the particular substantive goods of my own world-view, my own communitarian affiliations, and lend support to the other? Because that other is Anyone, like me. I could have become other than I did; I could become other than I am. Hence, in sanctioning the freedoms of Anyone, politesse sanctions me. Anyone benefits from politesse. In my self-ishness I discover the human and engage with the human whole'.

Politesse recognizes, sanctions and celebrates the process of selfhood, a continual and creative effecting in which substance is variable and capacity constant and universal. Its understanding of virtue is not accommodating extant cultural traditions or current personal identifications but respecting and accommodating individual actors as bearers of contingent presents and unknown and unknowable futures. Anyone is accommodated within politesse not on the basis of who he or she appears to be or have been but on the basis of their potential becoming: their innate, embodied possession of a precious, unique futurity. Anyone's life is a thing-in-itself, now and forever: its capacity for self-fulfilment is its own and its own kind. And Anyone accommodates himself or herself to politesse on this basis. 'I respect the other and do not wish to deny them because I recognize the human potential to become other than one is, to become Anyone. I can become Anyone and vice versa. Futurity is our common human birthright'.

Conclusion: Good Manners

I began by defining politesse as a kind of 'superficial polite engagement'. Politeness phenomena were naturally occurring aspects of social milieux, I suggested, where interactional norms oversee a routine engagement between individual partners to an exchange. Politesse amounted to a mannered and mannerly surface: a kind of public language or restricted code whose routine-ness and ambiguity might safely encompass Anyone's irreducible difference; a kind of equivalence structure, mediating between the discrete lives of different individuals and affording them space to flourish. I have ended by depicting politesse as a moral means to engage with Anyone on a potentially global scale, a methodology for configuring social integration and instituting human rights universally. To contract into politesse was a moral act in which Anyone might both perfect his or her own self-fulfilment and play a part in securing anyone else's rights to an autonomous futurity. Is this a sleight of hand? If politeness is an ambiguous social form can it do the work of a cosmopolitan ethos, serving as a lever of global civil society? Can a general form vouchsafe particular lives? Can a symbolic contract vouchsafe a moral vision? Can politesse carry so much weight?

It must be granted that in and of itself politeness is meaningless. A key insight into symbolic exchange has been the way in which individual interpretation is responsible for public languages being given significance and being maintained as features of social settings – symbolic forms do not possess their own agency – and yet individual interpretation remains intrinsically diverse. Interactional routines are maintained for a diversity of reasons and deployed to effect a diversity of purposes, interest, agendas and projects. But then the phatic nature of symbolic exchange should not be overlooked. Politesse becomes more than an empty gesture (and a sleight of hand), I conclude, insofar as it is intentionally and continually adopted as an ethos by Anyone.

The form comes to serve as a mnemonic, its regular usage instructive of what symbolically, ritualistically, it stands for. I am considering politesse as having 'perlocutionary effects' (Austin 1962: 101) on Anyone who remains a self-conscious participant. Politesse cannot cause a civil milieu in which Anyone flourishes; politesse cannot cause anything. But by way of the mannered style of interaction individuals might remind themselves routinely of imperatives basic to cosmopolitanism as an ethos.

'Manners maketh man' was the celebrated phrasing of William of Wykeham (1324–1404), the pedagogue responsible for the founding of Winchester College and of New College, Oxford. Others have followed in inferring a connexion between social form and civil ethos, suggesting that manners be practised as a civil duty. 'Manners are one of the greatest engines of influence ever given to man', concluded Richard Whately; for, 'Manners easily and rapidly mature into morals' (Horace Mann); and indeed, 'Manners are stronger than laws' (Thomas Carlyle). There is even the anthropological colouration: 'I have a respect for manners as such, they are a way of dealing with people you don't agree with or like' (Margaret Mead). But then contrariwise, 'Manners are the hypocrisy of a nation' (Honore de Balzac); and, 'No softening of manners, no reform or revolution has ever brought human equality a millimeter nearer' (George Orwell).

My contention would be that the very decorousness of manners is the source of their possible effectiveness as a particular code of interaction. Manners bring a distinctive decorative quality to exchange, and while this quality is 'merely' decorative (and literally meaningless) and hence liable to abuse – as hypocrisy and obfuscation – the symbolic decoration is also the aid to manners' mnemonic function. Manners stand out for their being mannered, 'merely' mannerisms, seeming fripperies in the face of harsh inequalities and hard lives. ('Nowadays, manners are easy and life is hard' – Benjamin Disraeli.) But Anyone is made conscious of what is merely mannerly each time he or she is called upon to engage in this superficial, 'frivolous' form of exchange, and hence the invitation to consider the nature of such politesse and to contract into its moral ethos is repeated.

Virginia Woolf makes the case convincingly in her novel *The Waves*, a masterpiece of humane ethnography in which a medium is found to recount six distinct lives: as individuals alone, as friends, and as inhabitants of a paradigmatically human existence. Considering letter writing as a coded form of exchange, she writes:

> [O]ne begins letters 'Dear Sir,' ends them 'yours faithfully'; one cannot despise these phrases laid like Roman roads across the tumult of our lives, since they compel us to walk in step like civilized people with the slow and measured tread of policemen though one may be humming any nonsense under one's breath at the same time – 'Hark, hark, the dogs do bark,' 'Come away, come away, death,' 'Let me not to the marriage of true minds,' and so on. (Woolf 1969: 223)

The point is that politesse might serve as an 'engine of influence', that the mannerly can 'mature' into the moral, giving rise to an ethos 'stronger than laws', if its habitation by *Anyone* is self-conscious.

I have depicted 'virtue' by way of perfectionism and 'morality' as crucially concerning space: the 'good society' is one where Anyone can come into his or her own. Cosmopolitan politesse I have seen as a proportionate figure, anticipating that Anyone will occupy certain social spaces – that an individual human life represents a transition between certain social spaces – but not expecting to know what Anyone's purposes might be or might become. It is 'good manners' to anticipate the possibility of Anyone entering into social exchange with anyone else; and it is 'good manners' to anticipate Anyone becoming anyone else.

Good manners is the encoding of Anyone's right to take part in routine social exchange but also to occupy space in his or her own way. The effect of good manners is to safeguard a public space for Anyone to occupy, irrespective of the private significance they give to their behaviour, the roles they might contract for themselves in family and community. It is Anyone's right to have his or her voice heard and behaviour observed, should they so wish, and to occupy a public space beyond the personal preserve of their private consciousness (beyond their unvoiced interior dialogue) and also beyond the habituses of their familial or communitarian belongings (beyond the proprieties of their communal role playing).

The mannerisms of politesse can be a significant mnemonic mechanism. Anyone is routinely brought to mind of a cosmopolitan ethos which recognizes himself or herself and anyone else universally to be the constituent units of human society, the repositories of meaning and value in human life.

AFTERWORD:
JEWISH COSMOPOLITANISM

'Rootless cosmopolitan' (безродный космополитт) was an expression first coined by Soviet literary critic Vissarion Belinsky to describe writers who lacked Russian national character and did not possess appropriate patriotic allegiance to the Soviet Union. The term came to be widely used during Stalin's anti-Zionist campaign of 1948 to 1953 as a euphemism for Jewish intellectuals. 'Cosmopolitan' deviants and parasites were now also seen to be 'Zionist' traitors working powerfully and surreptitiously in league with foreign bodies to overcome socialism for their particular nefarious purpose.

A *Pravda* article of 28 January 1949 initiated the aggressive stage of the state-wide campaign. It identified: 'unbridled, evil-minded cosmopolitans, profiteers with no roots and no conscience ... Grown on the rotten yeast of bourgeois cosmopolitanism, decadence and formalism ... non-indigenous nationals without a motherland poison with stench ... our proletarian culture' (*Pravda* 1949: 3). Cosmopolitans were reactionary and anti-Marxist, opposing Soviet patriotism, defaming Soviet socialist culture, threatening to corrupt Soviet literature, film and graphic arts, the great Russian traditions in philosophy, history and law, and to negate the Communist Party policy of attaching significance to the national characters, qualities and traditions of peoples. 'National nihilism', as Stalin (1953: 94) himself put it, was injurious to the cause of socialism, acting as a tool for the anti-patriotic ideology of bourgeois cosmopolitanism. The campaign was therefore justified in its seemingly contradictory ends: that which was deemed 'Jewish' should be suppressed by the Soviet authorities, and the word 'Jew' disappear from Soviet media, since Jewishness polluted the purity of Soviet nationalities; 'anti-Zionism' surfaced, however, as a legitimate means to identify and attack continuing Jewish conspiracies. Many individuals were prosecuted, imprisoned and executed.

Before ending this book I want to reflect more explicitly on the concept of cosmopolitanism as a focus of personal engagement and on the contradictions this appears to throw up. What of elective affinities towards cosmopolitanism? While Anyone's birthright has been portrayed as the futurity of an individually authored identity and life-project – such that 'History is more or less bunk' (John Ford) – I also know that my own birth was based on the historical contingency of a family, designated as Jewish, that happened to move to Britain from Eastern Europe in the late nineteenth century, thus escaping both Stalinism and Nazism. In personally querying, over much of a lifetime, how and whether to be a Jew, I have kept Israel alive as an 'inner kingdom'. According to Alain Finkielkraut (1994: 117), this is typical for the Jewish diaspora. I have done this for the sake of the people I have known there in the times I have spent there – 'a screaming assembly of five million prophets and prime ministers' (Oz 1992) – but also for the sake of what Finkielkraut (1994: 125) depicts as a vengeance on oppression: 'Every aspect of Israel was a bit of dignity returned to the Jews as a whole ... Israel: a redemptive country that rescues Jews from the influence of their detractors'. Indeed, a deal of my engagement with cosmopolitanism, as a concept and a project, can be said to be entwined with the question of Israel and the mortal challenges it faces, not least from cultural fundamentalism. This book is a speculation upon an end to category-thinking – upon a politics of identity that deals not in essential classes, collectivities and communities but in human beings as individual things-in-themselves – but its immediate dedication is to individuals in Israel. I identify with cosmopolitanism but I reconcile this, to my own satisfaction, with also being a Zionist who remembers the Holocaust. Is my satisfaction delusional?

Jew, Israeli, Cosmopolitan

'Cosmopolitan' is a 'glorious noun', writes George Steiner (1997b: 62–63), with its promise of the unalienated and inalienable: All are human, all are validated in their being and becoming. And yet, Steiner (1997a: 234) also asserts that a Kantian universalist vision of cosmopolis is illusionary in the face of today's tribalism and religious fundamentalisms.

Included within such expressions of tribalism Steiner locates the present State of Israel: even its foundational secular Zionist ideology is riven by the logical flaw of a supposed Abrahamic contract to the 'Holy Land'. Albeit that the signal enigma of Jewish survival after the Holocaust makes Israel an 'indispensable miracle', it is nevertheless the case that ending the two-thousand-year history of genocide of Jews in a nation-state as normal as Israel – armed, itself persecuting to survive, surrounded by cynical and pitiless enemies – is 'scandalous'

(Steiner 1997b: 60, 174). The Jews' 'true mission' cannot be that of 'a nation state, as abominable or brave, as corrupt or inventive as any other' (Steiner 1998: 15). The riddle of Jewish diaspora and survival must surely have another calling.

Steiner's solution is that the Jew continues the historical role – the voluntary telos – of playing the 'moral irritant' among humanity, a kind of conscience: continuously calling to mind the fact that time, not space, is the native ground of truth; that land is for wandering, for moving through; that we are all guests of a small Earth and that mutual hospitality is the only path to peace and the sustainability of the species. Steiner elaborates:

> It was, owing to his peregrine, powerless condition, the nobility of the Jew, his true 'election', not to torture other human beings, not to make them homeless as he so often was. [Is not therefore the true election of Jews to be] guests (be they unwelcome) among men? For only as a guest of each other, as of this small planet, will man escape destruction. (Steiner 1998: 15)

The 'dignity' of the diasporic Jew – of Judaism universally moving among the Gentile – was that he or she was too weak to make another as wretched as himself or herself. The lesson of the torment and of the resilience of the diaspora is that we learn to be one another's guests: 'guests of life' (Steiner 1997b: 60). The truth is that our hatreds are territories of the mind and that our arsenals guard these fictional territories. We must transcend this ideology, understand that we have legs not roots, and that there is no particular physical space that is not worth either improving or leaving. The phenomenon of the Wandering Jew translates into a celebration of the status of visitor, and the virtue in making welcome: intrusion is the Jew's calling, affording others the opportunity to make the practice of hospitality habitual.

If the Wandering Jew has come to find that nothing human is alien to him or her – that fate is as strange as anything else he or she encounters – then by virtue of that experience all can learn to be one another's guests-in-life. And while the constant reminder – in the Jew's physical presence – against the naturalness of territorialism breeds loathing – from the counter-Enlightenment of de Maistre, Herder and Hegel to the murderous totalitarianism of Stalin and Hitler to contemporary Islamo-fascisms – still, the duty is to be 'errant': committed to physical transience, motivated by temporal ideals concerning the possibilities for human progress. Here is a meaning to Jewishness far more universal than the terminus of the State of Israel. To be this wandering kind of Jew is an honour: a club not to resign from however much prejudice it attracts (Steiner 1997b: 69).

Now hear the voice of David Grossman (2008), the Israeli novelist (who lost a son fighting Hezbollah in southern Lebanon), as he wonders aloud concerning the distance between, and yet the possible synthesis of, two very different versions of contemporary Jewishness: the cosmopolitan who has a universal moral mission to fulfil, as against the Israeli living in and on his own land.

Grossman recalls reading stories about the *shtetl*, such as Sholom Aleichem's *Tevye and his Daughters* (the basis for *Fiddler on the Roof*), as a young boy growing up in Israel in the 1950s and 1960s. The tenuousness of diasporic existence he found strange, and the suffering within the everyday: the fear of pogrom, the dependency on despots, the fatalism, the intimacy with calamity whose imminence was never in doubt. The young Grossman could not understand why Jews lived with these dangerous Gentiles; nor how it was possible for a Gentile to uproot a Jew, to tell him 'Go' with a sweep of the arm.

When the Holocaust is invoked in Israeli Hebrew, Grossman explains, the designation is of something that happened not 'back then' but 'over there': it is a foreign but coeval place. Israel coexists with an absence 'over there'; Israel embodies escape, survival and a learning from experience. Notwithstanding, a suspiciousness remains. Even in Israel there is the 'constant quiver of a profound lack of confidence in the possibility of [Jews'] existence', not only among Gentiles but anywhere (Grossman 2008: 73). Is not the continuous work needed to 'weave the thin fabric of everydayness over the horrors beneath' a superhuman one: 'an effort to convince ourselves that despite everything we know, despite everything engraved on our bodies and souls, we have the capacity to live on, and to keep choosing life and human existence' (Grossman 2008: 74). Even in Israel, it seems, Jewish fatalism makes 'death the immediate interlocutor' and, given the fragility of the body, of the family and of life, all one's energies have to be expended to escape its dread. 'Death is true, all else is an illusion' (Grossman 2008: 15).

The Zionist dream was to create a 'natural home', Grossman continues: a physical space for the Jewish individual and nation where one was not a guest, a stranger to be merely tolerated or a parasite, but a landowner living where one was safe and unquestioned. This was also an escape from the diasporic Jew as symbol or metaphor or parable – whether good or bad. For both demonization and idealization deny humanity to the Jew by refusing to see the thing itself: a person and nation among others. The eternal other, the archetypal alien, is not flesh and blood. Jews have been existentially foreign among others throughout the diaspora.

And yet Israelis overwhelmingly feel that they are yet fully to 'arrive': to transcend the Jewish fate of victimhood and persecution, to overcome a sense of loneliness and alienation. Israel is 'a tortured country, drugged to the point of overdose by history, by emotions beyond what humans can contain, by an extreme excess of events and tragedy, by an excess of fear and a crippling sobriety, by an excess of memory, by dashed hopes, by a fate unique among nations' (Grossman 2008: 67). No Israeli has ever known a time without an enemy: Israel has never known fixed borders or a territory not under violent threat: 1947, 1948, 1956, 1967, 1973, 1977, 1982, 1993, 1994, 2006, 2008 saw violence at its borders; no future can be taken for granted.

The 'failing' left among Israelis by history is that life is 'latent death' and that a Holocaust is ready to colonize this land also (Grossman 2008: 118). But then Israel remains a manifest fact and what is necessary is to abide by what Grossman terms an 'acquired naïveté', continuing to maintain the utopian ideal of the Jew in and on his land, ordinary among men (Grossman 2008: 107).

The speculation on cosmopolitanism which I have undertaken in this book might be said equally to be naive, utopian. Even amid a politics of identity dominated by culturally fundamentalist discourses it continues to prescribe that Kantian, liberal ideal vision of a humanity that recognizes its global singularity, with the individual as its universal exemplar. I have disparaged a dilution of the Kantian project that would see a pluralizing, rooting, indigenizing or relativizing of the concept of the 'cosmopolitan'; that would detach cosmopolitanism from a Western heritage and Enlightenment deemed incapable of treating radical cultural difference. 'Difference', I have maintained, pertains ontologically only to individuality. All other claims to difference can be treated analytically, and should be treated morally, as epiphenomenal. They are symbolic constructions whose validity depends on their voluntaristic character: lifestyle options freely undertaken by the individual and ironically inhabited.

Alongside this treatment of cosmopolitanism, however, the Holocaust has formed a historical backdrop, and not only to Rickey Hirsch's personal biography. From the book's epigraph (Primo Levi) onwards, a kind of zigzag has been traversed between a transcendent humanity and transcendent individuality and a perspective informed by the interests of a personal ethnicity not so far removed from Steiner's or Grossman's. Have I shown integrity as a narrator? Has my stance as a social scientist been sufficiently scrupulous if my conceptual argument possesses an elective affinity with a personal identification? Am I merely rehearsing a 'Jewish cosmopolitanism'?

I believe my motives are honest. And I think I can specify my problem. The point of departure into a cosmopolis is hard to identify with confidence, hard to secure or ensure. It seems like a leap of faith to trust in a vision of Anyone-in-the-world when category-thinking is still so prevalent, when its violent adjuncts (anti-Semitism and anti-Zionism) are not only historically recent but ongoing, and when liberal enclosures – from the defensive borders of democratic nation-states, to the acquired sophistication of interpretive communities (say, the readership of the *Times Literary Supplement* or the audience of the BBC), to gated residential communities – appear to be the necessary guardians of liberal freedoms. How to begin towards cosmopolis when one appears to depend, periodically, on boundaries, defending civil liberties and exchanges – indeed, life itself – from the forces of totalitarianism and reaction, religious, political, communitarian? Can one begin towards cosmopolis except from liberal institutions that continue to be anchored in traditions of civil society? One needs a certain confidence if one is to render history 'bunk' when its 'dead generations weigh like a nightmare on the brains of the living' (Marx 1934: 10).

Steiner and Grossman offer very different responses here. But both would retain 'Jew' vis-à-vis a cosmopolitan ideal. For Steiner, one accommodates to 'Gentile' and 'Jew', to a categorial and teleological structuration of identities and relations, because the long and recent history of persecution is too terrible to remain unredeemed. After the horrors of the twentieth century the distinctiveness of Jewish identity may not be 'casually' sloughed off, whether through assimilation or in nationalism. Both the 'illusion' that is cosmopolitanism today and the 'indispensable miracle' that is the State of Israel bespeak unfinished business: a human need towards whose fulfilment there is a continuing Jewish mission. The 'business' of Judaism will end only when we recognize the fictional nature of all territorial sentimentality and also instrumentality, and transition towards a new ideology of mutual guesthood on the earth's surface and of universal hospitality – Kant's key term. Until then, categorial Jewishness is a necessary means: a role with a humanistic and humanizing function.

For Grossman, meanwhile, Jewish fatalism appears inescapable. History is so close and continuing – 'coeval' – that one is drawn to despair. There appears no possible move to a new territory that can be made except in the accompaniment of old fears and foes, just as there appears no final secure home for frail human bodies, families and lives except in the constant accompaniment of death. And yet such sobriety or cynicism – living in the Israeli war zone – in time rots the soul. One must therefore act with the naivety of supposing that an ideal solution *is* possible: the Jew secure in his or her own land who is at the same time a cosmopolitan in possession of a universal moral sensibility. The metaphorical and categorial Jew is finally transcended in the cosmopolitan Israeli.

I find myself torn. Intellectually I would side with the prognosis of Stanislas de Clermont-Tonnerre, liberal member of the new French Assembly of 1789, endeavouring to codify Enlightenment principles of rational human universalism and British principles of the rule of law into a new French constitution: 'To the Jews as individuals one must grant everything; to the Jews as a "race" one must grant nothing' (cited in Ackerman 1977: 240). In emancipating the Jews (and Protestants) and granting them citizenship, post-Revolutionary France would also insist that there are no ontological identities that must legally, politically and morally be guaranteed besides individuality and humanity. Clermont-Tonnerre's is a cosmopolitan vision of overcoming the fiction of culture as collective essence and identity. Even as collective belonging (ethnic, religious, sexual, political), culture is recognized solely as an individual lifestyle choice. There can be no essential 'Jewish' territory, then, any more than there can be 'Muslim' or 'male' or 'Mill-ian'; nor can there be a teleological 'Jewish' mission. History starts afresh with each individual life. Collective identities under any dispensation – historical 'redemption', 'pragmatic' nationalism – are dangerous warping fictions that must be thoroughly eschewed: there can be no compromise, no strategic essentialism. The only true categories are 'human' and 'individual', and the polythetic nature of these – the ways in which they can be substantiated only through particularity – it has been the project of this book to elucidate.

At the same time I have my sentimental attachment to Israel. I carry with me the memories of, and a respect for (and anxiety concerning), a country of kibbutzim and academies – Amos Oz's 'fiery collection of arguments' (Oz 1992) – of rehabilitation after persecution, of a citizen army resolute against intimidation. I cannot detach from my mind the seven million people who exist precariously in a territory almost exactly the same size as my native Wales (20,770 square kilometres), beleaguered by cultures of ignorance, enmity, mendacity and violence. My sentimental attachment is maintained alongside an awareness of the tensions inherent in Israeli everyday life, that the very character and the procedures of the state are internally disputed and that the political process contains chauvinistic, fundamentalist and even non-democratic elements (Amos Goldberg, personal communication, 2011).

By what criteria of right do I not negate this attachment in myself, then? It hardly seems cosmopolitan or 'revolutionary' (after Clermont-Tonnerre). It is perhaps 'absurd'. Thomas Nagel (1971: 718–20) suggests defining 'absurdity' as that universal human condition in which pretension and reality can be recognized as clashing. Anyone steps back and surveys the life to which he or she is committed, with its arbitrariness and contingency, its habits that cannot be defended without circularity, but still Anyone does not disengage from it. Taking a dispassionate look at themselves, human beings nevertheless keep on being themselves; this is sentimentalism, and absurd.

I would not define my stance on Israel as absurd, however. It concerns an intellectual awareness of historical persecution and violence (anti-Semitic and anti-Zionist) for which there is no evidence of cessation. It concerns an intellectual awareness of the stereotyping and misinformation concerning Jews and Israelis that I would be loath to allow to proceed unmarked and unchecked. It concerns an intellectual awareness of the civil society that exists in Israel, the institutions that sponsor freedom of expression, democratic representation, social security, education and the progress of knowledge. It concerns, too, that sentimental awareness of a number of the individual lives whose homes are now in Israel and whose right it is to achieve fulfilment: a futurity that begins in a present space.

David Grossman's 'acquired naïveté' entails engaging with Israel's enemies – including enemies of the 'Zionist entity' who do not recognize 'Israel' – and endeavouring to find compromise. One grants them unilaterally the dignity of a voice that might deliberate with one's own. This does not strike me as absurd either. Grossman is disengaging from the contingency of particular habits and loyalties – from everyday, practical concerns for Israeli security and the routines of vigilance, military efficiency and sacrifice which that security have since 1948 necessitated – in order 'naively' to plan for the possibility of peace. He is prepared to abjure his 'pretensions' for the sake of realpolitik.

Let me, however, deliberately push my attachment to Israel into the realm of absurdity by hypothesizing upon habits and loyalties that do become simply arbitrary. Let me imagine that I would wish Israel to remain in its current statal form even could the security of Israel's population and liberal sociality be assured: I would wish Israel to exist for its own sake. Even should cosmopolis become a reality I would wish for Israel to continue to exist, mediating between Anyone and a global society – and thus imperfectly reflecting the nature of the paradigmatic relationship between the individual human being and humankind – because of my sense of attachment and loyalty. In this hypothetical situation I love Israel purely *as* Israel, a historically specific symbolic construction; I love Israel because it is as it is and not other, I love Israel as something that is mine and not others'. Is this, then, what I feel? Do I have this kind of 'tribal' attachment to Israel: a historical rootedness that I value for its own sake? If so, this is not cosmopolitan as I have described the term. A sentimental attachment to Israel ceases to be cosmopolitan at that point at which one prefers its existence to a human wholeness and the continual newness of individual creations of identity and identification. A 'communitarian cosmopolitanism' or 'rooted cosmopolitanism' is a contradiction in terms, and awareness of it constitutes an absurdity.

This book began with the voice of Martha Nussbaum (1996) exhorting Americans to recognize a duty to a greater belonging: to the human species over against the American nation. The extra resources at Anyone's disposal should so far as possible ensure the nourishment of human beings everywhere, anywhere on the globe, and not be deployed wholly or primarily or firstly to fellow nationals. This is a cosmopolitan virtue. As this book draws to a close let me draw on Nussbaum again as a source for self-exhortation. The cosmopolitan vision is a kind of ending of history; if the birthright of Anyone is their futurity, as an ongoing process of becoming, then history begins and rebegins in each individual life. No thing-in-itself, 'Israel' is the name of an ongoing association between some (at present) seven million individuals. 'Cosmopolis' is an ideal of liberal-democratic institutions that ensure for all individual members of the human species equally a space of security and development. It is for Anyone to nurture an 'acquired naïveté' to throw over attachment to nationality (also ethnicity, religiosity, gender, class, and so on) in the name of the individual and the human. This is something I must practice: disengage from the place in which Israel is an 'indispensable miracle' in order for the global space of Anyone to be achieved.

REFERENCES

Ackerman, W. (ed.) 1977. *Out of Our People's Past*, New York: United Synagogue of America.

Agamben, G. 1998. *Homo Sacer*, Stanford CA: Stanford University Press.

Amit, V., and N. Rapport. 2002. *The Trouble with Community: Anthropological Reflections on Movement, Identity and Collectivity*, London: Pluto.

Anderson, B. 1998. 'Nationalism, Identity, and the World-in-Motion: On the Logics of Seriality', in P. Cheah and B. Robbins (eds), *Cosmopolitics*, Minneapolis: University of Minnesota Press.

Anderson, E. 1999. 'What Is the Point of Equality', *Ethics* 109: 287–337.

———— 2004. 'The Cosmopolitan Canopy', *Annals of the American Academy of Political and Social Science* 393: 14–31.

Appiah, K.A. 1998. 'Cosmopolitan Patriots', in P. Cheah and B. Robbins (eds), *Cosmopolitics*, Minneapolis: University of Minnesota Press.

———— 2007. *Cosmopolitanism*, New York: Norton.

Arendt, H. 1959. *The Human Condition*, Garden City NY: Doubleday Anchor.

Austin, J. 1962. *How To Do Things with Words*, Oxford: Oxford University Press.

Avelar, I. 2004. *The Letter of Violence*, New York: Palgrave Macmillan.

Baert, P. 2005. 'Towards a Pragmatist-inspired Philosophy of Social Science', *Acta Sociologica* 48(3): 191–203.

Baier, A. 1995. *Moral Prejudices*, Cambridge MA: Harvard University Press.

Barber, B. 1996. 'Constitutional Faith', in J. Cohen (ed.), *Love of Country*, Boston: Beacon.

Barry, B. 1999. 'Statism and Nationalism: A Cosmopolitan Critique', in I. Shapiro and L. Brilmayer (eds), *Global Justice*, New York: New York University Press.

———— 2001. *Culture and Equality*, Cambridge: Polity.

Barzun, J. 1959. *The House of Intellect*, London: Secker and Warburg.

Bateson, G. 1972. *Steps to an Ecology of Mind*, Frogmore: Paladin.

———— 1980. *Mind and Nature*, Glasgow: Fontana.

Bateson, G., and J. Ruesch. 1951. *Communication*, New York: Norton.

Bauböck, R. 2000. 'Political Community beyond the Sovereign State, Supranational Federalism, and Transactional Minorities', in S. Vertovec and R. Cohen (eds), *Conceiving Cosmopolitanism*, New York: Oxford University Press.

Bauman, Z. 1998. 'Postmodern Religion?' in P. Heelas (ed.), *Religion, Modernity and Postmodernity*, Oxford: Blackwell.

Beck, U. 1998. 'The Cosmopolitan Manifesto', *New Statesman*, March 20, pp. 28–30.

———— 2002. 'The Cosmopolitan Society and Its Enemies', *Theory, Culture and Society* 19(1–2): 17–44.

———— 2006. *Cosmopolitan Vision*, Cambridge: Polity.

Bell, K. 2001. *Stanley Spencer*, London: Phaidon.

Benhabib, S. 2006. *Another Cosmopolitanism*, New York: Oxford University Press.

Benjamin, W. 1968. 'Theses on the Philosophy of History', in *Illuminations*, New York: Shocken.

Bergson, H. 1972. 'La Politesse', in A. Robinet (ed.), *Henri Bergson: Mélanges*, Paris: Presses Universitaires de France.

Berlin, I. 1990. *The Crooked Timber of Humanity*, London: Murray.

Bernstein, B. 1964. 'Aspects of Language and Learning in the Genesis of the Social Process', in D. Hymes (ed.), *Language in Culture and Society*, New York: Harper and Row.

Bok, S. 1996. 'From Part to Whole', in J. Cohen (ed.), *Love of Country*, Boston: Beacon.

Boon, J. 1982. *Other Tribes, Other Scribes*, Cambridge: Cambridge University Press.

Bowie, M. 2000. 'Humanism Refitted', *Times Literary Supplement* 5094, p. 20.

Breckenridge, C., S. Pollock, H. Bhabha and D. Chakrabarty (eds). 2002. *Cosmopolitanism*, Durham NC: Duke University Press.

Brock, G., and H. Brighouse (eds). 2006. *The Political Philosophy of Cosmopolitanism*, Cambridge: Cambridge University Press.

Brown, P., and S. Levinson. 1978. 'Universals in Language Usage', in E. Goody (ed.), *Questions and Politeness*, Cambridge: Cambridge University Press.

Burke, E. 2005. *Burke: Select Works*, Oxford: Clarendon.

Butler, J. 1996. 'Universality in Culture', in J. Cohen (ed.), *Love of Country*, Boston: Beacon.

Caglar, A. 2000. 'Media Corporatism and Cosmopolitanism', in S. Vertovec and R. Cohen (eds), *Conceiving Cosmopolitanism*, New York: Oxford University Press.

Calhoun, C. 2000. 'The Class Consciousness of Frequent Travellers: Towards a Critique of Actually Existing Cosmopolitanism', in S. Vertovec and R. Cohen (eds), *Conceiving Cosmopolitanism*, New York: Oxford University Press.

Cawley, C. (ed.) 1970. *Everyman and Medieval Miracle Plays*, London: Dent.

Chakrabarty, D. 2002. 'Universalism and Belonging in the Logic of Capital', in C. Breckenridge, S. Pollock, H. Bhabha and D. Chakrabarty (eds), *Cosmopolitanism*, Durham NC: Duke University Press.

Chamberlain, L. 1996. 'A Spoonful of Dr Liebig's Beef Extract', *Times Literary Supplement* 4871, pp. 14–15.

———— 1997. *Nietzsche in Turin*, London: Quartet.

Cheah, P. 1998. 'Rethinking Cosmopolitical Freedom in Transnationalism', in P. Cheah and B. Robbins (eds), *Cosmopolitics*, Minneapolis: University of Minnesota Press.

Cheah, P., and B. Robbins (eds). 1998. *Cosmopolitics*, Minneapolis: University of Minnesota Press.

Clifford, J. 1998. 'Mixed Feelings', in P. Cheah and B. Robbins (eds), *Cosmopolitics*, Minneapolis: University of Minnesota Press.

Cohen, A. 2008. 'The Ultimate Kantian Experience: Kant on Dinner Parties', *History of Philosophy Quarterly* 25(4): 315–36.

Cohen, A.P. 1994. *Self Consciousness*, London: Routledge.

Cohen, A.P., and N. Rapport (eds). 1995. *Questions of Consciousness*, London: Routledge.

Cohen, J. (ed.) 1996. *Love of Country*, Boston: Beacon.

Collis, M. 1962. *Stanley Spencer*, London: Harvill.

Colson, E. 2008, 'The Founding Moment: Sixty Years Ago', in P. Werbner (ed.), *Anthropology and the New Cosmopolitanism*, Oxford: Berg.

Conley, V. 2002. 'Chaosmopolis', *Theory, Culture and Society* 19(1–2): 127–38.

Conrad, J. 1925. *The Nigger of the Narcissus*, New York: Doubleday.

Crapanzano, V. 2003. *Imaginative Horizons*, Chicago: University of Chicago Press.

Derrida, J. 1997. *Cosmopolites des tous les pays, encore un effort!* Paris: Galilée.

Devereux, G. 1978. *Ethnopsychoanalysis*, Berkeley CA: University of California Press.

Dreitzel, H. 1970. 'Introduction', in H. Dreitzel (ed.), *Patterns of Communicative Behaviour*, London: Collier-Macmillan.

Dworkin, R. 1977. *Taking Rights Seriously*, London: Duckworth.

Edelman, G. 1992. *Bright Air, Brilliant Fire*, Harmondsworth: Penguin.

Emerson, R.W. 1981. *The Portable Emerson*, Harmondsworth: Penguin.

Esteva, G., and M. Prakash. 1998. *Grassroots Post-modernism*, London: Zed.

Etzioni, A. 2002. 'Thickening the Soup', *Times Literary Supplement* 5175, pp. 8–9.

Falk, R. 1996. 'Revisioning Cosmopolitanism', in J. Cohen (ed.), *Love of Country*, Boston: Beacon.

Fardon, R. 2008. 'Cosmopolitan Nations, National Cosmopolitans', in P. Werbner (ed.), *Anthropology and the New Cosmopolitanism*, Oxford: Berg.

Featherstone, M. 2002 'Cosmopolis: An Introduction', *Theory, Culture and Society*, special issue, 19(1–2): 1–16.

Feyerabend, P. 1995. *Killing Time*, Chicago: University of Chicago Press.

Fine, R., and R. Cohen. 2000. 'Four Cosmopolitan Moments', in S. Vertovec and R. Cohen (eds), *Conceiving Cosmopolitanism*, New York: Oxford University Press.

Finkielkraut, A. 1994. *The Imaginary Jew*, Lincoln: University of Nebraska Press.

Freud, S. 1997. *The Interpretation of Dreams*, Ware: Wordsworth.

Furbank, P.N. 1999. *Behalf*, Lincoln: University of Nebraska Press.

Gellner, E. 1973. *Cause and Meaning in the Social Sciences*, London: Routledge and Kegan Paul.

———— 1993a. *Postmodernism, Reason and Religion*, London: Routledge.

————— 1993b. 'The Mightier Pen? Edward Said and the Double Standards of Inside-out Colonialism', *Times Literary Supplement* February 19, pp. 3–4.

————— 1995a. 'Anything Goes: The Carnival of Cheap Relativism which Threatens to Swamp the Coming *fin de millenaire*', *Times Literary Supplement* June 16, pp. 6–8.

————— 1995b. 'A Case of the Liberal's New Clothes', *Guardian*, November 4, p. 29.

————— 1995c. *Anthropology and Politics*, Oxford: Blackwell.

————— 1998. *Language and Solitude*, Cambridge: Cambridge University Press.

Gewirth, A. 1998. *Self-Fulfilment*, Princeton NJ: Princeton University Press.

Giddens, A. 1991. *The Consequences of Modernity*, Cambridge: Polity.

Gilman, S. (ed.) 1987. *Conversations with Nietzsche*, Oxford: Oxford University Press.

Gilsenan, M. 1976. 'Lying, Honour and Contradiction', in B. Kapferer (ed.), *Transaction and Meaning*, Philadelphia: ISHI.

Goffman, E. 1978. *The Presentation of Self in Everyday Life*, Harmondsworth: Penguin.

Golding, W. 1988. *Close Quarters*, London: Faber.

Goodenough, W. 1963. *Cooperation in Change*, New York: Sage.

Goody, E. 1978. 'Introduction', in E. Goody (ed.), *Questions and Politeness*, Cambridge: Cambridge University Press.

Greene, G. 1979. *The Quiet American*, Harmondsworth: Penguin.

Grossman, D. 2008. *Writing in the Dark*, London: Bloomsbury.

Gumperz, J. 1970. 'Linguistic and Social Interaction in Two Communities', in E. Hammel and W. Simmons (eds), *Man Makes Sense*, Boston: Little, Brown.

Gupta, A. 1995. 'Blurred Boundaries: The Discourse of Corruption, the Culture of Politics, and the Imagined State', *American Ethnologist* 22(2): 375–402.

Gutmann, A. 1996. 'Democratic Citizenship', in J. Cohen (ed.), *Love of Country*, Boston: Beacon.

Habermas, J. 1989. *The Structural Transformation of the Public Sphere*, Cambridge: Polity.

Hage, G. 1998. *White Nation*, Sydney: Pluto.

Hall, S. 2008. 'Cosmopolitanism, Globalisation and Diaspora', in P. Werbner (ed.), *Anthropology and the New Cosmopolitanism*, Oxford: Berg.

Hann, C. 2008. 'Towards a Rooted Anthropology: Malinowski, Gellner and Herderian Cosmopolitanism', in P. Werbner (ed.), *Anthropology and the New Cosmopolitanism*, Oxford: Berg.

Hann, C., and E. Dunn (eds). 1996. *Civil Society*, London: Routledge.

Hannerz, U. 1990. 'Cosmopolitans and Locals in World Culture', *Theory, Culture and Society* 7(2–3): 237–51.

————— 2004. 'Cosmopolitanism', in D. Nugent and J. Vincent (eds), *Companion to the Anthropology of Politics*, Oxford: Blackwell.

————— 2006. *Two Faces of Cosmopolitanism: Culture and Politics*, Barcelona: CIDOB.

———— 2007. 'Foreign Correspondents and the Varieties of Cosmopolitanism', *Journal of Ethnic and Migration Studies* 33(2): 299–311.

Harvey, D. 2000. 'Cosmopolitanism and the Banality of Geographical Evils', *Public Culture* 12(2): 529–64.

Hegel, G. 2008. *Lectures on the Philosophy of Religion*, Vol. 2: *Determinate Religion*, Oxford: Oxford University Press.

Held, D. 2000. 'Culture and Political Community: National, Global, and Cosmopolitan', in S. Vertovec and R. Cohen (eds), *Conceiving Cosmopolitanism*, New York: Oxford University Press.

———— 2006. 'Principles of Cosmopolitan Order', in G. Brock and H. Brighouse (eds), *The Political Philosophy of Cosmopolitanism*, Cambridge: Cambridge University Press.

Hendry, J., and C.W. Watson (eds). 2001. *The Anthropology of Indirect Communication*, London: Routledge.

Herzfeld, M. 1993. *The Social Production of Indifference*, Oxford: Berg.

Himmelfarb, G. 1996. 'The Illusions of Cosmopolitanism', in J. Cohen (ed.), *Love of Country*, Boston: Beacon.

Hirsch, E. 2008. 'Paradoxes of the Cosmopolitan in Melanesia', in P. Werbner (ed.), *Anthropology and the New Cosmopolitanism*, Oxford: Berg.

Hodgson, D. 2008. 'Cosmopolitics, Neoliberalism and the State: The Indigenous Rights Movement in Africa', in P. Werbner (ed.), *Anthropology and the New Cosmopolitanism*, Oxford: Berg.

Hollinger, D. 2000. 'Not Universalists, Not Pluralists: The New Cosmopolitans Find their Own Way', in S. Vertovec and R. Cohen (eds), *Conceiving Cosmopolitanism*, New York: Oxford University Press.

Hughes–Freeland, F. 2001. 'Dance, Dissimulation and Identity in Indonesia', in J. Hendry and C.W. Watson (eds), *The Anthropology of Indirect Communication*, London: Routledge.

———— 2008. *Embodied Communities: Dance Traditions and Change in Java*, Oxford: Berghahn Books.

Humphrey, C. 2004. 'Cosmopolitanism and *Kozmopolitizm* in the Political Life of Soviet Citizens', *Focaal* 44: 138–54.

Humphrey, N. 1997. 'What Shall We Tell the Children?' Amnesty Lecture, 21 February, Oxford.

Hurka, T. 1993. *Perfectionism*, Oxford: Oxford University Press.

Hymes, D. 1973. 'Towards Ethnographies of Communication: The Analysis of Communicative Events', in P. Giglioli (ed.), *Language and Social Context*, Harmondsworth: Penguin.

Irving, A. 2009. 'The Color of Pain', *Public Culture* 21(2): 293–319.

Jackson, M. 1989. *Paths Toward a Clearing*, Bloomington: Indiana University Press.

———— 2002. *The Politics of Storytelling*, Copenhagen: Museum Tusculanum Press.

———— 2004. *In Sierra Leone*, Durham NC: Duke University Press.

———— 2008. *Excursions*, Durham NC: Duke University Press.

James, A. 2005. 'The Standardized Child: Issues of Openness, Objectivity and Agency in Promoting Childhood Health', in N. Rapport (ed.),

Democracy, Science and the 'Open Society', New Brunswick NJ: Transaction.

Jones, C. 2001. *Global Justice: Defending Cosmopolitanism*, Oxford: Oxford University Press.

Jones, S. 1996. 'In the Blood', BBC 2, 10 June.

Josephides, L. 1999. 'Disengagement and Desire: The Tactics of Everyday Life', *American Ethnologist* 26(1): 139–59.

———— 2003. 'The Rights of Being Human', in R. Wilson and J. Mitchell (eds), *Human Rights in Global Perspective*, London: Routledge.

———— 2008. *Melanesian Odysseys: Negotiating the Self, Narrative, and Modernity*, Oxford: Berghahn.

Kahn, J. 2003. 'Anthropology as Cosmopolitan Practice?', *Anthropological Theory* 3(4): 403–15.

———— 2008. 'Other Cosmopolitans in the Making of the Modern Malay World', in P. Werbner (ed.), *Anthropology and the New Cosmopolitanism*, Oxford: Berg.

Kant, I. 1974. *The Philosophy of Law*, Clifton NJ: Kelley.

———— 1991. *Kant: Political Writings*, Cambridge: Cambridge University Press.

———— 1993. *Grounding for the Metaphysics of Morals*, Indianapolis IN: Hackett.

———— 1996. *'Toward Perpetual Peace' and Other Writings on Politics, Peace, and History*, New Haven CT: Yale University Press.

Kateb, G. 1984. 'Democratic Individuality and the Claim of Politics', *Political Theory* 12(3): 331–60.

———— 1991. 'Democratic Individuality and the Meaning of Rights', in N. Rosenblum (ed.), *Liberalism and the Moral Life*, Cambridge MA: Harvard University Press.

Kaufmann, W. 1976. 'Introduction', in *The Portable Nietzsche*, Harmondsworth: Penguin.

Kersten, C. 2011. *Cosmopolitans and Heretics*, London: Hurst.

Kierkegaard, S. 1941. *Concluding Unscientific Postscript*, Princeton NJ: Princeton University Press.

———— 1958. *The Journals of Kierkegaard 1834–1854*, Glasgow: Fontana.

———— 1959. *Either/Or*, New York: Doubleday.

Klemperer, V. 2000. *The Language of the Third Reich*, London: Athlone.

Knapp, J. 1994. *An Empire Nowhere*, Berkeley CA: University of California Press.

Kwon, H. 2008. 'The Ghosts of War and the Spirit of Cosmopolitanism', *History of Religions* 47(4): 22–42.

Kymlicka, W. 2006. 'Liberal Nationalism and Cosmopolitan Justice', in S. Benhabib, *Another Cosmopolitanism*, New York: Oxford University Press.

Lamb, S. 2009. *Aging and the Indian Diaspora: Cosmopolitan Families in India and Abroad*, Bloomington: Indiana University Press.

Larkin, P. 1990. *Collected Poems*, London: Faber.

Latour, B. 2004. 'Whose Cosmos, Which Cosmopolitics?' *Common Knowledge* 10(3): 450–62.

Leach, E. 1977. *Custom, Law and Terrorist Violence*, Edinburgh: Edinburgh University Press.

Leavis, F.R. 1972. *Nor Shall My Sword*, London: Chatto and Windus.

Legros, D. 2008. '0.45% Cosmopolitan', *St Thomas Law Review* 20(3): 490–512.

Lewis, G. 2000. *A Failure of Treatment*, Oxford: Oxford University Press.

McConnell, M. 1996. 'Don't Neglect the Little Platoons', in J. Cohen (ed.), *Love of Country*, Boston: Beacon.

McKinnon, C. 2006. 'Cosmopolitan Hope', in G. Brock and H. Brighouse (eds), *The Political Philosophy of Cosmopolitanism*, Cambridge: Cambridge University Press.

Maistre, J. de. 1797. *Considérations sur la France*, London: Bâle.

Malcolmson, S. 1998. 'The Varieties of Cosmopolitan Experience', in P. Cheah and B. Robbins (eds), *Cosmopolitics*, Minneapolis: University of Minnesota Press.

Malkki, L. 1995. *Purity and Exile*, Chicago: University of Chicago Press.

Mandle, J. 2006. 'Tolerating Injustice', in G. Brock and H. Brighouse (eds), *The Political Philosophy of Cosmopolitanism*, Cambridge: Cambridge University Press.

Marx, K. 1934. *The Eighteenth Brumaire of Louis Napoleon*, Moscow: Progress.

Meskimmon, M. 2010. *Contemporary Art and the Cosmopolitan Imagination*, London: Routledge.

Mill, J.S. 1957 [1873]. *Autobiography*, New York: Library of Liberal Arts.

——— 1874. *A System of Logic*, New York: Harper.

——— 1950. *Mill on Bentham and Coleridge*, ed. F.R. Leavis. London: Chatto and Windus.

——— 1963. *The Six Great Humanistic Essays of John Stuart Mill*, New York: Washington Square.

——— 1972. *Utilitarianism, on Liberty, and Considerations on Representative Government*, London: Dent.

Miller, A. 2008 'The Soviet Union they Couldn't Break', *Observer* (features and reviews section), 29 June, p. 25.

Murdoch, I. 1970. *The Sovereignty of Good*, London: Routledge and Kegan Paul.

Murphy, R. 1972. *The Dialectics of Social Life*, London: Allen and Unwin.

Nagel, T. 1971. 'The Absurd', *Journal of Philosophy* 68(20): 716–27.

Narayan, K. 2007. 'Moving Stories: Beyond the Local in Ethnography and Fiction', in K. Robinson (ed.), *Asian and Pacific Cosmopolitans*, Basingstoke: Palgrave.

Nietzsche, F. 1968. *The Will To Power*, New York: Random House.

——— 1974. *The Gay Science*, New York: Vintage.

——— 1979a. *Beyond Good and Evil*, Harmondsworth: Penguin.

——— 1979b. *Ecce Homo*, Harmondsworth: Penguin.

——— 1979c. *Twilight of the Idols and the Anti-Christ*, Harmondsworth: Penguin.

——— 1994. *Human, All Too Human*, Harmondsworth: Penguin.

Nussbaum, M. 1996. 'Patriotism and Cosmopolitanism', in J. Cohen (ed.), *Love of Country*, Boston: Beacon.

———— 2006. 'Beyond the Social Contract: Capabilities and Global Justice', in G. Brock and H. Brighouse (eds), *The Political Philosophy of Cosmopolitanism*, Cambridge: Cambridge University Press.

Observer. 1994. 'Hitler's Heirs Incite Islamic Students', *Observer*, 13 March, p. 25.

Ong, A. 1998. 'Flexible Citizenship among Chinese Cosmopolitans', in P. Cheah and B. Robbins (eds), *Cosmopolitics*. Minneapolis: University of Minnesota Press.

Oz, A. 1983. *In the Land of Israel*, London: Fontana.

———— 1992. 'Israeli Literature', Raymond Williams Lecture, Hay Festival, 31 May.

Paine, R. 1992. 'The Marabar Caves, 1920–2020', in S. Wallman (ed.), *Contemporary Futures*, London: Routledge.

Parry, J. 2008. 'Cosmopolitan Values in a Central Indian Steel Town', in P. Werbner (ed.), *Anthropology and the New Cosmopolitanism*, Oxford: Berg.

Peterson, M. 2011. *Connected in Cairo: Growing Up Cosmopolitan in the Modern Middle East*, Bloomington: Indiana University Press.

Pinsky, R. 1996. 'Eros against Esperanto', in J. Cohen (ed.), *Love of Country*, Boston: Beacon.

Piot, C. 1999. *Remotely Global*, Chicago: University of Chicago Press.

Pollock, S. 2002. 'Cosmopolitan and Vernacular in History', in C. Breckenridge, S. Pollock, H. Bhabha and D. Chakrabarty (eds), *Cosmopolitanism*, Durham NC: Duke University Press.

Pople, K. 1991. *Stanley Spencer*, London: Collins.

Popper, K. 1980. *The Open Society and Its Enemies*, London: Routledge.

———— 1997. *The Myth of the Framework*, London: Routledge.

———— 1998. 'Karl Popper on God: The Lost interview (1969)', ed. E. Zerin, *Skeptic* 6(2): 47–48.

Popper, K., and J. Eccles. 1977. *The Self and Its Brain*, Berlin: Springer.

Post, R. 2006. 'Introduction', in S. Benhabib, *Another Cosmopolitanism*, New York: Oxford University Press.

Pravda. 1949. 'About One Anti–patriotic Group of Theatre Critics', *Pravda*, 28 January, p.3. Retrieved 29 November 2010 from: http://www.cyberussr.com/rus/kritikov–e.html.

Propp, V. 1968. *Morphology of the Folk Tale*, Austin TX: University of Texas Press.

Putnam, H. 1996. 'Must We Choose Between Patriotism and Universal Reason?' in J. Cohen (ed.), *Love of Country*, Boston: Beacon.

Rabinow, P. 1986. 'Representations Are Social Facts: Modernity and Post-modernity in Anthropology', in J. Clifford and G. Marcus (eds), *Writing Culture*, Berkeley CA: University of California Press.

Rapport, N.J. 1986. 'Cedar High Farm: Ambiguous Symbolic Boundary. An Essay in Anthropological Intuition', in A.P. Cohen (ed.), *Symbolising Boundaries*, Manchester: Manchester University Press

———— 1987. *Talking Violence: An Anthropological Interpretation of Conversation in the City*, St John's, Newfoundland: Institute of Social and Economic Research Press, Memorial University.

————— 1992. 'Connexions with and within a Text: From Forster's *Howards End* to the Anthropology of Comparison', *Bulletin of John Rylands University Library of Manchester*, special issue, 73(3): 161–80.

————— 1993. *Diverse World-views in an English Village*, Edinburgh: Edinburgh University Press.

————— 1994. *The Prose and the Passion: Anthropology, Literature and the Writing of E. M. Forster*, Manchester: Manchester University Press.

————— 1997a. *Transcendent Individual: Towards a Literary and Liberal Anthropology*, London: Routledge.

————— 1997b. 'The "Contrarieties" of Israel: An Essay on the Cognitive Importance and the Creative Promise of Both/And', *Journal of the Royal Anthropological Institute* 3(4): 653–72.

————— 1999. 'Context as an Act of Personal Externalization: Gregory Bateson and the Harvey Family in the English Village of Wanet', in R. Dilley (ed.), *The Problem of Context*, Oxford: Berghahn.

————— 2001. 'Random Mind: Towards an Appreciation of Openness in Individual, Society and Anthropology', *Australian Journal of Anthropology* 12(2): 190–220.

————— 2002. 'Em louvor do cosmopolita ironico: nacionalismo, o "judeu errante" e a cidade pos-nacional', *Revista de Antropologia* 45(1): 89–130.

————— 2003. *I Am Dynamite: An Alternative Anthropology of Power*, London: Routledge.

————— 2004. 'Envisioned, Intentioned: A Painter Informs an Anthropologist about Social Relations', *Journal of the Royal Anthropological Institute* 10(4): 861–81.

————— 2005. 'Nietzsche's Pendulum: Oscillations of Humankind', *Australian Journal of Anthropology* 16(2): 1–17.

————— 2006a. 'Diaspora, Cosmopolis, Global Refuge: Three Voices of the Supranational City', in S. Coleman and P. Collins (eds), *Locating the Field*. Oxford: Berghahn.

————— (ed.) 2006b. *Democracy, Science and the Open Society: A European Legacy?* Piscataway NJ: Transaction.

————— 2006c. 'Anthropology as Cosmopolitan Study', *Anthropology Today* 22(1): 23–24.

————— 2007. 'An Outline for Cosmopolitan Study, for Reclaiming the Human through Introspection', *Current Anthropology* 48: 257–83.

————— 2008. 'Gratuitousness: Notes Towards an Anthropology of Interiority', *Australian Journal of Anthropology* 19(3): 331–49.

————— 2009a. '*Quiconque*: vers une moralité anthropologique pour l'individu global', *Anthropologica* 51: 121–31.

————— 2009b. 'Power and Identity', in S. Clegg and M. Haugaard (eds), *The Handbook of Power*, London: Sage.

————— 2010a. 'Apprehending *Anyone*: The Non-indexical, Post-cultural and Cosmopolitan Human Actor', *Journal of the Royal Anthropological Institute* 16(1): 84–101.

——— 2010b 'Afterword: the Cosmopolitan Justice of A Direction Home,"
in C. Trundle and B. Bonisch–Brednuch (eds), *Local Lives: Migration
and the Politics of Place*, Aldershot: Ashgate.

——— 2010c. 'Human Capacity as an Exceeding, a Going Beyond', in N.
Rapport (ed.), *Human Nature as Capacity: An Ethnographic Approach*,
Oxford: Berghahn.

——— 2011. 'The Liberal Treatment of Difference: An Untimely Meditation
on Culture and Civilization', *Current Anthropology* 52(5): 687–710.

——— 2012a. 'Emancipatory Cosmopolitanism: A Vision of the individual
Free from Culture, Custom and Community', in G. Delanty (ed.),
Handbook of Cosmopolitan Studies, London: Routledge.

——— 2012b. 'Shy and Ticklish Truths as Species of Scientific and
Artistic Perception', *Indo-Pacific Journal of Phenomenology*.

Rapport, N.J., and J. Overing. 2007. *Social and Cultural Anthropology: The Key
Concepts*, 2nd edn, London: Routledge.

Rapport, N.J., and R. Stade. 2007. 'A Cosmopolitan Turn – Or Return?', *Social
Anthropology* 15(2): 223–35.

Rapport, N.J., and H. Wardle (eds), 2010. 'A Cosmopolitan Anthropology',
Social Anthropology, special issue, 18(4).

Rawls, J. 1971. *A Theory of Justice*, Oxford: Oxford University Press.

Redfield, P. 2005. 'Doctors, Borders and Life in Crisis', *Cultural Anthropology*
20(3): 328–61.

Ree, J. 1998. 'Cosmopolitanism and the Experience of Nationality', in P.
Cheah and B. Robbins (eds), *Cosmopolitics*, Minneapolis: University
of Minnesota Press.

Robbins, B. 1998. 'Actually Existing Cosmopolitanism', in P. Cheah and B.
Robbins (eds), *Cosmopolitics*, Minneapolis: University of Minnesota
Press.

Robertson, R. 1995. 'Glocalization: Time-space and Homogeneity-
heterogeneity', in M. Featherstone, S. Lash and R. Robertson (eds),
Global Modernities, London: Sage.

Robinson, K. 2007. 'Asian and Pacific Cosmopolitans: Self and Subject in
Motion', in K. Robinson (ed.), *Asian and Pacific Cosmopolitans*,
Basingstoke: Palgrave.

Rorty, R. 1980. *Philosophy and the Mirror of Nature*, Princeton NJ: Princeton
University Press.

——— 1992. *Contingency, Irony, and Solidarity*. Cambridge: Cambridge
University Press.

——— 1998 'Justice: A Larger Loyalty', in P. Cheah and B. Robbins (eds),
Cosmopolitics, Minneapolis: University of Minnesota Press.

Sapir, E. 1956. *Culture, Language and Personality*, Berkeley CA: University of
California Press.

Sartre, J.-P. 1956. *Being and Nothingness*, New York: Philosophy Library.

Scarry, E. 1996 'The Difficulty of Imagining Other People', in J. Cohen (ed.),
Love of Country, Boston: Beacon.

Schreiner, O. 1998. *The Story of an African Farm*, Oxford: Oxford University
Press.

Schwartz, T. 1978. 'The Size and Shape of a Culture', in F. Barth (ed.), *Scale and Social Organisation*, Oslo: Greig.

Sen, A. 1996. 'Humanity and Citizenship', in J. Cohen (ed.), *Love of Country*, Boston: Beacon.

Sennett, R. 2000. 'Cosmopolitanism and the Social Experience of Cities', in S. Vertovec and R. Cohen (eds), *Conceiving Cosmopolitanism*, New York: Oxford University Press.

Sichone, O. 2008. 'Xenophobia and Xenophilia in South Africa: African Migrants in Cape Town', in P. Werbner (ed.), *Anthropology and the New Cosmopolitanism*, Oxford: Berg.

Simmel, G. 1971. *On Individuality and Social Forms*, Chicago: University of Chicago Press.

———— 1991. *Schopenhauer and Nietzsche*, Urbana: University of Illinois Press.

Simpson, E., and K. Kresse. 2007. 'Cosmopolitanism Contested: Anthropology and History in the Western Indian Ocean', in E. Simson and K. Kresse (eds), *Struggling with History: Islam and Cosmopolitanism in the Western Indian Ocean*, London: Hurst.

Smith, A. 1990. 'Towards a Global Culture?', *Theory, Culture and Society* 7(2–3): 171–91.

Solomon, R. 1978. *From Rationalism to Existentialism*, Brighton: Harvester.

Spencer, S. 2001. *Stanley Spencer: Letters and Writing*, ed. A. Glew. London: Tate.

Stade, R. 2006. 'Cosmos and Polis: Past and Present', in J. Scholte and R. Robertson (eds.), *Encyclopedia of Globalization*, London: Routledge.

———— 2007. 'Cosmopolitans and Cosmopolitanism in Anthropology', *Social Anthropology* 15(2): 226–29.

Stalin, J. 1953. *Works*, Vol. 4, Moscow: Foreign Languages Publishing House.

Steiner, G. 1997a. *No Passion Spent*, London: Faber.

———— 1997b. *Errata: An Examined Life*, New Haven CT: Yale University Press.

———— 1998. 'War, Terrorism and Chaos: God's Idea of Keeping a Promise', *Observer Review*, 22 February, p. 15.

———— 2003. *Lessons of the Masters*, Cambridge MA: Harvard University Press.

Stern, J.P. 1981. *A Study of Nietzsche*, Cambridge: Cambridge University Press.

Stivens, M. 2008. 'Gender, Rights and Cosmopolitanisms', in P. Werbner (ed.), *Anthropology and the New Cosmopolitanism*, Oxford: Berg.

Stocking, G. 1982. *Race, Culture and Evolution*, Chicago: University of Chicago Press.

———— 1992. *The Ethnographer's Magic and Other Essays in the History of Anthropology*, Madison: University of Wisconsin Press.

Strawson, G. 1997. 'In Deepest Sympathy: Towards a Natural History of Virtue', *Times Literary Supplement* 4887, pp. 3–4.

Sznaider, N. 2010. 'A Jewish Comment on Cosmopolitan Citizenship in the Middle East', *Open Democracy*, 10 August. Retrieved 29 November 2010 from: http://www.opendemocracy.net/natan-sznaider/jewish-comment-on-cosmopolitan-citizenship-in-middle-east.

Szwed, J. 1966. *Private Cultures and Public Imagery*, St. John's Newfoundland: ISER Press, Memorial University.

Taylor, C. 1992. 'The Politics of Recognition', in A. Gutmann (ed.), *Multiculturalism*, Princeton NJ: Princeton University Press.

Thin, N. 2001. 'Indirect Speech: Heteroglossia, Politeness and Rudeness in Irula Forest Festivals', in J. Hendry and C.W. Watson (eds), *The Anthropology of Indirect Communication*, London: Routledge.

Thomas, W.I., and D.S. Thomas. 1928. *The Child in America*, New York: Knopf.

Tully, J. 1995. *Strange Multiplicity*, Cambridge: Cambridge University Press.

Turner, B. 1990. 'The Two Faces of Sociology: Global or National?', *Theory, Culture and Society* 7(2–3): 343–58.

——— 2002. 'Cosmopolitan Virtue, Globalization and Patriotism', *Theory, Culture and Society* 19(1–2): 45–63.

Turner, J.S. 2000. *The Extended Organism*, Cambridge MA: Harvard University Press.

Vertovec, S., and R. Cohen (eds). 2000. *Conceiving Cosmopolitanism*, New York: Oxford University Press.

Waldron, J. 2006. 'Cosmopolitan Norms', in S. Benhabib, *Another Cosmopolitanism*, New York: Oxford University Press.

Wallace, A.F.C. 1961. 'The Psychic Unity of Human Groups', in B. Kaplan (ed.), *Studying Personality Cross-culturally*, New York: Harper and Row.

——— 1962. 'Culture and Cognition', *Science* 135: 351–57.

——— 1964. *Culture and Personality*, New York: Random House.

Walzer, M. 1994. *Thick and Thin*, Notre Dame IN: University of Notre Dame Press.

——— 1996. 'Spheres of Affection', in J. Cohen (ed.), *Love of Country*, Boston: Beacon.

Wardle, H. 2000. *An Ethnography of Cosmopolitanism in Kingston, Jamaica*, Lampeter: Mellen.

——— 2010. 'A Cosmopolitan Anthropology?' *Social Anthropology*, special issue, 18(4): 381–8.

Weissbrodt, D. 1988. 'Human Rights: An Historical Perspective', in P. Davies (ed.), *Human Rights*, London: Routledge.

Werbner, P. 1999. 'Global Pathways: Working-class Cosmopolitans and the Creation of Transnational Ethnic Worlds', *Social Anthropology* 7(1): 17–35.

——— 2008a. 'The Cosmopolitan Encounter: Social Anthropology and the Kindness of Strangers', in P. Werbner (ed.), *Anthropology and the New Cosmopolitanism*, Oxford: Berg.

——— (ed.) 2008b. *Anthropology and the New Cosmopolitanism*, Oxford: Berg.

Werbner, R. 2007. 'Oceanic Visions: Situated Practices and the New Cosmopolitanism', in K. Robinson (ed.), *Asian and Pacific Cosmopolitans*, Basingstoke: Palgrave.

——— 2008. 'Responding To Rooted Cosmopolitanism: Patriots, Ethnics and the Public Good in Botswana', in P. Werbner (ed.), *Anthropology and the New Cosmopolitanism*, Oxford: Berg.

Wilson, Richard. (ed.) 1997. *Human Rights, Culture and Context*, London: Pluto Press.

Wilson, Rob. 1998. 'A New Cosmopolitanism Is in the Air: Some Dialectical Twists and Turns', in P. Cheah and B. Robbins (eds), *Cosmopolitics*, Minneapolis: University of Minnesota Press.

Winch, P. 1970. *The Idea of a Social Science, and Its Relation to Philosophy*, London: Routledge and Kegan Paul.

Wittgenstein, L. 1978. *Philosophical Investigations*, Oxford: Blackwell.

———— 1980. *Culture and Value*, Chicago: University of Chicago Press.

Wood, A. 1998. 'Kant's Project for Perpetual Peace', in P. Cheah and B. Robbins (eds), *Cosmopolitics*, Minneapolis: University of Minnesota Press.

Woolf, V. 1969. *The Waves*, Harmondsworth: Penguin.

Wulff, H. 2009. *Dancing at the Crossroads*, Oxford: Berghahn.

Zizek, S. 2005. 'Against Human Rights', *New Left Review* 34: 115–32.

Zolo, D. 1997. *Cosmopolis: Prospects for World Government*, Cambridge: Polity.

INDEX

www.ingramcontent.com/pod-product-compliance
Lightning Source LLC
Chambersburg PA
CBHW072105040426
42334CB00042B/2335